This book is about the biological conquest of the New World. It explores the idea that the transformation of the biological regime associated with the introduction of Old World species into New World ecosystems enabled the conquest of indigenous populations and the domination of vast areas of rural space. It uses the sixteenth-century history of a region of highland central Mexico as a case study and focuses on the changes associated with the introduction of Old World grazing animals. The study spells out in detail the processes by which the grazing animals and their human minders entered and dominated a semiarid New World region, in the process transforming the physical environment and, as a result, the traditional natural resources of the indigenous communities. It demonstrates how these processes aided the Spanish takeover of land, and clarifies the role of environmental change in the evolution of the colonial society. Deterioration of the soil–water regime, marginalization of the indigenous majority, and the formation of latifundia were reflected in the formation of an archetypically New World landscape that has mystified the history both of the land and its inhabitants, and led to policies that treat the symptoms of environmental degradation rather than the cause.

STUDIES IN ENVIRONMENT AND HISTORY

A Plague of Sheep

STUDIES IN ENVIRONMENT AND HISTORY

Editors

Donald Worster   *University of Kansas*
Alfred W. Crosby   *University of Texas at Austin*

Advisory Board

Reid Bryson   *Institute for Environmental Studies, University of Wisconsin*
Raymond Dasmann   *College Eight, University of California, Santa Cruz*
E. Le Roy Ladurie   *Collège de France*
William McNeill   *Department of History, University of Chicago*
Carolyn Merchant   *College of Natural Resources, University of California, Berkeley*
Thad Tate   *Commonwealth Center for the Study of American Culture, College of William and Mary*

Other Books in the Series

Donald Worster   *Nature's Economy: A History of Ecological Ideas*
Kenneth F. Kiple   *The Caribbean Slave: A Biological History*
Alfred W. Crosby   *Ecological Imperialism: The Biological Expansion of Europe, 900–1900*
Arthur F. McEvoy   *The Fisherman's Problem: Ecology and Law in the California Fisheries, 1850–1980*
Robert Harms   *Games Against Nature: An Eco-Cultural History of the Nunu of Equatorial Africa*
Warren Dean   *Brazil and the Struggle for Rubber: A Study in Environmental History*
Samuel P. Hays   *Beauty, Health, and Permanence: Environmental Politics in the United States, 1955–1985*
Donald Worster   *The Ends of the Earth: Perspectives on Modern Environmental History*
Michael Williams   *Americans and Their Forests: A Historical Geography*
Timothy Silver   *A New Face on the Countryside: Indians, Colonists, and Slaves in the South Atlantic Forests, 1500–1800*
Theodore Steinberg   *Nature Incorporated: Industrialization and the Waters of New England*
J. R. McNeill   *The Mountains of the Mediterranean World*

A Plague of Sheep

Environmental Consequences
of the Conquest of Mexico

Elinor G. K. Melville

CAMBRIDGE
UNIVERSITY PRESS

Published by the Press Syndicate of the University of Cambridge
The Pitt Building, Trumpington Street, Cambridge CB2 1RP
40 West 20th Street, New York, NY 10011–4211, USA
10 Stamford Road, Oakleigh, Melbourne 3166, Australia

First published 1994

Printed in the United States of America

Library of Congress Cataloging-in-Publication Data
Melville, Elinor G. K.
   A plague of sheep : environmental consequences of the conquest of
Mexico / Elinor G. K. Melville.
   p.   cm.
Includes bibliographical references (p.   ) and index.
ISBN 0–521–42061–X
   1. Sheep – Mexico – Mezquital Valley (Hidalgo) – Ecology – History —
16th century.   2. Animal introduction – Environmental aspects – Mexico
– Mezquital Valley (Hidalgo) – History – 16th century.   3. Grazing –
Environmental aspects – Mexico – Mezquital Valley (Hidalgo – History –
16th century.   4. Pastoral systems – Environmental aspects – Mexico –
Mezquital Valley (Hidalgo) – History – 16th century.   5. Human ecology
– Mexico – Mezquital Valley   (Hidalgo) – History – 16th
century.   6. Indians of Mexico – Mexico –   Mezquital Valley (Hidalgo) –
History – 16th century.   7. Mezquital Valley (Hidalgo, Mexico) –
Environmental conditions – History.   8. Mexico – History – Conquest,
1519–1540.   9. Mexico – History – Spanish colony, 1540–1810.   I. Title.
SE375.5.M6M45   1994
304.2'7'097246 – dc20   93–10662
                                                                   CIP

A catalog record for this book is available from the British Library

ISBN 0–521–42061–X hardback

*In Memory of my mother, Helen,
and my teacher, Charles Gibson*

"God struck and chastened with ten terrible plagues this land and all who dwelt in it, both natives and foreigners...
The first was a plague of smallpox...
The second was the great number of those who died in the conquest of New Spain...
The third plague was a very great famine which came immediately after the taking of Mexico...
The fourth plague was that of the calpixques or overseers, and the negroes...
The fifth plague was the great taxes and tributes that the Indians paid...
The sixth plague was the gold mines...
The seventh plague was the building of the great city of Mexico, which, in the first years employed more people than the building of Jerusalem...
The eighth plague was the slaves whom the Spanish made in order to put them to work in the mines...
The ninth plague was the service of the mines...
The tenth plague was the divisions and factions which existed among the Spanish of Mexico..."

Motolinia (Toribio de Benavente),
History of the Indians of New Spain
Elizabeth Andes Foster, translator and editor

"Your sheep," I answered, "which are usually so tame and so cheaply fed, begin now, according to report, to be so greedy and wild that they devour human beings themselves and devastate and depopulate fields, houses, and towns."

St. Thomas Moore, *Utopia*

CONTENTS

ILLUSTRATIONS AND TABLES

PREFACE

This is a study of the environmental consequences of the European invasion of the New World. It uses the sixteenth-century history of the Valle del Mezquital, Mexico (1530–1600) as a case study and focuses on the changes associated with the introduction of Old World grazing animals into New World ecosystems. It attempts to show how the ecological and social changes associated with this process brought about the conquest and domination of territory.

The study builds on Alfred Crosby's insight that the conquest of the New World was as much a biological conquest as a political one, and involved the transformation of New World environments. But whereas Crosby is interested in the processes by which Europeans came to dominate the temperate latitudes, I am interested in the nature of the conquest in the tropics, where the indigenous populations have remained to shape landscapes, society, and culture. At first sight these "indigenous" landscapes appear to reflect a continuity of ecosystems, as well as culture and society. But this apparent continuity is misleading: the presence of chickens, pigs, donkeys, goats, sheep, cattle, horses, and mules are all evidence of an ecological revolution brought about by the European invasion, and while the persistence of Indian culture and society is remarkable, a profound shift in the modes of production from horticulture to some form of agropastoralism occurred in almost all parts of the New World as a result of the European invasion. It has long been argued that the development of pastoralism in the New World was a major factor in the evolution of the distinctive colonial regimes; in this study I explore the idea that the expansion of pastoralism enabled the conquest of the indigenous populations and the domination of vast areas of rural space, as well as the corollary to this idea – that the evolution of colonial society itself constituted the conquest.

Topics I deal with in the following chapters, such as the expansion of Spanish modes of land use, the development of Spanish landholding, and the formation of the hacienda system, are staples of the tradition of Mexican rural history. But the approach taken to these topics falls within the genre of environmental history: the physical environment itself is the object of study. I draw on the biological literature dealing with plant–herbivore systems, especially the introduction of herbivores into new ecosystems, grazing ecology, and soil–water relationships, in order to understand the nature of the changes brought about by the introduction of Old World grazing animals. Further, I propose that the natural resource base was not simply a passive constraint on initial choice, but an active variable in the process of social change. This is not sociobiology, however, where biological imperatives are thought to drive human behavior. Nor is it environmental determinism, where human society is determined by its physical environment. Rather, it is an exploration of the reciprocal nature of environmental and social change within the context of the European conquest of the New World.

This book has been many years in the making, and I have accumulated debts along the way that I am very pleased to acknowledge. I have been most fortunate in the help I have received from people who have read various drafts of the manuscript. William Taylor's detailed critique of the first draft of the original dissertation provided me with ideas I have tried to address in this final version, and much needed encouragement – his generous advice to an unknown graduate student was much appreciated. Charles Gibson, Juan Carlos Garavaglia, and John Frederick Scwhaller read the completed thesis and encouraged me to publish it. Recent drafts have benefited immeasurably from Joseph Ernst's critical reading, Mary Hodge's help with the Introduction, and Sam Lanfranco's comments on market formation in the final chapter. Any omissions are, of course, my own responsibility.

The support extended to workers in the field of Latin American history by established scholars and students is extraordinary. It would be impossible to acknowledge all those who took time to suggest a source, an alternative analysis, or who simply listened. I would, however, like to acknowledge some people with whom I have had a continued dialogue over the years: Christon Archer, Adán Benavides, Dawn Bazely, Elizabeth Brumfiel, Charles Frederick, Elizabeth Graham, Mary Hodge, Herman Konrad, Colin MacLachlan, Roberto Salmón, John Schwaller, Rebecca Scott, William Taylor, and Eric Van Young. I would also like to thank Richard Tucker for introducing me to the world of environmental history.

The staff of the Archivo General de la Nación (Mexico) have made my work in their archive a pleasure and I would especially like to thank the *porteros* of Galeria 4, Armando Juárez, Jesús López Martínez, Arturo Librado Galicia, Serafín Villagómez Zavala, and Joel Zúñiga Torres, who have brought me endless volumes with unfailing courtesy; and the Department of Technical Support, directed by Lic. Leonardo González and aided by Alejandro Pérez Santiago and Alejandro Barrera, who have provided me with excellent microfilm. I would also like to acknowledge the work of the staff of the Archivo General de Indias (Seville), the Mitchell Library in Sydney, Australia, the library at the Commonwealth Scientific and Industrial Research Organization in Canberra, Australia, the Nettie Lee Benson Library at the University of Texas at Austin, and last but not least, the librarians in the Department of Inter Library Loan at York University. I would especially like to thank the editors of Cambridge University Press; they have reduced the trouble of revisions and corrections to the bare minimum, and made the whole process a fascinating education in the minutiae of publishing. I am indebted to Charles Frederick for the maps and Susan Rainey for the tables.

My heartfelt thanks go to the groups who have supported me through the long period of research and writing. Canada Council doctoral fellowships supported the first three years of dissertation research, and the Centre for Continuing Education of Women, the Rackham School of Graduate Studies, and the Alumni Association of the University of Michigan all provided much-appreciated support. During the period of rewriting I have been supported by post doctoral and Canada research fellowships from the Social Sciences Research Council of Canada.

Finally, I would like to thank my neighbors in Tlayacapan, Morelos, Mexico who have come to know much more about sheep grazing and the Valle del Mezquital than they probably ever thought they would – or perhaps even wanted to.

1

INTRODUCTION

The Biological Conquest of the New World

What happened after the military defeat of the Aztecs, the Incas, and the myriad towns and city states of the New World? How did the Spaniards and the Europeans who followed them into the New World extend their control over the countryside? This more prosaic, less swashbuckling, less colorful aspect of conquest is crucial for a lasting result, and overall the Europeans were as successful in this as they had been in the military conquests.

The Europeans' success can, in great part, be ascribed to the fact that they did not come alone to the New World, but brought with them animals and plants; weeds, seeds, and diseases. In Alfred Crosby's evocative terminology they traveled with their "portmanteau biota."[1] The Spaniards, for example, did not travel with just their horses and war dogs – they also brought more ordinary animals such as pigs, chickens, sheep, goats, and cattle. They imported grains like wheat and barley, as well as fruit trees, grapevines, and flowers. Weeds came attached to fur and hair and in the seedstock; and pests such as rats came in ships' holds. The conquistadors also carried with them Old World pathogens. The invaders had brought with them more means than they knew to conquer a continent.

The introduced species did not discreetly move into unoccupied niches – they exploded into huge populations that in one way or another transformed the biological and social regimes of the New

---

[1] Crosby, *Ecological Imperialism*, p. 89. Crosby suggests that the secret of the Europeans' success lies in the "ecological component" of European imperialism. In several books and articles he has described how the Europeans left on their voyages with the means to reproduce their culture and their landscapes wherever they landed. The demographic and environmental changes brought about by the ensuing introduction of alien Old World species constituted a major element of the conquest and domination of the New World; see Crosby, *Ecological Imperialism, Columbian Exchange,* "Ecological Imperialism."

1

World. The success of the biological conquest of the New World, of "ecological imperialism,"[2] depended to a great degree on the comprehensiveness of the portmanteau biota (i.e. the number and variety of species) and the extraordinary facility with which they expanded into and transformed the New World environments. It also depended on the transformation of indigenous landscapes and societies, and the formation of new systems of production. The extreme rapidity of the changes, their immense scale, and above all the combination of many different types of change brought about by the multiplicity of introduced species made the Europeans almost invincible.

The thesis of ecological imperialism is supported by clear evidence that the Europeans did best in temperate regions where climates similar to Europe meant that their grazing animals and crops were able to thrive, and where the indigenous populations were sparse at contact. Those regions where Europeans have been most successful, such as Argentina, Canada, and the United States, are today distinguished by populations of predominantly European extraction, by the economic predominance of Old World flora and fauna (wheat, cattle, sheep), and by European-like landscapes and societies.[3] The apparent lack of success in those areas where the Europeans' portmanteau biota did not flourish, the hot, humid tropics for example, or where dense indigenous populations far outnumbered them, as in Mexico, also seems to support this thesis; the tropics are still, after all, dominated by New World peoples, flora, and fauna.

But the apparent environmental continuity in the American tropics is misleading. Despite that the Europeans did not biologically dominate in much of what we know today as Latin America, they did manage to politically dominate vast areas of the hinterlands of the high civilizations in Mexico and the Andes in a remarkably short time, and to control, albeit more slowly and somewhat insecurely, much of the tropical lowlands. It is clear, moreover, that although European-like landscapes did not develop in the hinterlands of Latin America's high civilizations, the biological status quo was not maintained either. The indigenous species of the New World did not triumph over the invaders as in Asia, where the Europeans and their animals and plants barely gained a foothold.[4] On the contrary, the native biological re-

---

[2] Rappaport, "The Flow of Energy," p. 275. Crosby, *Ecological Imperialism* especially, pp. 1–7.
[3] Crosby calls these regions "neo-Europes"; *Ecological Imperialism*, p. 2.
[4] In Chapter 6 of *Ecological Imperialism*, Crosby discusses the various reasons Europeans and their portmanteau biota were unsuccessful in the humid tropics and in the densely populated zones, except as traders or as extractors of primary products.

gimes underwent radical changes following the introduction of Old World species, and new landscapes that we now think of as typically New World were formed. The expansion of Old World grazing animals and the demographic collapse of the indigenous populations were major processes in this transformation. Diseases endemic to Europe such as smallpox, measles, and influenza, when introduced into the New World exploded into terrifying and unpredictable epidemics that swept through the Americas leaving communities decimated. The epidemics were repeated regularly throughout the first hundred years and reduced the indigenous populations to ever-lower plateaus; sporadic outbursts continued throughout the colonial period. The combination of the virulent nature of the epidemics themselves and the collapse of the indigenous populations meant that the Europeans were able to move quickly into even densely populated and highly organized regions. An epidemic of smallpox decimated the defending population of the city of Tenochtitlán, contributing to the fall of the Aztec Empire in 1521. Another epidemic in the Andes paved the way for the Spanish conquest of the Inca. It is possible, as well, that epidemic disease swept ahead of the Europeans into the interior of North America, clearing the way for the European conquest.[5] The demographic collapse was such an effective ally that some Europeans saw the epidemics as divine intervention on their behalf, as witness the statement made by John Winthrop, first governor of Massachusetts Bay Colony: "For the natives, they are neere all dead of small Poxe, so as the Lord hathe cleared our title to what we possess."[6] In apparent confirmation of this point of view, the introduced grazing animals increased exponentially (at least at first) to truly extraordinary numbers; as they expanded into the countryside, they transformed the ecosystems of the New World and played a crucial role in the domination of the countryside by the Spaniards.

How, exactly, *did* these alien species – the disease organisms and the grazing animals – expand into the New World ecosystems? Did

[5] The precontact indigenous population of North America and the extent of its collapse is a hotly debated topic, as is the means by which it was infected; see, for example, the debate carried on in the *Latin American Population History Bulletin* by Whitmore and Henige.

[6] Cited in Crosby, *Ecological Imperialism*, p. 208. See Crosby's discussion of the role of epidemic disease in the defeat of the Aztec and Inca Empires, and his discussion of the diseases introduced into the New World, and the Pacific, in Chapter 2 of *The Columbian Exchange* and Chapter 9 of *Ecological Imperialism*. See also McNeill, *Plagues and Peoples*.

they have some sort of competitive advantage? Were New World species somehow inferior, not as tough or aggressive? The answers to these questions can be found in two biological processes with wonderfully exotic names: virgin soil epidemics – the process by which disease organisms move into new populations; and ungulate irruptions – or, how grazing animals move into new ecosystems. The great advantage of both these processes as explanatory tools is that they are universal phenomena. They are not exclusive to the New World, they do not depend on genetic differences, nor can they be ascribed to imagined cultural or physical superiority. They occur wherever and whenever the circumstances are suitable.

Virgin Soil Epidemics

Virgin soil epidemics are characterized by an immunologically defenseless host population (hence their name), extremely rapid spread, and almost universal infection. Old-World pathogens were successful because the New World populations had never been infected by them and had no defenses. They spread with shocking speed, infecting entire communities and resulting in appalling death rates. All these new diseases were repeated every few years until the indigenous populations gained some immunity, a process that seems to have taken four to six generations. The successive epidemics resulted in a massive demographic collapse: the estimated population decline in Mexico, for example, was 90–95 percent between 1519, when the Spaniards arrived, and 1620, when the indigenous population began its slow recovery.[7]

In an article on virgin soil epidemics in America, Alfred Crosby discusses several factors that account for the high mortality rate among the New World indigenes. First, he points out that our designation of these diseases as mild childhood infections gives a misleading idea of their virulence. Modern medicine does not cure diseases such as measles and influenza; it can keep down the normally high mortality rates characteristic of these diseases only by defending the infected individual against other infections. Where help is not available, the

---

[7] See Crosby, "Virgin Soil Epidemics," for a succinct description of the New World virgin soil epidemics and the consequences for the indigenous population of North America. See also Crosby's *Columbian Exchange* and Chapter 9 of *Ecological Imperialism*. See Whitmore, "Population Decline," for a recent evaluation of the demographic collapse and an argument for the lower figure of 90 percent; and David Henige "Native American Population," for a discussion of the debate over the original population and its collapse.

mortality rates are very high, even in populations where these diseases are endemic. Second, the diseases carried to the New World, such as smallpox, measles, influenza, plague, and tuberculosis,[8] are characterized by very high mortality rates in the age group 15–40 years; that is, the group most involved in the production and preparation of food, shelter, and so on. When a high percentage of this group dies, those who might otherwise survive are neglected and die from untreated complications or starvation. Third, the Amerindians were rarely infected by a single disease; it was much more likely that they would be faced with a barrage of new infections. Where several virgin soil epidemics occur at the same time, the mortality rate soars; it also rises where other infections exacerbate the effects of the new infection. Modern experience has demonstrated that repeated virgin soil epidemics can effectively destroy societies. Fourth, epidemic disease was spread by apparently healthy people fleeing their villages, only to carry the contagion to new communities, and by a complete lack of quarantine. Finally, Crosby notes that a fatalistic attitude toward the inevitability of death often meant the loss of entire families.[9]

The demographic collapse of the New World populations was reflected in a declining labor pool, altered settlement patterns, and changes in the exploitation of the natural resources.[10] In agricultural

[8] For a discussion of why the same or similar diseases had not evolved in the New World, see Crosby, Chapter 11 of *Ecological Imperialism* and Chapter 2 of *The Columbian Exchange.*

[9] Crosby, "Virgin Soil Epidemics," p. 29.

[10] The demographic collapse was clearly one of the major forces shaping the colonial societies. The historiography of sixteenth-century Mexico includes a broad range of studies that have as their focus the epidemics and their social and economic consequences. Scholars have used biological, environmental, cultural, and social factors to demonstrate the size and health of the New World populations at contact. See, for example, Cook and Borah, *Essays in Population History.* See also Dobyns, "Estimating Aboriginal American Population: An Appraisal of Techniques with a New Hemispheric Estimate"; Whitmore, "Population Decline"; and Zambardino, "Mexico; Population in the Sixteenth Century: Demographic Anomaly or Mathematical Illusion?" For a discussion of the arguments concerning the susceptibility of the aboriginal populations to the Eurasian disease organisms, and the nature and course of the epidemics, see Crosby, *The Columbian Exchange;* also McNeill, *Plagues and Peoples.*

A number of social and economic historians have addressed the consequences of the demographic collapse for the evolution of the colonial political economy, taking as their focus the role played by a rapidly dwindling labor pool in the formation of the colonial systems of production. See, for example, Assadourian, "La despoblación indígena en Perú y Nueva España durante el siglo xvi y la formación de la economía colonial"; Bakewell, *Silver Mining and Society;* Borah, *New Spain's Century of Depression;* Chevalier, *La formación;* Florescano, *Estructuras y problemas agrarias* and "La formación

regions, for example, cultivated fields were reduced and fallow ones extended. In a seminal study of land exploitation in sixteenth-century Mexico, Lesley Byrd Simpson proposed that the lands freed by the demographic collapse of the indigenous populations allowed for the expansion of the domestic grazing animals introduced by the Spanish. In a famous graph, Simpson inversely correlated the human population decline with a steady increase in the animal population up to about 1620, when the Indian population began to stabilize.[11] The animal and human populations are seen as dependent variables, both competing for space. As will be demonstrated later in this book, however, the densities of the two populations in fact changed independently of one another: the animal populations peaked in advance of the decline of the human populations, then crashed before the human populations reached the nadir of their collapse. The decline of the human populations did not trigger the extraordinary increase of the introduced grazing animals; rather, the abundance of New World vegetation and the complete absence of competition from indigenous domesticated grazing animals, except in the Andes, did.

Ungulate Irruptions

Whenever ungulates (herbivores with hard horny hooves[12]) are faced with more food than is needed to replace their numbers in the next generation, an ungulate irruption is the result. The animals react to the excess of food in a manner similar to pathogens encountering virgin soil populations: they increase exponentially until they overshoot the capacity of the plant communities to sustain them (the carrying capacity); their populations crash, then reach an accommodation with the now-reduced subsistance base at a lower density. The plant

de los trabajadores en la época colonial"; Frank, *Mexican Agriculture;* Gibson, *Aztecs;* Konrad, *A Jesuit Hacienda;* MacLeod, *Spanish Central America;* Taylor, *Landlord and Peasant.*

The striking variability in the relations of production uncovered by these studies, together with evidence of the growth and differentiation of the nonindigenous populations, the development of commercial agriculture, and the growth of regional markets and commerce – to name a few of the processes involved in the evolution of the colonial political economy – have radically changed our ideas about the nature and complexity of the colonial regime.

[11] Simpson, *Exploitation of Land.*
[12] Undomesticated ungulates include deer, caribou, and bison. Goats, pigs, sheep, cattle, donkeys, mules, and horses are the common domesticated ungulates of the Old World.

communities follow a reciprocal trajectory: the original standing crop of vegetation is severely reduced by grazing, reaching its lowest density and height just before the animal populations reach their greatest density; when the animal populations crash and grazing pressure is removed, the plant communities begin to recover, reaching an accommodation with the animal population at a lower density, height, and species diversity than that present at the beginning of the process. Animal and plant communities will oscillate around this level of accommodation unless there is some radical change in the conditions of plant growth leading to a marked increase in the carrying capacity,[13] at which time the whole process will begin again. The increase of the animal populations is known as an ungulate irruption; the combined reciprocal trajectories of the plant and animal populations are known as an irruptive oscillation (see Figure 2:1).[14] The entire process is extremely rapid, taking between thirty-five and forty years.[15] (The details of the stages making up an irruptive oscillation will be discussed in more detail in Chapter 2.)

During the course of an ungulate irruption plant communities are changed beyond recognition. Selective browsing simplifies species diversity and reduces the height and density of the vegetation; species unable to withstand the pressures of heavy grazing are relegated to relic stands in out-of-the-way places, and are replaced by others that are either browse-resistant or unpalatable. A new biological regime develops that is reflected in a radically changed landscape.[16] These changes occur whether humans are present or not. Nevertheless, as with virgin soil epidemics, the outcome of the introduction of Old World ungulates into the New World was influenced by human initiative – that is, by ideas, and by the cultures that shaped them.[17]

---

[13] Carl L. Johannessen writes that the "carrying capacity of the range may be described as the number of animals it can support in health, during the period when grass is palatable and nutritious, without reducing forage production in subsequent years ...Overgrazing occurs when the number of stock exceeds the carrying capacity of the range." *Savannas of Interior Honduras*, p. 106.

[14] See N. Leader-Williams, *Reindeer on South Georgia*, pp. 19–24 for a discussion of the model of ungulate irruptions and supporting research. I am indebted to my colleague in biology, Dawn Bazely, for bringing the literature on ungulate irruptions to my notice.

[15] Caughley, "Overpopulation," p. 10.

[16] Caughley, "Wildlife Management," p. 197; Leader-Williams, *Reindeer*, p. 241.

[17] Domestic stock undergo the same general process of irruption, crash and accommodation with their subsistance base as do nondomesticated stock; plant communities follow a reciprocal trajectory as in nondomestic ungulate irruptions.

Ideas and Environmental Change

The members of the portmanteau biota, it must be remembered, did not come alone, they came with humans. The ungulates that irrupted into the New World environments were domestic grazing animals that were part and parcel of a culturally defined system of animal and range management – pastoralism. Their diet, their daily wanderings in search of food and water, even their life span, were often subject to human choice and decision making. The lands they grazed also were subject to human choice. Humans are not content to simply graze their animals; they invariably manipulate the environment in order to achieve the maximum return from them. The form the manipulation takes is dictated by both culture and past experience. Where pastoralism is introduced for the first time, therefore, the cultural and social landscape is transformed along with the biological regime. This was especially true in the New World where (apart from in the Andes) society had evolved in the absence of domestic grazing animals. Pastoralism had no recognizable social counterparts in the preconquest world outside of the Andes, and its introduction involved not only the addition of exotic species but also a completely alien perception of the natural resources and their use; indeed, it involved the formation of completely new systems of production. The landscapes not only looked different, with new and different animals that radically changed the vegetative cover, but access to and exploitation of the natural resources were changed as well.

When considering the implications of the introduction of pastoralism, the problem is to ascertain what was "natural" environmental change and what was human-induced; and, where environmental change was the result of human action, to elucidate the ideas behind the actions. The biologists who study ungulate irruptions know only too well how difficult it is to separate the effects of human action from purely biological processes. For that reason studies of ungulate irruptions have been carried out on remote islands using nondomesticated ungulate populations in an attempt to exclude human influence and to control the parameters of the study.[18] These studies demon-

---

[18] See Bergerud, Jakinchuk and Carruthers, "The Buffalo of the North," and Peek, "Natural Regulation of Ungulates" on the difficulty of isolating human influence; see also Leader-Williams, *Reindeer*, pp. 244–5, 271, for a discussion of the utility of island studies.

strate that almost invariably the result of human interference in irruptive oscillations is environmental degradation such as erosion or the irretrievable loss of plant species.

Environmental degradation is not a necessary consequence of ungulate irruptions. Plant communities, for example, will regenerate if nondomesticated ungulates are removed, and erosion can generally be ascribed to friable soils, steep slopes, and rainfall. Where domestic stock is involved, however, the vegetation changes may be irreversible because pastoralists "sometimes hold stock at densities higher than would be possible if the stock arranged their own bionomics."[19] That is, pastoralists amplify the effects of the irruption of the animal populations, accelerating the degradation of vegetation. Humans may further destabilize the ecosystem by manipulation of the physical environment of pastoralism, for example by deforestation to free lands for grazing, burning in order to stimulate grass growth, and by other activities such as plowing, logging, or road building. The result is a loss of plant species, extinction of animals, or erosion.[20]

The introduction of grazing animals into new environments produces what we can think of as universal baseline changes in the biological regime. Environmental transformation over and above these changes can generally be ascribed to human activity interacting with the physical characteristics of specific regions. In the New World, therefore, there was a continuum of environmental responses to the introduction of Old World domesticates that ranged from changes in the biological regime associated with feral animals to changes associated with the introduction of pastoralism in combination with other activities such as cropping, mining, logging, lime manufacture, charcoal making, road building, and so on. In the present study I use the model of ungulate irruptions first as an independent model for comparison with historical case studies of the introduction of pastoralism in order to clarify the causes of environmental degradation in a region notorious for its degraded landscape; second, to demonstrate the reasons for overgrazing and the perceptions that shaped the Spaniards' actions and the environmental and social consequences of them; and third, to show how a rapidly changing environment influences perception and choice.

[19] Caughley, "Overpopulation," p. 14.
[20] Howard, "Introduced Browsing Animals and Habitat Stability in New Zealand," pp. 425, 429; Peek, "Natural regulation," pp. 218, 219, 224; Caughley, "Overpopulation," p. 14.

Colonial Society and Environmental Change

Whereas the biological changes brought about by the introduction of Old World species into New World ecosystems are examples of universal phenomena, the social context and consequences of these changes belong to a specific historical process: the European conquest of the New World and the evolution of European colonies.

Traditional histories of the New World colonies viewed local developments as the outcome of events in Europe, each colony being shaped by its relationship with its "mother country." But research carried out over the past twenty to thirty years has uncovered complex socioeconomic systems whose center of gravity was America rather than Spain, and that have resulted in an awareness of the role played by local realities in shaping colonial regimes. As a result, our understanding of the internal development of individual colonies and their position vis-à-vis other Latin American regions, as well as to Spain, has changed enormously. Colonial Mexico, for instance, is no longer viewed primarily as a source of Spanish silver; it is also seen as the center of a large trading region that included the Caribbean and extended south to Peru and west to the Philippines. The society that emerged out of the chaos of the conquest period was diverse, healthy, remarkably stable, and expansionist to boot.

The Eurocentric, essentially imperialist approach of the traditional histories is not yet dead, however – it lives on in new and more sophisticated guises. One of these "new" explanations is modern world-system theory.[21] In this approach the colonies are no longer seen as discrete units; rather, they are grouped together in the periphery of an evolving world system. Instead of being shaped by a specific relationship with their metropolis, the individual colonies are thought to have been shaped by their relationship with the center of the world system, Europe, for the greater part of the history of this system. The basic premise of modern world-system theory is that an international system of unequal exchange exists whereby the natural resources and labor force of the peripheral nations are exploited for the benefit of the center. Theorists argue that this system of unequal exchange, and the underlying distinction between the center and the periphery, is a distinguishing characteristic of the modern world system dating from its inception in the early modern era. The study of

---

[21] See Immanual Wallerstein, *The Modern World-System: Capitalist Agriculture and the Origins of the European World-Economy in the Sixteenth Century*, and *The Modern World-System II: Mercantilism and the Consolidation of the European World-Economy.*

local processes involved in the development of the political economies of both Europe and the New World during the sixteenth century is therefore crucial for development of realistic models of the growth of the modern world system. To date, however, lack of attention to local processes in the New World in the formative sixteenth century has led students of the modern world system to produce simplistic models of the colonial political economies. The imposition of an export-oriented extractive economy as an immediate result of conquest and settlement is seen to have been accompanied by exploitative systems of production which, from the first, characterized the New World societies.[22]

By contrast, the debate within Latin American historical circles over the dominant mode of production during the colonial era – whether it was capitalist, feudal, or something new and different – has hinged on the relative importance of local versus external realities for the development of colonial relations of production. As evidence has mounted regarding the role played by colonial realities in shaping systems of production, belief in the necessary preeminence of external factors and a developmental process that apes the European has waned;[23] indeed, when local processes are examined in detail, the distinction between the social organization of production in the center and the periphery becomes less clear. By analyzing developments in the New World as action taken in response to local realities as well as reaction to external stimuli, historians have replaced the essentially passive concept of adaptation with the idea that the inhabitants of the New World colonies were actors in their own history – that they controlled to a great extent the context within which they made choices, planned, and put their plans into action.[24] What, then, of the

---

[22] Wallerstein agrees that "each actor opting for a given alternative in fact alters the framework of the whole," but places the emphasis for effective change on the European-centered context, arguing that "the alternatives available to each unit are constrained by the framework of the whole"; cited in Schwartz, "Indian Labor and New World Plantations," p. 43.

[23] For example, Schwartz writes that "colonial slavery had emerged as the dominant mode of production [in Northeastern Brazil], and the process of its emergence was not dictated by the market so much as by the organization of production. The system of labor and nature of the labor force was determined not only in the court at Lisbon or in the counting houses of Amsterdam and London but in the forests and canefields of America." "Indian Labor and New World Plantations," p. 79.

[24] This does not mean that historians of Latin America deny the presence of a world system, nor its importance for the formation of New World societies and economies. There are, however, problems with seeing it as *the* motor for change and development in the New World. Stern, for example, writes that "the emerging world-system

biological changes that so transformed the New World context? What price knowledge of the land, or of animal husbandry, if the environment changes unpredictably – that is, if the context within which knowledge is applied is transformed?

Neither the Spaniards nor the Indians were prisoners of history, but their initiatives often had unexpected results, and the new societies that evolved as a result of the Spanish conquest and settlement of the New World were, to a remarkable degree, shaped by the unplanned, the unexpected, and the unwanted consequences of the European presence. That events were unpredictable should not be surprising; this was, after all, a new world to the Spaniards, and the Spaniards themselves were alien to the indigenous populations. Our own experience with a rapidly changing physical environment clearly demonstrates that the Spaniards could neither accurately assess the nature of the New World resources nor predict the outcome of adding new species. Our understanding of the process by which herbivores expand into new ecosystems, for example, is recent, as is a great deal of our understanding of the relationship between human societies and their environment. And yet, with the exception of the epidemics and the resulting demographic collapse, and in spite of the fact that the natural resource base is a crucial variable in analyses of regional development, environmental change is rarely taken into consideration as a factor in decision making, nor is it treated as an active variable in the evolution of colonial society – probably because the environment is not seen to change.[25]

As we have already noted, however, the environment *did* change. In some cases the environment was degraded and the productivity of the land destroyed – thus radically changing the natural resource base and forcing further choices. In the case we will be considering, the

remains important as a concept explaining America's subjugation to mercantile exploitation. But its power to reduce the periphery to a functionally optimal role serving the core of international capitalism proves more contingent – more constrained, buffeted, and driven by the force of independent causal "motors" and by internal contradictions – than is suggested by Wallerstein's theoretical framework." "Feudalism, Capitalism and the World-System," p. 857.

Stern provides an invaluable history of the development by Latin American intellectuals of dependency theory (which predates the world-system model and provides its inspiration) and its spread to other regions, including Africa and the United States. He also discusses the reasons for the lack of interest on the part of the Latin Americans in world-system theory.

[25] There are of course exceptions to this statement; see Chapter 6, note 3, for an indication of some of the historians of Mexico who have taken the changing environment into consideration in their analyses.

productivity of the indigenous modes of resource exploitation masked the fragility of the ecosystems, leading the Spaniards to make choices based on production levels current at the time of the conquest rather than on the capacity of the land to support new and different regimes. As a result of their initiatives, the natural resource base for both indigenous agriculture and the introduced modes of land use deteriorated rapidly, forcing the development of extensively grazed latifundia rather than the smaller, more intensively worked holdings found in other regions of apparently rich resources. That is, changing New World realities constrained the Spaniards' choices, if not their expectations.

That the Spaniards could not accurately assess the nature of the New World resources or predict the outcome of modifying them, and the possibility that their initiatives had destructive consequences, calls into question the idea that the Spaniards maximized the resources of the New World *as they found them.* Ignorance of the New World conditions and inappropriate strategies could and, as we will see, did bring about totally unexpected changes in the natural resource base, thus changing the context of choice. The invasion of Old World species put in motion a vast number of changes that were augmented and complicated by the settlement process. Only when the processes of rapid change had run their course, and when the Spaniards had gained knowledge and understanding of the nature of the environment, were they sufficiently in control to be able to develop the best means possible to exploit the riches of this new land.

A Case Study of the Biological Conquest

In the pages that follow we will examine the environmental and social consequences of the European entrance into a region of highland central Mexico, the Valle del Mezquital. The invasion of this region brought about an ecological revolution – that is, an abrupt and qualitative break with the processes of environmental and social change that had developed in situ.[26] During the second half of the sixteenth

---

[26] The idea of an ecological revolution is taken from Carolyn Merchant's paper, "The Theoretical Structure of Ecological Revolutions." Merchant writes that "ecological revolutions are major transformations in human relations with non-human nature. They arise from changes, tensions, and contradictions that develop between a society's mode of production and its ecology, and between its modes of production and reproduction. Those dynamics in turn support the acceptance of new forms of consciousness, ideas, images, and worldview." In the case of New England, the colonial ecological revolution in the seventeenth century "resulted in the collapse of

century the relationships between humans and the physical environment of the Valle del Mezquital were completely changed: intensive irrigation agriculture shifted to extensive pastoralism; the region was transformed from a complex and densely populated agricultural mosaic into a sparsely populated mesquite desert; and the indigenous populations were economically marginalized while land and regional production passed into the hands of large landowners who were socially (if not always ethnically) Spanish. The processes of transformation, and the evolution of the colonial regime, meant the conquest and domination of the indigenous societies and their physical world;[27] it is this dual process of conquest and colonization, of transformation/ formation and the consequences for the future development of the region, that concern us here.

The narrative moves from the relationship between the landscapes of the Valle del Mezquital and the populations that shaped them, to the processes of environmental change that underlay the shift from a human-centered landscape to an animal-centered landscape, and finally to a discussion of the role of environmental change in the Spanish takeover of the means of production, the marginalization of the indigenous communities, and the formation of the colonial re-

indigenous Indian ecologies and the incorporation of a European ecological complex of animals, plants, pathogens, and people. It was legitimated by a set of symbols that placed cultured Europeans above wild nature, other animals, and 'beastlike savages.' It substituted a visual for an oral consciousness and an image of nature as female and subservient to a transcendent male God for an animistic fabric of symbolic exchanges between people and nature." Merchant, "Theoretical Structure," pp. 365–6.

There is no doubt that the indigenous peoples of New Spain manipulated their world, and in so doing set in motion processes of environmental and social change that continued through the colonial era. Equally, it is clear that the arrival of the Europeans and their portmanteau biota initiated a new dynamic. The addition of pastoralism, for example, meant not only the addition of new species of herbivores that transformed the biological regime, it also required the addition of a new form of land management and social organization of production to those already in place. Because each type of animal (cattle, sheep, pigs, horses, and goats) requires a different regime (both biological and management), the changes associated with their introduction were wide ranging and complex. If we also consider the political, social, and economic consequences of the demographic collapse, we see that the addition of only two groups of Old World species brought about an environmental revolution in the sense proposed by Merchant.

[27]   Richard Salvucci makes the same point in his discussion of the ways in which Spanish *obraje* owners obtained labor in *Textiles and Capitalism*, p. 98; as do James Lockhard and Stuart Schwartz in their study of Ibero-America, *Early Latin America*, p. 86.

gime. I have used several approaches: descriptive, narrative, and comparative history, as well as simple quantitative analyses. In Chapter 2, I attempt to reconstruct the environment of the Valle del Mezquital at contact and its transformation over the course of the sixteenth century. The chapter begins with a discussion of the related problems of regional definition and formation; it goes on to examine the environmental changes brought about by epidemic disease and the irruption of Old World domesticates, and to discuss the consequences for future development. The Valle del Mezquital is interesting because what we are studying, in effect, is the evolution of an archetypical landscape that mystifies the nature of the environment of the region, making it seem as if regional underdevelopment is caused by inherent barrenness. In Chapter 3 the nineteenth-century history of the highlands and tablelands of New South Wales is used as a case study of the environmental consequences of the introduction of pastoralism into new ecosystems. In Chapter 4 we examine the environmental processes that underlay the degradation of the environment of the Valle del Mezquital and "fixed" the ecological revolution, making a return to prior modes of resource exploitation and production impossible and prejudicing future development. The environmental transformation of each such sub-area of the Valle del Mezquital is examined in detail, and the relationship between pastoralism and environmental degradation in this region is clarified. In Chapters 5 and 6 I demonstrate the socioeconomic consequences of the ecological revolution and associated changes in the mode of production: in Chapter 5 we follow the process of Spanish land takeover, and in Chapter 6 the evolution of the classic colonial system of production – the hacienda. We see how the changes put in motion by this invasion disabled indigenous resistance and aided the Spaniards in their domination of the region by restricting indigenous control and use of the land, thus allowing the Spaniards to dominate politically and economically even where they did not dominate biologically.

These analyses are developed within certain constraints. Although it is true that the long-term consequences of initiatives taken in the sixteenth century are still being played out today, the study ends in 1600. The expansion of intensive pastoralism (specifically sheep grazing) in the Valle del Mezquital was a major variable in the transformation of the environment. But intensive pastoralism had a very short life in this region. By the late 1570s it was on the wane, and by 1600 regional production was dominated by extensive pastoralism. Whereas continued grazing meant that the land could not recover, the major damage had already been done by the end of the sixteenth century.

Thus both cause (intensive pastoralism) and effect (rapid and profound environmental degradation) had played themselves out by then.

This study is primarily concerned with processes that occurred within the boundaries of the Valle del Mezquital. The processes underlying the transformation of this region did not occur in isolation, but were initiated by the Spanish conquest – the external influence par excellence – and they occurred within the context of the developing political economy of New Spain and were thus subject to continual external influence.[28] I argue, however, that once the train of events initiated by the introduction of Old World grazing animals into the fragile, semiarid ecology of this region was underway, the end result – the development of an archetypically barren region – had very little to do with external developments.

Finally, humans, although they are seen as the initiators of change, take a back seat to the environment in this study. Whereas the evidence of environmental change is described in detail, social change, that is, the development of colonial organization of production, is simply outlined. This is not due to any philosophical bias on my part toward the environment, but quite simply because this sort of study takes time, and the detailed history of human society in the region remains to be written.

[28] In this case external refers to the extraregional context, that is the regions that make up New Spain, as well as the international context that includes the colonies of the Spanish Empire, Spain itself, and the international market.

2
ALIEN LANDSCAPES

Sometime in the late seventeenth century the lands lying to the north of the Valley of Mexico received the sobriquet "el Valle del Mezquital," or simply "el Mezquital," the valley or place where mesquite grows. The Valle del Mezquital was an almost mythologically poor place renowned for its aridity, for the poverty of its indigenous inhabitants, and for exploitation by large landowners; it became the archetype of the barren regions of Mexico. Despite its notoriety, however, the Valle del Mezquital remained an ill-defined area that did not exhibit the characteristics of a region. It was not a specific administrative or a political unit, it was not associated with a clearly defined economic or agricultural system, and it was not even clearly associated with a specific geographic area. Although centered on the Tula River Valley, its boundaries could be expanded to include distinct regions such as the Tulancingo Valley to the east and Meztitlan to the north. It was not until the twentieth century that the Valle del Mezquital came to refer to a specific region.[1]

---

[1] "[A region may be] a geographical space with boundaries determined by the effective reach of some kind of system whose parts interact more with each other than with outside systems." Van Young, *Hacienda and Market*, pp. 3–4.

According to current folk definition, the Valle del Mezquital includes Pachuca, sometimes Tulancingo, and at times the whole of the State of Hidalgo. The map of the State of Hidalgo produced by the state tourist agency centers the Valle del Mezquital in Huichiapan. Researchers have adopted an equally wide range of definitions: the biologists Lauro González Quintero and Signoret Poillon limited the region to the valley of the River Tula for their studies of the flora of the region; for the historian Miguel Orthón de Mendizábal and the geologist Blazquez, the region coincided with the entire drainage basin of the Tula River; Canabal and Martínez Assad incorporated the pre-Hispanic provinces of Xilotepec and Teotlalpan in the region; while recently the archaeologist Jeffrey Parsons has adopted the extended version that includes the whole of the State of Hidalgo; González Quintero, "Tipos de Vegetación"; Poillon, "Datos sobre Algunas Caracteristicas Ecologicas del Mezquite," p. 78; Mendizábal, *Obras Completas*, vol. 6, pp. 36, 40–3, 80; Blazquez, "Hidrogeología"; Canabal and Martínez Assad, *Explotación;* Parsons and Parsons, *Maguey Utilization*, see map, p. 8.

In 1900 the floodwaters that had regularly inundated Mexico City were channeled north and fed into the Tula River and its tributaries, the Salado and Tepexi rivers. In the 1930s an irrigation district was created that used these waters, together with the waste from Mexico City, to irrigate lands in the Tula River Valley. As the effluent from Mexico City increased in volume the irrigation district grew in extent and importance; in time the Valle del Mezquital became more than a convenient place to get rid of the city's waste and is now a major producer of vegetables for the Mexico City market. As the importance of these lands as a source of agricultural products (and profits) grew, the protection of local rights of access to water and land became an urgent issue. Organizations were formed to protect the interests of the inhabitants of the Valle del Mezquital – a region clearly determined by the lands encompassed by the current irrigation system or its future extension.[2]

The modern region represents an extraordinary reversal of the image presented by the barren landscape traditionally associated with the Valle del Mezquital. The irrigated lands are no longer barren. They are no longer exploited extensively for grazing or the cultivation of the maguey for production of the quintessentially Mexican drink, pulque, or for rope; rather, they are intensively exploited and highly productive. The Valle del Mezquital nevertheless remains in the popular imagination as a barren place,[3] and this image coexists with the

---

[2] The Tula River has captured the San Juan del Río River and together they form the upper drainage basin of the Moctezuma River. Tamayo, "Hydrography," p. 91. The overarching administrative unit is known as the Patrimonio Indígena del Valle del Mezquital (PIVM), and includes Meztitlan to the north; Medina and Quesada, *Panorama de los Otomíes*, p. 39.

[3] This image of the Valle del Mezquital is still so widely disseminated in Mexican culture that it is used in newspaper cartoons exposing exploitation and imperialism. In a cartoon entitled "Marginación IV," for example, a vulture perches on a rock that bears the words "mezquital valley"; it watches while starving peasants struggle to free themselves from the earth so that they can celebrate the "grito de Dolores," the anniversary of the call to arms that initiated the independence movement in 1810. A smaller rock bears the words "año de Hidalgo". (Vázquez Lira, *Unomásuno*, Mexico City, 15 September 1981.) In this cartoon, marginalization and exploitation are symbolized by reference to the Valle del Mezquital, the starving peasants, and by the vulture – possibly the Mexican eagle, symbol of the Mexican State, as seen from the peasants' point of view. External U.S. domination is indicated by writing the name of the region in English; and present dependence is contrasted with past independence by placing the action in the context of the independence celebrations.

Research by scholars from a wide variety of disciplines has generally served to confirm the popular image. An entire volume of Miguel Orthón de Mendizábal's collected works, published in 1946–7, was devoted to the Valle del Mezquital. This

very different, almost lush, landscape of the modern region, inform-ing and shaping policy and land use. (It is an indication of the power of the image of the Valle del Mezquital as a poor, unproductive place that untreated waste could be thought to improve it.)[4] Indeed, the extraordinary productivity of the irrigated soils *do* seem to indicate that the waste waters of Mexico City have made this region fertile – that modern technology has improved a poor indigenous landscape.[5]

A closer look at the history of the Valle del Mezquital challenges this interpretation. First, far from being the original indigenous land-scape of the region, the archetypical barren landscape is relatively recent; in the last quarter of the sixteenth century it replaced a densely populated and complex agricultural mosaic that was in place when the Spaniards arrived. Second, there is a crucial difference between the water regimes of the modern irrigated landscape and the one the

comprehensive and detailed history by an eminent Mexican scholar ranges from the preconquest era to the 1940s, and, because the author understood that the natural resources of the region were inherently poor, has done much to provide a historical basis for the region's image. In the 1960s and 1970s this region was studied by a large interdisciplinary group of social scientists under the auspices of the Patrimonio Indígena del Valle del Mezquital, the Instituto de Investigaciones Sociales, the Instituto de Investigaciones Económicas, and the Instituto de Investigaciones Históricos (which included a group of anthropologists) as the prime example of the socially, economically, and politically disadvantaged regions of Mexico; see, for example, Medina and Quesada, "Panorama de los Otomíes"; and Canabal and Martínez Assad, *Explotación y Dominio en el Mezquital*. More recently, a congress of social scientists and historians met to discuss the disadvantaged situation of the Otomí Indians; Congreso Sobre la Situación Otomí, Pachuca, Hidalgo, October, 1987.

[4] The ambivalent attitude of the Mexicans toward the use of Mexico City's waste to irrigate the Valle del Mezquital is evident in the title of an article by Anselmo Estrada Albuquerque: "Valle del Mezquital: las aguas negras matan la fauna y dan vida agrícola" ("Valle del Mezquital: The Black Waters Kill Animals and Give Life to Agriculture") in *Unomásuno*, Mexico City, 15 August 1983, p. 22. But on the whole, irrigation of the Valle del Mezquital with Mexico City's effluent was generally perceived as progress, as improvement of a barren region, until the past decade. Environmen-talists now query the suitability of irrigating with untreated human and chemical waste. It is interesting to note, however, that the concern is with the health of the consumers, not with the possibility that these chemicals might impoverish the soils of the Valle del Mezquital; indeed, the Valley is seen as a vast treatment plant for Mexico City's waste. For more recent commentary on the use of Mexico City's waste in the Valley, see Matilde Pérez Urbe, "Rechazan suspender el uso de aguas negras en Hidalgo," *La Jornada* (Mexico City) 23 September 1991, pp. 1, 14; and "Se reducirá el uso de aguas negras en el Mezquital: CNA," ibid. 24 September 1991, pp. 1, 16.

[5] See Finkler, "A Comparative Study," who noted that there had been a ninefold increase in productivity in some areas: from 535 kg of maize per hectare of nonir-rigated land to 4,828.91 kg of maize per hectare of land irrigated with untreated sewage; p. 105

Spaniards encountered. Sufficient water was generated within the region up to the middle of the sixteenth century to supply extensive systems of irrigation. By contrast, in the twentieth century insufficient water is generated within the region to supply more than a very limited irrigation system, and the region is dependent on the "black waters" imported from the Valley of Mexico. That is, the barren landscape reflected a process of desertification that occurred after the arrival of the Europeans. The region is not inherently poor, as the extraordinary fertility of the soils clearly demonstrates; and the current practice of importing water is a technological "fix" that does nothing to correct the underlying problems.

The archetype of a barren Valle del Mezquital has mystified the nature of this region and the history of its inhabitants, the Otomí. It has masqueraded as the indigenous landscape when in reality it was as alien to the indigenes as it was to the Spaniards. It was, in fact, a conquest landscape. By exploring the development of this landscape, we will understand something of the way in which the ecological revolution associated with the European invasion served to conquer the indigenous communities by changing their world.

Regional Boundaries and Internal Divisions

The Valle del Mezquital is defined for the purposes of this study as encompassing the catchment area of the Tula and Moctezuma rivers, that is, the present irrigation system and its planned extension, and falls within the coordinates longitude 98°45′–104°W and latitude 19°35′–20°55′N; the total surface area is approximately 10,139 square kilometers. The modern municipalities lying within this broad geographic region have been used to calculate the final definition and extent of the region.[6] (See Map 2:1.)

Although the Valle del Mezquital does not seem to have been perceived as a distinct entity until the formation of the modern irrigation

---

[6] I have followed the noted historian of the region, Miguel Orthón de Mendizabal, and included the drainage basin of the Moctezuma River and thus the colonial province of Xilotepec, since the political and sentimental affiliations and location of this province have been intimately associated with the province of Tula, both prior to the conquest and after. The surface area was obtained from the 1970 censuses published by the Secretaría de Indústria y Comércio, Dirección General de Estadística, IX Censo General de Población, 1970, (Mexico City, 1971). The modern municipalities appear to coincide fairly well with the colonial *cabeceras*. See also Johnson, "Do As the Land Bids," p. 238.

system,[7] geopolitics and history prefigured the modern region in several ways. It is roughly bounded on three sides by high mountains: the Sierra de Pachuca to the east, the Sierra de Juárez to the north and, to the south, the mountain range separating Xilotepec from Toluca together with the Sierra de las Cruces. In the past these mountain ranges prevented easy communication with the neighboring regions of Tulancingo, Meztitlan, and Toluca, allowing the formation of regions with distinctive political orientations and economic systems. Indeed, where there are no such obvious barriers as high mountain ranges, the role of history and the development of neighboring regions were as important as internal developments in defining regional boundaries. For example, the division between the Bajío and the Valle del Mezquital – the two regions that are symbolic of the rich and the poor regions of Mexico – were prefigured by several events in the 1550s that involved developments in geopolitical jurisdictions, administration, *encomienda* tenure, the ethnic composition of the inhabitants, and land use.

At contact the lands encompassed by the Valle del Mezquital and the eastern half of the Bajío were divided among thirty-two Otomí provinces all paying tribute to the Triple Alliance centered in Tenochtitlán (Mexico City) in the Valley of Mexico.[8] After the conquest of Tenochtitlán in 1521 the Spanish state replaced the Triple Alliance and the indigenous provincial (possibly state) level of organization disappeared. Although a middle organizational level between the Spanish state and the local populations – the *Alcaldía Mayor* – replaced the provincial level in theory, in practice the *cabeceras*, or head towns, developed into the more important locus of Spanish control of the countryside in the colonial era. The *cabeceras* were the basis on which the Spaniards organized Indian tribute and labor for their own use; the *cabeceras*, in turn, drew on their subject villages in order to meet the tribute and labor quotas imposed by the *encomenderos* (the recipients of Indian tribute and labor) or the crown.

The redefinition by the Spaniards of pre-Columbian geopolitical units effected shifts in their political orientation and reinforced internal trends toward regional differentiation. The political jurisdictions of the colonial *cabeceras* and villages in this region corresponded

---

[7] The southeastern quarter of the Valle del Mezquital (the southeastern sector of the North–South Plain, the Southern Plain, the Central Valley and the Northern Valley) encompassed the prehispanic region known as the Teotlalpan; but this name was not much used in the colonial era.

[8] Gerhard, *Guide*, pp. 44, 154–5, 295–7, 332–3, 383–4; Canabal and Martínez Assad, *Explotación*, chapter 1.

to the preconquest divisions and hierarchies, and in most cases the geographic limits of the colonial towns coincided with the preconquest boundaries as well.[9] The major exception to this rule in the Valle del Mezquital concerns the jurisdiction of the province of Xilotepec. During the first three decades of the colonial era the jurisdiction of Xilotepec extended as far north as Queretaro, although the bulk of the population appears to have been centered in the south. In 1524 the Xilotepec province was given in *encomienda* to four men, but it was almost immediately reassigned to Juan Jaramillo, husband of Marina, Cortes's interpreter.[10] By 1552 this huge *encomienda* had been divided between Jaramillo's widow (his second wife Beatriz de Andrada) and his daughter (Maria Jaramillo, daughter of Marina). Beatriz de Andrada retained the half known from then on as the "Xilotepec half" while Maria Jaramillo kept the "Queretaro half."[11] The northwestern boundary of the *cabecera* of Xilotepec was moved south to lie in the hills east of San Juan del Río, along the future boundary between the Bajío and the Valle del Mezquital.

The distinction between the two regions was further reinforced by two events that resulted in differences in land use: the movement south of the nomadic Indians, the Chichimecs, and the expulsion of cattle out of the Valle del Mezquital to the northern plains. In 1521 the Otomí provinces formed a densely settled border region lying between the agricultural populations of the Valley of Mexico and the hunters and gatherers of the north, the Chichimecs. Spanish conquest and settlement upset the balance of power between the nomadic and sedentary populations, and following the opening of the northern silver mines in Zacatecas in 1546 the war between the Spaniards and the Chichimecs began. The long route to the north became a battleground as the Chichimecs pushed down closer to the Valley of Mexico to plunder the mule trains moving between Mexico City and Zacatecas.[12] The northern half of the Valle del Mezquital, along with Cimapan on its northern border, became known as the *tierra de guerra*

---

[9] The great number of court cases between villages and towns over the correct placing of boundary markers clearly indicates a precise conception of the geographic jurisdictions of the municipalities. But in spite of the continuity between the pre- and postconquest jurisdictions at the level of the *cabeceras* (indeed it can be argued that they have lasted to the present day), the *cabeceras* were not perceived by the Spaniards (nor by the Indians, apparently) as forming part of a distinct region in the sixteenth century.

[10] AGIJ, leg. 129, no. 5; leg. 148, no. 1; leg. 168.

[11] AGIJ, leg. 168. Gerhard, *Guide*, pp. 383–4.

[12] Powell, *Soldiers*, p. 15.

(war zone), and Spanish settlers and Otomí fought the Chichimecs throughout the sixteenth century. The frontier between the nomadic and sedentary populations (the so-called Chichimec frontier) moved south to much the same area as the division between the Queretaro and Xilotepec halves, that is, the future northwest boundary of the Valle del Mezquital.

The southward movement of the Chichimec Indians and the formation of a frontier between the agricultural Indian communities and the nomadic bands added an element of terror and violence to social change in this region, and up to the end of the sixteenth century there was a sense of crossing a line between civilization and savagery when travelers left the relative safety of the road across the Valle del Mezquital and reached San Juan del Río, lying just to the northwest, to prepare for the long journey north.[13] But the southward migration of the Chichimecs does not seem to have greatly affected either Spanish settlement or Indian production during most of the century. When the viceroy sent the *alcalde mayor* of Actopan to see if a fort was really necessary to protect the lime workings of a Spaniard in Mizquiaguala in the North–South Plain in 1587, the tone of the order makes it clear that such defenses were not considered necessary.[14] Even the Huichiapan Plateau, which bore the brunt of the Chichimec raids and for that reason was settled by the Spanish somewhat later than the rest of the region, was a singularly productive agricultural and pastoral region nevertheless – although a Spanish farmer said that he always had his arquebus by his side in case of trouble.[15] The most obvious effect of the Chichimec raids was seen in the buildings and settlement patterns: Spanish houses were often forts, Tecozautla in the extreme northwest of the Huichiapan Plateau was a walled town, and in 1576 a group of Otomí, who had been colonists in Queretaro and now wanted to return home, suggested that by pooling the resources of several small populations to make one large village they would be able to resist the assaults of the nomads.[16] By such means the locals appear to have been able to contain the raids; the gun-toting Spaniard, for example, complained that someone stole his gun at a party – not that he needed more guns or more protection.[17] It was not deemed necessary to have soldiers in the region, and there was no presidio. In-

---

[13] AGNT, vol. 1867, exp. 1, fol. 1r. Powell, *Soldiers*, p. 31. Gerhard, *Guide*, p. 383.
[14] AGNG, vol. 3, exp. 495, fols. 232v–233r.
[15] AGIM, leg. 111, ramo 2, doc. 12, fol. 27v.
[16] AGNT, vol. 79, exp. 6, fol. 3r. AGNG, vol. 1, exp. 883, fol. 164.
[17] AGIM, leg. 111, ramo 2, doc. 12, fol. 27v.

stead, all the male inhabitants of Tecozautla on the frontier (including Indians) carried arms at all times.[18]

The number and extent of the raids increased in the last decades of the sixteenth century and early seventeenth century, however, just when the Chichimec "problem" was at last being resolved. The increase in hostilities coincided with a dramatic population decline of the indigenous populations. Towns no longer functioned as the centers of densely populated agricultural regions. Mesquite-dominated desert scrub separated and virtually isolated them and provided a haven for brigands and escaped slaves. The demographic collapse of the Indian communities may actually have prolonged the invasions by simply thinning out the defending population, thus making easier the guerrilla raids favored by the Chichimecs.[19]

The second event in the separation of the Bajío and the Valle del Mezquital, the expulsion of cattle from the densely populated central regions of New Spain during the 1550s, was carried out by order of Viceroy Velasco in an attempt to protect the Indians' agricultural lands and the Spaniards' food supply.[20] Cattle were moved from the (future) Valle del Mezquital northwest into "the Chichimecs," the southern extension of the northern plains – that is, the future Bajío. In the early colonial period, therefore, the Bajío was grazed by *ganado mayor* (cattle and horses) and was inhabited by nomadic and bellicose Indians. The Valle del Mezquital, in contrast, remained a settled region grazed by *ganado menor* (sheep, goats, and pigs).[21]

The boundary between the Valle del Mezquital and the Valley of Mexico to the south was not prefigured by events in the colonial era and remained vague until the waste waters of Mexico City were pumped into the tributaries of the Tula River, and the irrigation district serving the Valle del Mezquital was formed. This boundary now lies along the watershed between the drainage basins of the Valley of Mexico and the Tula River.

This is a large and complex region, and the data used as evidence for the processes discussed in the following chapters is extensive and varied. In order to facilitate the management of this data, and to make

---

[18] Spaniards were fined and Indians were flogged if they did not carry arms. AGNT, vol. 79, exp. 6, fol. 7r.

[19] The raids did not stop until the Spaniards moved into and colonized the northern lands, and either pacified the Chichimecs or pushed them farther north. Powell, *Soldiers*, p. 204.

[20] Chevalier, *La formación*, pp. 133–5.

[21] Dairy cattle and draught animals used for agricultural purposes were also grazed in small numbers on agricultural lands.

comparisons of the history of land use and environmental change in different parts of the region, I divided the region into sub-areas: the Southern Plain, the North–South Plain, the Central Valley, the Northern Valley (these four sub-areas compose the preconquest region known as the Teotlalpan[22]) and Ixmiquilpan, Alfaxayuca, Huichiapan, Xilotepec, Chiapa de Mota, and Tula (see Map 2:1). The divisions are based on geographic criteria: the first eight sub-areas are wide, flat plains and valleys; the Tula sub-area encompasses the headwaters of the Tula River in the foothills of the Sierra de las Cruces; and Chiapa de Mota includes the high mountain Valleys of the Sierra de las Cruces. The final geographic boundaries and extent of the sub-areas, as for the region as a whole, are taken to be coterminous with the lands under the jurisdiction of the modern municipalities located within their borders. Pueblo lands falling within the jurisdiction of a specific *cabecera*, whether in *encomienda* or *corregimiento*, were considered as subject to that *cabecera;* hence all documentation having to do with land (its ownership and use), or with *encomienda* and *corregimiento* affairs, refers to the appropriate *cabecera*. Thus it was quite a simple matter to assign documents – and therefore information about changes in land use, land tenure, and the environment etc. – to the appropriate sub-areas. The sub-areas, however, have no counterpart in political or administrative divisions and exist solely for the purposes of analysis.

Landscapes and Populations

The present-day landscape of the Valle del Mezquital exhibits extraordinary contrasts: lush, seemingly eternally green, irrigated lands contrast sharply with the sere aspect of those places where the "black waters" do not yet reach. As the irrigation water is pumped ever higher, the piedmont comes increasingly under cultivation and the green creeps up the bare, high, steep-sided hills. Even the eroded hardpan flats are being bulldozed and broken up, formed into terraces, and farmed.[23] In those places not yet part of the irrigation system, however, moonscapes of exposed hardpan, enormous gullies (carefully terraced to catch the runoff from the heavy summer rainfall),

---

[22] I have used Sherburne F. Cook's nomenclature for these sub-areas. Cook, *Historical Demography* pp. 3–4.
[23] In the twenty-four years during which I have been observing the Valle del Mezquital there has been an extraordinary extension of irrigated lands, even the ten years since I first wrote up this material has seen a vast expansion of irrigation.

Map 2.1. Geographic reference map: The Valle del Mesquital showing sub-areas and *cabeceras*

and scattered mesquite and cactus growing in stony soils, remind one
of the landscape that gave the Valle del Mezquital its name and notoriety.

This is a high, cool, arid region, part of the so-called *tierra fría*, the
cold lands. The basin of the valley (actually eight separate valleys)
slopes down to the north from 2,300 meters in the Southern Plain
and Central Valley, 2,200 meters at the outflow of the Tepexi River (a
tributary of the Tula River) from the Taxhimay Dam, and 2,650
meters in the foothills separating Xilotepec from the Toluca Valley,
to 1,700 meters in Ixmiquilpan, Tasquillo, and Tecozautla.[24] The

---

[24] Excellent maps have been distributed by the Secretaría de la Presidéncia, Comisión

region lies in the rain shadow of the Sierra Madre Oriental, and the overall picture is one of increasing aridity from south to north and east to west.[25] The highest temperatures occur just before the rainy season, which lasts from May to October (when the temperatures drop slightly); nights are always cool to cold; and in the coldest season (December to February) the area is subject to frosts (see Table 2.1). This is not an easy area to farm, and rainfall agriculture on the slopes of the Sierra de Juárez to the north come to harvest only one in every five to ten years.[26]

The geological underpinnings of this region are characteristic of the Mesa Central, or neovolcanic plateau. Basalt and andesite form the high hills and mountains, whereas conglomerates or combination layers of sedimentary and volcanic rocks underlie the lower slopes. The wide, flat plains and valleys that form the most conspicuous land forms of the region result from two different types of formation: the Southern Plain, North–South Plain, Central Valley, Northern Valley, and parts of Ixmiquilpan, as well as the Acambay Valley and the Huapango lake bed in western Xilotepec, are sites of old lake beds with alluvial soils of extraordinary depth; on the other hand, Ixmiquilpan, the Alfaxayuca Valley, and the Huichiapan and Xilotepec Plateaus are formed of basalt and andesite, with conglomerates, combination layers, sandstone, and residual soils forming isolated areas. Limestone formations in the southeast sector of the region provide raw materials for the cement industry.[27] Throughout the region the major towns, and many of the smaller ones, are sited on conglomerate rock formations near springs at the foot of basalt outcrops, and are fronted by arable lands in alluvial or residual soils. The geological siting of the towns is thus very distinctive; indeed, the towns in the Huichiapan and Xilotepec Plateaus appear in the geological maps as islands in a sea of volcanic rock.[28]

Soil erosion is a prominent feature of the landscape. A high pro-

---

de Estudios del Territorio Nacional (CETENAL) and the the Secretaría de Programación y Presupuesto, Coordinación General de Servicios Nacionales de Estadística Geográfica e Informática, Dirección General de Geografía del Territorio Nacional. Hereafter, references to maps will be cited as follows: Government maps, 1:50,000: (type of map used, i.e. Soil Use, Geology, etc.); or, Atlas 1:1,000,000: (Type of map used). Government maps, 1:50,000: Topographic.

[25] West, "The Natural Regions," p. 371.

[26] Parsons and Parsons, *Maguey Utilization*, p. 11. See also, Johnson, "Do As the Land Bids," p. 131, for Otomí reasons for planting in areas of low rainfall.

[27] West, "Surface Configuration," pp. 40–53.

[28] Government maps, 1:50,000: Geology.

Table 2.1. *Annual precipitation and average temperatures*

Sub-area	Annual Precipitation		Avg. Temperatures	
Southern Plain	East: West:	7–800mm 562mm		16.0
North–South Plain	South: Center: North:	508.8mm 508.8mm 455.5mm	South: Center:	15.2 17.4
Central Valley	 South–facing hills:	7–800mm 600mm	information not available	
Northern Valley	Southeast: Northeast: West:	6–70mm 500mm 568mm	Northeast:	16.0
Ixmiquilpan	Northeast: Southwest:	600mm 360.5mm	Southwest:	18.4
Alfaxayuca	South: North:	500.3mm 400mm	South:	17.2
Huichiapan		5–600mm	North:	19.1
Xilotepec	Central Plateau: Northwest: Southern mountains:	7–800mm 617.2mm 8–1,000mm	Plateau:	16.2
Tula	South: North: West:	7–800mm 6–600mm 5–600mm	South: North: West:	15.5 16.0 16.0
Chiapa de Mota		8–1,000mm		16.0

Avg. Temperatures = Average annual temperatures (degrees Celsius)

Sources: HMAI vol. 1, pp. 208–10. Government Maps 1:1,000,000 (Climate). Climate data was obtained from the censuses: IX Censo General de Población, 1970. Secretaría de Indústria y Çomércio, Dirección General de Estadística, México, D.F., 1971.

portion of waterborne erosion has occurred in areas where soils overlie the combination volcanic–sedimentary layers. Far more noticeable, however, is the erosion associated with unstable soils, especially in Chapantongo, western Xilotepec, and Huichiapan.[29] Rain falls in hard showers during the summer and erosion generally follows the line of

[29] See Melville, "The Pastoral Economy," Appendix C.

arroyos, which carry swift-flowing, heavy currents. High in the mountains and hills, where water begins to collect, there is practically no erosion (at least, of sufficient severity to be recorded on the government soil maps), whereas lower hillsides and undulating lands often exhibit extensive sheet erosion and gullying. Only in the center of the flat-bottomed valleys and plains, where the alluvial soils are so deep that the underlying rock is not exposed, does erosion seem absent. But when the land is prepared for planting these areas are subject to wind erosion; and in many places bottomlands are covered with waterborne slope-wash eroded off nearby hills.[30] Terracing and almost continual cropping of the irrigated lands has meant a reduction in wind and waterborne erosion; but these problems have been replaced by those associated with long-term irrigation, such as salinization.

This is primarily an agricultural region. Tourism is growing to serve the weekend exodus from Mexico City. Pemex (the national petroleum company) and cement manufacturers have refineries here, and there are nuclear power plants and cement manufacturies in the south. For the majority of the population, however, agriculture forms the basis of subsistence and trade. Peasants still take their small flocks of sheep and goats, as well as a few cattle, out daily to forage in the lush grass growing along the edges of the irrigated fields, if they are fortunate, or into the thorn-scrub and thin grasses of the piedmont and hillsides if they are less so; but this is more in the nature of insurance than the core of the subsistence base.[31] Some new towns have developed to serve modern needs, but most are based in old colonial *cabeceras*. They are generally tightly nucleated, leaving the precious agricultural lands free for cultivation, and almost all retain the grid pattern of streets around a central square that is typical of Spanish colonial town design.

How does this landscape compare with the landscape the Spaniards encountered? Perhaps the most obvious difference lies in land use. Although the land is irrigated, and modern agricultural methods are intensive, they are very different than those practiced by the indigenous populations at contact. Monoculture has replaced mixed horticulture, the plow has replaced the digging stick, pastoralism is an integral part of subsistence, and rather than being sold in the weekly markets, the produce is trucked daily to Mexico City. The landscape

---

[30] Stevens, "The Soils," pp. 265–90, 293–6. Government Maps, 1:50,000: Soils. Atlas, 1:1,000,000: Soils.

[31] I have to thank Carlos Rincón of the Geography Department at the University of Texas at Austin for this insight.

is very different as a result: the fields have straight lines to accommodate the plow; one crop is grown at a time in order to facilitate weeding and harvesting; in some places there are fences to prevent the free movement of animals; and the consumers in Mexico City determine to a great extent the type of crop grown – although in fact more indigenous crops are grown than are exotic ones.

The indigenous and modern landscapes differ in an even more crucial way, however, namely in the extent and types of forests and woodlands. Primary forest cover is now confined to the oak and pine forests in the Sierra de las Cruces and to coniferous forests in the hills to the north of Huichiapan and Alfaxayuca. The few remaining wooded hilltops in the Huichiapan area are covered with oaks (*robles*) and live oaks (*encinos*). Elsewhere there are isolated live oaks, mesquite, and Piru trees. Secondary vegetation composed of introduced grasses, thistles, thorn bushes, cacti, and the distinctive, introduced Piru has displaced the primary vegetation of the lower slopes (grass, cacti, and low trees, either thornless or only lightly armed).[32] The following quote sums up the relationship of the primary to the predominant secondary vegetation:

> Often, where there has been a long history of woodcutting and cattle or goats have grazed heavily in the past, the spaces between the occasional cacti are simply bare. The former cover of such places may be indicated by the pitiful clusters of unarmed shrubs and grasses cowering in the protective radiuses of the long-armed cacti, out of the reach of animals.[33]

Another marked difference, and one that arises out of the deforestation of the region, is in the water regime. Up to the last decades of the sixteenth century, water for extensive irrigation systems was generated within the Valle del Mezquital, and the soils were far more humid. Today the flow in the major rivers, the Tula and its tributaries (Tepexi, Coscomate, Suchitlan, and the Arroyo Rosas) and the Río Salado of Hueypostla – which joins with a tributary of the same name arising near Tequixquiac and flows north to the Tula River – is composed of Mexico City's waste. The region is not entirely without sources of internally generated water: there are the San Francisco and Tecozautla Rivers in the north west (tributaries of the Moctezuma River) and the so-called Alfaxayuca River, which is actually only an intermittent stream until it reaches Caltimacan north of Alfaxayuca.

---

[32] Wagner, "Natural Vegetation," pp. 251–2. Government maps, 1:50,000: Soil Use.
[33] Wagner, "Natural Vegetation," p. 257.

Water from springs, generally located in the areas of alluvial or residual soils at the base of conglomerate or combination sedimentary
and volcanic layers, is collected together with the runoff from the hills
in several large modern dams on the Tula River and in the Xilotepec
Plateau, and in many smaller dams scattered across the region. There
are, as well, artesian bores along the base of the mountains bounding
the south of the Xilotepec Plateau.[34] Streams no longer run all year,
however. The springs are fewer and give less water, and in areas not
served by the imported water there are no longer humid bottomlands.
The region is essentially arid.

The Otomí Landscape

When Europeans first entered these wide, flat valleys and plains they
saw a landscape that had been shaped by centuries of human occupation. It was a fertile, densely populated, and complex agricultural
mosaic composed of extensive croplands, woodlands, and native grasslands; of irrigation canals, dams, terraces, and limestone quarries.
Oak and pine forests covered the hills, and springs and streams supplied extensive irrigation systems.

For at least four hundred years before the arrival of the Spaniards,
the population that shaped this landscape was composed of Otomí
Indians.[35] Otomí speakers apparently migrated from the west following the fall of Tula in the twelfth century, and by the thirteenth
century they formed a powerful group in the north of the Valley of
Mexico. Their power declined during the fourteenth century, however, as a result of wars with Cuautitlan and the Mexica in the Valley
of Mexico, and they were dispersed to the north and east.[36] This
dispersal, Gibson writes, was so complete that "throughout the colonial
period [the Otomí] remained a diffused and subordinated people,
more densely distributed in the north than in the south, but always
lacking a fixed or integral territory."[37]

Judgments made throughout the centuries as to the capabilities and

---

[34] Government maps, 1:50,000: Topographic.
[35] There were a few communities of settled Chichimecs in the north, and here and
there a few Nahuatl speakers, but the Otomí formed the bulk of the population.
Gerhard, *Guide*, pp. 44, 155, 295, 332, 383, 401.
[36] Gibson, *Aztecs*, p. 10. A continuous sequence of ceramic types in the Tula River Basin
from the late postclassic to the colonial era indicates that the Otomí have predom-
inated here since at least the fall of Tula; Mastache and Crespo, "La Ocupación
Prehispánica," pp. 74–7.
[37] Gibson, *The Aztecs*, p. 10.

mode of life of the Otomí are part of the mythology surrounding the
Valle del Mezquital. The Aztecs seem to have despised them as mere
hunters and gatherers, as people without culture or civilization.
Cortés, seeing them from the vantage of the conquered Aztec capital,
described the Otomí as " 'mountain people' and as slaves of Tenoch-
titlan."[38] Nevertheless, an interesting indication of former Otomí importance survived into the early colonial period in the marriages
between the houses of the rulers of Tenochtitlán (the Aztec capital)
and of Tula (the former Toltec capital). Moctezuma II, the Aztec
emperor when the Spaniards arrived in 1519, was married to a daughter of the ruler of Tula. His son Don Pedro de Moctezuma also married a noblewoman of Tula,[39] and the ruler of the Otomí province of
Xilotepec at the time of the conquest was Moctezuma's cousin.[40] The
Aztecs believed that the Otomí were descended from the Toltecs, the
fabulous peoples who had dominated the highlands from the eleventh
to the thirteenth centuries and, despite their scorn for the Otomí as
conquered peoples, they needed the legitimation that marriage with
the descendants of the Toltecs conferred.

The Spaniards maintained the fiction that the Otomí were poor
mountain folk incapable of the arts of civilization, especially agriculture; it may have served them in their conquest of the hinterlands of
the Aztec Empire to do so. In fact their records indicate that they saw
something quite different. Around 1548, at the end of a disastrous
four-year epidemic, the crown ordered the completion of the first
geographic description of New Spain, the *Suma de Visitas*.[41] In accordance with the directions sent out to Spanish officials, the descriptions
of the provinces composing the Valle del Mezquital recorded the
natural resources of the region and their use by the Indian population
following the epidemic. More important for this study, however, they
also surveyed the economic potential of the region for Spanish exploitation, including the suitability of soils for wheat growing; water

---

[38] Gibson comments that the Otomí "were the only major Indian group in the Valley
possessing a separate, or non-Nahuatl, language, and Nahuatl speaking peoples
generally looked down on them"; ibid., p. 10. Throughout the sixteenth century the
Spaniards writing the geographic descriptions repeat the Aztec views on the character and intelligence, society and culture of the Otomí; see the comments in the
1579 geographic description, PNE, vol. 6.

[39] Alavarado Tezozomoc, *Crónica mexicayotl*, pp. 87–8, 135–8, 150–8; Gibson, *Aztecs*,
p. 50. I am indebted to Elizabeth Brumfiel for these citations.

[40] AGIJ, leg. 207, no. 2, ramo 3.

[41] This is known as the *Suma de Visitas* and is published in Volume 1 of *Papeles de la
Nueva España*. It will be cited hereafter as PNE vol. 1.

resources for agriculture, pastoralism, and milling operations; the presence (or absence) of precious metals; the availability of forest resources for mining and lime production; the extent and value of grasslands for grazing; and other resources such as quarries for limestone and building stone.[42] The Spaniards' categorization of lands in the Valle del Mezquital in 1548 provides a key to their perception of the natural resources and an idea of which were, in their view, of importance. For example, in the early decades mining obviously took precedence in the Spanish mind, and wooded areas (necessary to provide struts and beams, etc., for mine shafts) are generally mentioned in connection with potential mining operations, thus falling within the category of *tierras realengas* (royal or unappropriated lands),[43] rather than *tierras baldias* (vacant or public lands). The *tierras baldias*, on the other hand, were mentioned separately, and often in terms of their extent and suitability for grazing.[44]

The major obstacles to Spanish settlement of the Valle del Mezquital in the early decades were the frosts, the infrequent rainfall and, most especially, the dense Indian population.[45] Even though epidemics had caused a dramatic drop in the indigenous population by 1548, well-populated villages still covered the landscape. Some communities ordered their houses by streets and were approved of by the Spanish as following their renaissance ideal of the proper urban form. The inhabitants of other communities, perhaps the majority, were scattered across the lands of the municipality to be near their agricultural fields, and were looked on with disfavor.[46] In the densely settled

---

[42] PNE vol. 1, nos. 1, 2, 8, 9, 10, 106, 110, 111, 112, 235, 258, 293, 347, 397, 417, 498, 533, 534, 538, 546, 547, 548, 549, 550, 554, 555, 556, 771, 781, 838.

[43] PNE vol. 1, nos. 112, 548, 549, 550: the quote generally reads "no tienen montes ni minas."

[44] PNE vol. 1, nos. 533, 534. But in no. 347 woodlands and grasslands are mentioned together when talking of their scarcity (tiene pocos montes y pocos pastos); and in no. 550 the lack of mines and grazing lands is mentioned together with the lack of public lands (no tiene montes ni pastos ni tierras baldias).

[45] PNE vol. 1, nos. 1, 2, 8, 110, 235, 258, 293, 347, 533, 534, 546, 547, 548, 549, 550, 781. PNE vol. 3 pp. 68–9, 72.

[46] PNE vol. 1, no. 538; PNE vol. 3 p. 82; PNE vol. 6, p. 27, 32, 202. The following quote from the 1580 Relación de Atitalaquia demonstrates very well the Spanish attitude to scattered settlement patterns, and the reasons for them: "Estan poblados el dia de oy en poblaçones juntas, por dispusiçion del muy excelentisimo señor Don Martyn Enriquezz, bissorey desta Nueva España, avnque algunos yndios, como a urta cordel, se buelben a la antigua costumbre que tenian de bibir apartados vnos de otros, en choçuelas pajizos y en quebradas y en llanos, especialmente si para ello les ayuda la comodidad de magueyes que tienen a do se determinar de yr a uivir,

flatlands of the southeastern quarter of the region, the houses were almost contiguous.[47] Indian agricultural production in these provinces focused on the classic Mesoamerican triad of maize, beans, and squash, together with chilies, tomatoes, beans, amaranth, sage, and others. Local variations depended on the local flora and fauna, the microclimate, and the presence or absence of water for irrigation (or dependable rainfall). The Spaniards noted excellent soils, and the southern half of the region was famed as a productive agricultural area both before and immediately after the conquest.[48] As the Indians stated in court on various occasions, however, irrigation was necessary to secure harvests in this semiarid region.[49] Indeed, archaeological surveys of the Tula region and the northern end of the Valley of Mexico, as well as the documentary records, show extensive irrigation systems.[50]

The only large towns without at least some irrigated plots were five of the hillside *cabeceras:* Tlapanaloya, Tezcatepec, and Tuzantlalpa (Southern Plain), Tepetitlan and Sayula (Tula); and two located in the dry Northern Valley, Tecpatepec and Yetecomac.[51] The partic-

---

lo qual es enconbiniente digno de rremediar por algunas razones, espeçialmente por lo que toca la doctrina suya." PNE vol. 6, p. 202.

[47] Gerhard, *Guide,* p. 295, writes of the Alcaldia of Tetepango-Hueypustla that "there was an extraordinarily dense population at contact in this bleak countryside: settlements were practically contiguous, with houses everywhere." An investigation carried out in 1564 of the towns granted in *encomienda* to a son of Moctezuma shows that there was hardly any land between the towns in the Tula area, AGIJ, leg. 207 no. 2, ramo 3.

[48] PNE vol. 1, nos. 2, 111, 112, 347, 533, 538, 546, 548, 554, 555, 771, 781, 838. Cook, *Historical Demography,* pp. 38–41. Mendizábal, *Obras,* pp. 42–4.

[49] AGNT, vol. 3, exp. 1; vol. 64, exp. 1; vol. 79, exp. 6, fol. 11r; vol. 1486, exp. 8, fol. 17r; vol. 1487, exp. 1, fol. 15r; vol. 1693, exp. 2, fol. 42r. AGNM, vol. 5, fol. 122; AGIJ, leg. 207, no. 2, ramo 3. AGIE, leg. 161-C, fol. 250.

[50] Mastache, "Sistemas de riego." Sanders, Parsons, and Santley, *Basin of Mexico,* pp. 260–72.

[51] *Cabeceras with irrigation:*

Southern Plain: Tequixquiac, Apasco: PNE vol. 1, nos. 2, 533. AGIE, leg. 161-C, fol. 110v.

North–South Plain: Atitalaquia, Atotonilco, Chilcuautla, Mizquiaguala, Tezcatepec, Tlacotlapilco, Tlahuelilpa, Tlamaco: PNE vol. 1, nos. 1, 9, 112, 550, 555, 556. PNE vol. 6, pp. 200–1. AGIE, leg. 161-C. AGNM, vol. 2, exp. 622, fols. 246v–248r; vol. 16, fols. 106r–107r. AGNT, vol. 1519, exp. 4, fol. 145r; vol. 1628, exp. 3, fol. 4v; vol. 1640, exp. 2, fols. 25v, 33r; vol. 2717, exp. 10, fols. 6r–v; vol. 2720, exp. 18, 1r–7v.

Central Valley: Axacuba, Tlilcuautla, Tornacustla: PNE vol. 1, no. 8, PNE vol. 6, p. 17. AGNT, vol. 64, exp. 1, fols. 1–20.

Northern Valley: Tecaxique, Actopan: AGNT, vol. 1693, exp. 2, fol. 42.

Ixmiquilpan: Ixmiquilpan, Tlacintla: PNE vol. 1, no. 293. AGNT, vol. 1487, exp.

ularly dry regions bordering the northern section of the Tula River in Tlacotlapilco, Chilcuautla, and Ixmiquilpan were said to be suitable for "everything that can be irrigated"; Cotton and chilis are specifically mentioned (cotton was also grown in Xilotepec).[52] In areas without water for irrigation, subsistence was based on plant species typical of arid regions: maguey, nopal cactus, and mesquite, together with a striking number of wild animals, birds, reptiles, and grubs.[53] But it is

1, fol. 7r. AGNM, vol. 7, fols. 192r–193r.
Alfaxayuca: Alfaxayuca: AGIM, leg. 111, ramo 2, doc. 12.
Huichiapan: Huichiapan, Tecozautla, S. José Atlan: AGIM leg. 111, ramo 2, doc. 12. AGNT, vol. 3, exp. 1, fols. 1–8; vol. 3, exp. 2, fols. 1r–v, 10r; vol. 79, exp. 6, fols. 1–27; vol. 1867, exp. 1, fols. 2v, 4v.
Xilotepec: Xilotepec: AGNM, vol. 19, fols. 239r–v. AGIJ leg. 124, no. 1, fol. 19.
Tula: Atengo, Chapantongo, Nextlalpan, Otlazpa, Suchitlan, Tepexi, Tula, Zayanaquilpa, Xipacoya: PNE vol. 1, nos. 10, 106, 110, 417, 498, 538, 771, 781, 838. PNE vol. 6, p. 181. AGNM, vol. 2, exp. 347, fols. 141v–142r; vol. 5, fol. 122r; vol. 9, fols. 132v–133r; AGNT, vol. 45, exp. 1, fol. 10r; vol. 1486, exp. 8; vol. 1527, exp. 2, fol. 53v; vol. 2284, exp. 1, fols. 743r–744r; vol. 2337, exp. 1, fol. 395; vol. 2812, exp. 13, fols. 402v–410; vol. 3517, exp. 1, fol. 5r. AGNH vol. 410, fol. 77r–8or.
Chiapa de Mota: Chiapa de Mota: PNE vol. 1, no. 111.
Sources that refer to *acequias* (irrigation canals) and *canales* (canals) but not specifically to irrigation are:
Ixmiquilpan: AGN, Indios, vol. 6, pte. 1 exp. 291, fols. 79r–v; vol. 6, pte. 2, exp. 532, fol. 117r. AGNM, vol. 7, fols. 192v–193r.
Tula: Otlazpa, Tula, Xipacoya, Zayanaquilpa: AGIJ leg. 207, no. 2, ramo 3, fol. 55r. AGNT, vol. 45, exp. 1, fol. 10r; vol. 1529, exp. 1, fol 124. AGNM, vol. 2, exp, 347, fols. 141v–142r; vol. 11, fol. 64r.
North–South Plain: Atitalaquia, Mizquiaguala, Tlahuelilpa, Tlacotlapilco: PNE vol. 1, no. 550. PNE vol. 6, p. 201. AGNT, vol. 1520, exp. 5, fol. 49v; vol. 1628, exp. 3, fol. 14v; vol. 2720, exp. 18, fols. 1r–7v. AGNM, vol. 2, exp. 622, fols. 246v–248r.
Huichiapan: Huichiapan, Tecozautla: AGNT, vol. 3, exp. 2, fols. 1–10; vol. 3672, exp. 19, fol. 6r. AGNM, vol. 19, fols. 239r–v.
Chiapa de Mota: AGNM, vol. 20, fols. 78r–79r.
52 PNE vol. 1, no. 550. AGIJ, leg. 124 #1.

53 Animals	Birds	Reptiles & insects
adives ?coyotes	ansares blancos	cicadas
deer	aquilillas	crickets
field mice	barn owls	fish
gatos ?bobcats	buntings	lizards
hares	crows	lobsters
leones ?mountain lions	ducks	locusts
moles	eagles	maguey grubs
rabbits	eagle owl	snakes
skunks	gavilanes finos	toads
squirrels	?sparrow hawks	
topos ?moles	gavilanes sacres	
weasels	?lanner falcons	(continued)

evident from later documentation that towns in areas without surface water for canal irrigation often had recourse to humid bottomlands where they grew maize, chilis, and squash.[54] The maguey formed a consistent and important element in the economy of the region as a whole, except perhaps for Chiapa de Mota, and in some areas it too was irrigated.[55]

The extent of the irrigation systems in the Valle del Mezquital tells us a great deal about the environment in this early period. It not only indicates the essential aridity of the region's climate and its uncertain rainfall, but also the health of the watershed. That is, the soils were fertile but irrigation was necessary to secure crops. Irrigation, in turn, depended on a healthy catchment area, which meant the maintenance of vegetative cover on the hills. The extent and importance of spring-fed irrigation provides indirect evidence of a healthy watershed because adequate ground cover in the form of trees, shrubs, herbs, and grasses was necessary to ensure that rainwater soaked into the soil and recharged groundwater, thereby maintaining the water table at a level to supply the springs – and the irrigation systems.

Animals	Birds	Reptiles & insects
wolves	hawks	
	hawk owls	
	jackdaws	
	nightingales	
	pigeons	
	primas	
	quail	
	red owls	
	sernycalos	
	sparrows	
	swallows	
	thrushes	
	turtle doves	
	vultures	

Sources: PNE vol. 6, pp. 4, 16, 18, 21, 25, 30–4, 37, 206. The writer of the *Relación de Atitalaquia*, who appears to have been an observant and thoughtful type, noted the following: "No perdian ningun señor el autoridad de ser señor por comer todo esto que tengo dicho [sapos, culebras, rratones, langostas, lagartijas, cigarrones y gusanos]." PNE vol. 6, p. 206: "No gentleman loses his authority by eating all these things [i.e. toads, snakes, mice, lobsters (?), lizards, cicadas, and worms]."

[54] PNE vol. 1, no. 207, 533. AGNT, vol. 1486, exp. 2, fol. 3v. AGIJ, leg. 207 no. 2, ramo 3, fol. 55r. AGNM, vol. 4, fol. 122r. The presence of swamps indicates the possibility of a far wetter soil regime than is present today.

[55] AGNT, vol. 64, exp. 1, fol. 1r.

Direct evidence also suggests that adequate woodlands existed up to the 1560s despite the dense population and extensive croplands. The now-bare, high, steep-sided hills and mountainsides were tree-covered, most towns and villages had woodlands (*montes*), and streams and riverbeds were lined by trees. It is also clear that forest products (lumber, firewood for domestic use and the lime industry, herbs and roots for food and medicine) as well as forest-dependent wild animals were an important part of the indigenous economy.[56] At high altitudes the forests were composed of both oak and pine, while oak forests alone were more often found lower down. Nevertheless, a low-altitude pine forest near Zayanaquilpa is mentioned. The most heavily forested areas were found in the mountains that ring the Valle del Mezquital: those separating Xilotepec and Toluca, the Sierra de las Cruces, the high hills lying to the south of the Central Valley, the foothills of the Sierra de Pachuca, and the Sierra de Juárez.[57] There were woods in other areas as well, often quite extensive. For example, the now-barren hills behind Axacuba in the Central Valley were covered with an oak forest one by two leagues in extent, or approximately 35 square kilometers.[58]

In the Southern Plain, Tezcatepec was situated in a valley surrounded by forested hills, and Tlapanaloya and Apasco both had adequate woodlands.[59] The hills and valleys composing the southern half of the Tula sub-area appear to have been heavily forested, es-

---

[56] PNE vol. 1, nos. 111, 347. PNE vol. 3, p. 69. PNE vol. 6, pp. 15–16, 25, 33, 37, 206. AGIJ, leg. 124 no. 1, fol. 15; leg. 154 no. 3, 3a pte., fol. 404r. AGNM, vol. 7, fol. 87r; vol. 2, fol. 173v. AGNT, vol. 64, exp. 1, fol. 4v; 1525, exp. 1, fols. 55, 72v, 91.

[57] *Xilotepec:* AGNT, vol. 1872, exp. 10, fols. 2r–v. AGNM, vol. 1, exp. 37, fol. 20r.

    Sierra de las Cruces: PNE vol. 1, no. 111. AGNM, vol. 11, fol. 173r; vol. 12, fols. 303r–304r; vol. 14, fols. 27r, 77v, 249v–250v; vol. 19, fols. 202r–203r, 206v, 207v–208r, 210v–211r; vol. 20, fols. 66v–69r.

    Hills between the Valley of Mexico and the Central Valley: PNE vol. 1, nos. 8, 546. PNE vol. 3, p. 72. PNE vol. 6, pp. 17, 32. AGNM, vol. 2, fols. 95v–96v; vol. 5, fol. 7r; vol. 6, fol. 456r. AGNT, vol. 1525, exp. 1, fol. 91r; vol. 2672, exp. 15, fol. 25v; vol. 2674, exp. 10, fols. 307r–315r, 319r–329r.

    Sierra de Pachuca Foothills: PNE vol. 6, pp. 24. AGNM, vol. 5, fol. 70r; vol. 12, fols. 409v–410v, 443r; vol. 19, fols. 217v–218r. AGNT, vol. 64, exp. 1, fol. 7r.

    Sierra de Juárez/Ixmiquilpan: PNE vol. 1, no. 293. PNE vol. 3, p. 99. PNE vol. 6, p. 4. AGNT, vol. 2756, exp. 7, fols. 1r–16r.

[58] PNE vol. 1, no. 8.

[59] PNE vol. 1, nos. 2, 546. PNE vol. 6, p. 33. AGNM, vol. 2, fols. 95v–96r; vol. 6, fols. 455v–456r, 456r; vol. 8, fols. 227v–228r; vol. 12, fols. 409v–410v; vol. 21, fols. 79v–80r. AGNT, vol. 1525, exp. 1, fols. 43r, 91r; vol. 2697, exp. 10, fols. 308r–315r; vol. 2697, exp. 11, fols. 319r–329r. AGNI, vol. 5, exp. 762, fols. 203r–v; exp. 940, fols. 241v–242r.

pecially around Otlazpa. But while the town of Tula in the center of the sub-area had woods, Tepexi just to the south of it did not; and the densely populated and irrigated Tula River valley (the North–South Plain) had few wooded areas.[60] Ixmiquilpan was well wooded in the 1540s, apparently by mesquite, which was favored by the miners for use in lanterns and wagon wheels.[61] The Xilotepec province was not included in the geographic description of 1548, but sources for the early 1550s show that forests were plentiful and important in this sub-area.[62] Throughout the region stands of cedars grew along riverbanks, willows marked springs and water holes, and mesquites and native cherries formed part of the subsistence economy of the villages.[63] The only towns not supplied with adequate woodlands were found in the densely populated North–South Plain and the arid Northern Valley – although the mountain range to the east of the

---

[60] *Tula:* PNE vol. 1, nos. 106, 498, 538. AGNM, vol. 3, fols. 169r–v; vol. 5, fols. 258v–259r, 260r–v; vol. 13, fols. 182r–v. AGNT, vol. 45, exp. 1, fol. 7v; vol. 2735, 2a pte., exp. 8, fol. 1r; vol. 3670, exp. 19, fols. 1r–7v. AGI, Justicia, leg. 207 no. 2, ramo 3, fol. 67.

North–South Plain: AGNM, vol. 6, fols. 455v–456r. AGNT, vol. 2354, exp. 1, fol. 27.

[61] PNE vol. 1, no. 293. PNE vol. 3, p. 99. PNE vol. 6, p. 4.

[62] AGNT, vol. 1872, exp. 10, fols. 2r–v; vol. 2764, exp. 5, fol. 4v. AGNM, vol. 1, fol. 20r; vol. 3, fols. 283v–284r, 766; vol. 4, fol. 291v. In later years the province was still forested:

Xilotepec: AGNM, vol. 11, fols. 64r, 122v–123r; vol. 13, fols. 13r–14r, 61r, 210r–211r; vol. 14, fols. 84r–85r, 142v, 233v–234r; vol. 15, fols. 286r–v; vol. 16, fols. 129r–130r; vol. 17, fols. 38r–v, 39r–40r, 63r–64r, 103v–104r, 119r–120r; vol. 18, fols. 41r–42r, 81v–82r, 227r–v, 236r–v, 266r–v, 281r; vol. 19, fols. 85v–86v, 239v–240r; vol. 22, fols. 298v–299r. AGNT, vol. 2764, exp. 26, fol. 335; vol. 2742, exp. 10, fol. 3r. AGNI, vol. 2, exp. 46, fol. 11r; vol. 3, exp. 150, fol. 35r.

Alfaxayuca: AGNM, vol. 8, fol 8r. AGNT, vol. 2092, exp. 2, fol. 19v; vol. 2718, exp. 15, fol. 1r–v.

Huichiapan: AGNM, vol. 3, exp. 819, fol. 323; vol. 5, fols. 257v–258r; vol. 8, fols. 177v–178r; vol. 13, fols. 38r–v, 61r, 144v–145r; vol. 14, fol. 230v; vol. 15, fols. 221v–222r, 256v; vol. 16, fols. 5r–v, 25r–26r; vol. 17, fols. 39r–40r; vol. 18, fol. 264; vol. 22, fols. 268v, 447r–448v. AGNT, vol. 1791, exp. 1, fols. 135r–v; vol. 2092, exp. 2, fol. 2r; vol. 2105, exp. 1, fol. 2r; vol. 2683, exp. 2, fol. 1r; vol. 2703, exp. 2, fol. 1r; vol. 2762, exp. 11, fol. 125; vol. 2764, exp. 5, fol. 4v; vol. 3568, fols. 22r, 35r, 40, 42r.

[63] PNE vol. 1, nos. 112, 548, 549, 550, 556. PNE vol. 6, p. 18. AGNM, vol. 5, fols. 257v–258r; vol. 9, fols. 271v–272r; vol. 13, fols. 61r, 210v–211r; vol. 14, fols. 230v–231r; vol. 16, fols. 25r–26r; vol. 17, fols. 38r–v, 103r–v, 119v–120r, 218r–v, 224r–v; vol. 18, fols. 81v–82r, 278v–279r; vol. 19, fols. 85v–86r; vol. 20, fols. 67v–68r, 98r–v. AGIJ, leg. 207 no. 2, ramo 3, fol. 67. AGNT, vol. 1529, exp. 1, fols. 138r–v; vol. 1640, exp. 2, fols. 32r–33r; vol. 2177, exp. 1, fol. 2r; vol. 2742, exp. 12, fol. 1r; vol. 2762, exp. 11, fol. 125.

Northern Valley was heavily forested.[64] (See Chapter 4 for a discussion of the documentation for environmental change, and the use of the term *monte*.)

It is clear that the Otomí had evolved a very successful approach to living in this high region of little rainfall and frequent frosts. Although wild game and herbs from the forests and woodlands were important elements in the diet, this was true of all small rural Mexican towns in both the preconquest and colonial periods, as it is today. And though the maguey and the nopal cactus were important in subsistence and trade, the inhabitants of this region nevertheless were settled agriculturalists who produced large grain harvests. They appear as well to have maintained high levels of grain production up to the middle of the sixteenth century without sacrificing the forests in the greater part of the region; and although we have evidence from field observations made in 1949 that the A-horizon soils of the piedmont in several areas were eroded prior to the conquest (probably by wind erosion after the soils were prepared for planting),[65] the documentary record does not provide evidence of extensive sheet erosion or gullying until later in the century, when the indigenous population had declined (this point will be discussed further in this chapter). Indeed, the dense populations, the high levels of grain production, and the extensive forests of the early decades masked the fragility of the ecosystems of this semiarid region, and thus the nature of the relationship between the human populations and their environment, leading the Spaniards to make choices that led ultimately to the destruction of this way of life. By the end of the sixteenth century, only eight decades after the Spaniards arrived, the picture had changed. The Indian populations were decimated and their fields reduced. The once fertile flatlands were covered in a dense growth of mesquite-dominated desert scrub, the high, steep-sided hills were treeless, and the piedmont was eroded and gullied. Sheep grazing, not agriculture, took precedence in regional production. Sheep, not men, dominated the ecosystems of the Valle del Mezquital and shaped its landscapes.

The Conquest Landscape

Sheep did not simply replace men, however, although that was the final outcome; rather, they displaced them – ate them, as the saying goes. The processes by which sheep grazing displaced agriculture,

---

[64] PNE vol. 1, no. 9. AGNM, vol. 13, fols. 176r–v.
[65] Cook, *Historical Demography*, pp. 41–7.

and sheep displaced humans, resulted in the formation of a new and far less hospitable landscape within which the indigenous populations were marginalized and alienated, their traditional resources degraded or lost, and their access to the means of production restricted. Let us examine the major processes underlying the formation of this landscape and their temporal relationships, that is, the demographic collapse of the indigenous populations, the expansion of pastoralism, and the transformation of the environment.

By the end of the sixteenth century the indigenous human population of the Valle del Mezquital was a tenth its size at contact. Disease was not the only cause of this demographic collapse, but it was the primary one. Between 1521 and 1600 a series of epidemics with high mortality rates reduced the indigenous population of the Valle del Mezquital to ever-lower levels.[66] There seems to have been hope in the 1560s that the epidemics had come to an end, and the population may have shown signs of increasing; but the terrible epidemic known as the "Great Cocolistle" that raged throughout New Spain between 1576 and 1581 was followed by epidemics each decade until finally, by the 1620s, the indigenous population reached an accommodation with the introduced diseases, the downward slide stopped, and the population began slowly to increase.

The demands of work gangs in populations weakened by disease compounded the effects of the epidemics. The conditions of work were often horrific, and the food the men carried with them did not last or was inedible after a short time. Subsistence production was reduced because men were removed from their villages to work in the mines, on Spanish farms, and on government projects such as the *desague* (the draining of the lakes in the Valley of Mexico), usually when they were most needed to look after their own agricultural plots.[67] Flight and emigration also reduced the population in specific areas. Groups of Indians from the Xilotepec province were used by the Spanish to colonize the northern lands, in an attempt to pacify

---

[66] Gibson, *Aztecs*, Appendix 4, pp. 448–51, lists the epidemics that occurred in the Valley of Mexico for the whole of the colonial period; the records of the *Contaduría* of the AGI and the *Suma de Visitas* make it clear that the Valle del Mezquital was subjected to epidemics at the same time. See Appendix B for evidence of the population decline in the Valle del Mezquital.

[67] See Gibson, *Aztecs*, pp. 224–36, for a discussion of the history of the government-controlled allocation of Indian labor, the *repartimiento*. A census made in 1587–8 of the tributaries of the Huichiapan and Alfaxayuca valleys for the purposes of calculating the size of the work gangs to be supplied by each town, lists the number

the nomadic and bellicose Chichimecs by example. Others fled the ravages of cattle in their agricultural lands.[68] Evidence of the population decline in this region comes from the records of the *Contaduría*, the day-to-day accounts of the royal treasurers that start in the 1520s and continue throughout the colonial

of males required each week for work in Cimapan, Celaya, Tepozotlan, and the local sheep stations and agricultural holdings:

Valley & Pueblo	No. of tributaries	No. to be sent to:	No. used locally
Huichiapan Valley			
S. Mateo Gueychiapa	468	18 Cimapan	17
Santiago Tecuçautla	660	16 Celaya	17
S. Josepe Atlan	248	9 "	12
Sta. Maria Magdalena Nopala	252	6 "	15
S. Geronimo Acagualzingo	142	7 Tepozotlan	12
S. Lorenço Tlacotlaliztla	63	2 Celaya	7
Sta. Maria Tecçisapa	88	3 "	7
S. Francisco de Xolitlica	126	6 "	7
S. Miguel Caltepantla	74	3 "	11
S. Buenaventura Xonacapa	174	7 Cimapan	16
Santiago Acuçilapa	38	6 "	6
Sta. Maria Ameyalco	125	9 Tepozotlan	9
S. Marcos Tlatlapetonco	20	1 Cimapan	2
S. Sebastian Macatloholaya	20	1 Celaya	1
S. Sebastian Çontepeque	15	1 "	1
S. Bartolome Tlascalilla	81	3 "	7
S. Lucas Tecasapantonco	33	1 Cimapan	3
S. Antonio Vizpachquautla	13	1 Celaya	1
S. Jhoan Tlamimilolpa	10	2 "	1
Alfaxayuca Valley			
S. Martin Alfaxayuca	346	12 Cimapan	5
S. Augustin Tlalisticapa	119	4 "	4
S. Lorenço Tepectlacocolco	70	2 "	3
S. Juan Xochitlan	30	2 "	2
Sta. Maria Atlaucheo	18	1 "	2
S. Pablo Topozantla	13	5 "	5
S. Pedro Teoporcolco	96	2 "	4
Sta. Cruz Quiauac	28	8 "	1
S. Bernadino Tlasco	252	1 "	0
S. Pedro Tenextlacostla	30	5 "	0
S. Juan Caltimanca	104	5 "	0
S. Francisco Cocachichilco	165	0	0
S. Antonio Tecocicapa	145	5 "	4

Source: AGIM, leg. 111, ramo 2, doc. 12.

[68] AGNT, vol. 79, exp. 6, fol. 8v. AGNI, vol. 5, fols. 2v–3v. AGNM, vol. 3, fols. 283v–284v. It is not clear, however, where they fled to; see Whitmore's discussion of this point, "Sixteenth-Century Population Declines," p. 13.

period.[69] (See Appendix B for a discussion of these records and the population of each *cabecera* over the sixteenth century.) The use of the *Contaduría* poses many problems. For example, the royal treasurers counted people liable to pay tribute, rather than the entire population;[70] also, the *Contaduría* records of tribute assessments and payments are of no help in calculating the number of tributaries before the 1560s, even for towns under the crown's jurisdiction. Early royal tribute assessments, while to a certain degree simplified and adjusted to the needs of the Spanish community, were not based on individual head counts. Tribute did not become based on a head count until the 1550s and 1560s. At the same time tribute exemptions were dropped for the sub-*macegual* class (subordinate people owing tribute and service to a member of the Indian nobility) and in some cases for the *caciques* (Indian rulers) as well, thus including the bulk of the population in the tributary counts.[71] Cook and Borah note that the

[69] Especially interesting is the 1576 investigation into the records of Treasurer Portugal for the period 1553–69, in which the numbers of tributaries who died in the epidemics of 1564–6 were noted; AGIC, legs. 665 and 787, A & B. The reasons why a particular *corregimiento* could not pay its assessed yearly tribute are listed. For example, "Los naturales del pueblo dieron cuenta de la del año de 1558 y los dichos principales y el dicho Geronimo Mercado [corregidor] juran y firman del dicho no averse coxido en el dicho pueblo ningun maiz en el año 1558 aunque lo sembraron a causa de aver avido gran sequedad" AGIC leg. 665, *Relación de Izquinquitlapilco*. The promptness with which payments were adjusted to the capacity to pay, or to changes in population, is general throughout: "Que no se cobrare dellos por la esterilidad que avia avido el dicho ano [1566] en el dicho pueblo por lo qual razon no se les hase cargo dello sino tan solamente de 324 hanegas [of the 1567 harvest]" AGIC leg. 786-B (Atengo, 1567). Similar accountings are found for the years 1538– 53 in AGIC leg. 662-A; and for 1544–9 in AGIC leg. 664. Changes in the assessments (the history of the *tasaciones*) are given for 1553–69 in AGIC leg. 670; for 1531–64 in AGIC leg. 785; for 1573–84 in leg. 692; and for 1581–91 in leg. 668.

[70] The royal treasurers often based their assessments on counts carried out by the ecclesiastics. I have used the ecclesiastical records in the few cases where totals were not available in the *Contaduría*, and to check doubtful totals. The resulting tributary totals agree fairly well with those estimated for this region by Sherburne F. Cook and Woodrow Borah, and Peter A. Gerhard. Cook and Borah, "The Indian Population," Appendix; Gerhard, *Guide*, pp. 45, 155, 298, 333, 384.

[71] See Gibson *Aztecs*, pp. 194–205, for a discussion of the sixteenth century tribute history. Aspects of this history pertinent to the calculation of the tributary population have been extracted from his discussion.

Up to ca. 1550: "In an average community...the Indian criteria for liability in payment continued to prevail. This meant the exemption, in various degrees, of caciques and principales, or those who paid to private Indian recipients, of the aged and infirm, or children and youths still living with their families, and in some instances of merchants and craftsmen. Just as maceguales who supported the Aztec temples had paid no tribute in the pre-conquest period, so those serving in the

apparent rise in population between 1548 and 1569/70 indicates the increase in the numbers of individuals eligible for tribute payments rather than an increase in the population base.[72] The earliest tributary population total we can trust, therefore, is that for 1570, and estimates of the population at conquest are based ultimately on this total.

The number of tributaries in the Valle del Mezquital in 1570 was 76,946. After a series of terrible epidemics, the tributary population of the valley in 1600 was reduced to 20,447.5, a decline of 73.4 percent in only thirty years. Contemporaries estimated that the indigenous population of New Spain as a whole declined by a half to two-thirds by midcentury, and by two-thirds to five-sixths by 1565.[73] If we assume a decline of 66 percent for the period 1521–70 as related to the 1570 total, the number of tributaries present in the region in 1519 would have been 226,311. Assuming an 83 percent decline gives 452,623. If we accept contemporary estimates, then, the tributary population declined from between 226,311 and 452,623 to 20,447.5 over the period 1519–1600 – an overall rate of decline of 90.9–95.4 percent. Whereas a population decline of 95.4 percent for the highlands is excessive, 90.9 percent is in line with contemporary estimates of the overall population decline by the end of the sixteenth century.[74]

The factor by which the tributary count is to be multiplied to give the total population has been debated for decades. Estimates of the total population are inexact and it is possible to gain only an approximate idea of the order of magnitude of the demographic disaster.

Christian monasteries and churches – including singers and players of musical instruments – were commonly exempted from early colonial tribute" (p. 197).

In the 1550s and 1560s common plantings were abandoned and each tributary was assessed directly, although "towns were still held liable for bulk amounts in a form of assessment that would continue up to the end of the colonial period, but the amounts were now determined by population counts and each tributary was expected to contribute an equal payment" (p. 199). Multiple commodity payments gave way to stated amounts of money and maize: nine-and-a-half *reales de plata* and one-half *fanega* of maize per tributary, half this amount for half-tributaries. In the 1560s the exemptions were dropped as a result of the Valderrama *visita*, for sub-*macegual* classes and sometimes *caciques*. Full exemptions "were now limited to the aged, children, the blind, the crippled, the sick, and bachelors and spinsters (*solteros*) living with their parents. The phrase 'even though they have lands' (*aunque tengan tierras*), frequently attached to the exemption regarding bachelors and spinsters, sought to separate the new system completely from Indian landholding" (p. 200).

[72] Cook and Borah, *Indian Population*, p. 6.

[73] Motolinía, *History*, p. 302; Gibson, *Aztecs*, p. 138.

[74] In a recent article, Thomas Whitmore presents the results of simulation of the sixteenth-century population decline in the Valley of Mexico and concludes that the decline was about 90 percent; Whitmore, "Population Decline," p. 11.

Because it is possible to gain the same idea from the tributary totals, no attempt has been made here to calculate the total population for any period.[75] However, sixteenth century descriptions of the Valle del Mezquital make it clear that the region contained many more people and was more intensively cultivated up to the middle of the sixteenth century than it was in the last quarter of that century. The *Suma de Visitas*, for instance, presents a picture of a very dense population that derived more than sufficient produce from the region for subsistance, trade, and tribute. Later descriptions of villages in the Tula sub-area (1561) give the impression of still-densely populated settlements and extensive croplands, and the writers of reports collected in a geographic relation written in 1579–81 note that formerly the land had been intensively cultivated and densely populated. These reports have been confirmed by archaeological surveys that demonstrate very dense populations in the Tula River basin and headwaters up to the mid–sixteenth century. The records dating from the last decades of the sixteenth century make it equally clear that there had been massive depopulation of the region during the first eighty years of settlement.[76]

The demographic collapse of the indigenous populations was one of the major variables in transforming the structural position of the Indian communities in the colonial society. By the end of the sixteenth century the bulk of the population of New Spain was still Indian; but the Indians were no longer in possession of the land, as they had been during the first generation after the conquest. The colonial society had changed from the early postconquest decades, when tiny groups of Spaniards represented the new political order in a predominantly indigenous culture and civilization. By the end of the century the Indian population was an impoverished peasantry in a new political economy.

The first Spaniards to enter the Valle del Mezquital came as *encomenderos*, missionaries, and royal officials – the classic troika of Spanish conquest and settlement. These representatives of the Spanish regime redefined the hierarchy of towns and villages and fixed their bound-

---

[75] See, for example, the recent discussion by Whitmore and the response by Feldman, over the problems involved in calculating contact populations; Whitmore, "Population Decline"; Feldman, "Comment." See also, Henige "Native American Population."

[76] PNE vol. 1, nos. 1, 2, 8–10, 106, 110–12, 235, 258, 293, 347, 397, 417, 498, 533, 534, 538, 546–50, 554–6, 771, 781, 838; see also, note 47. AGNT, vol. 1529, exp. 1. PNE vol. 6, pp. 15, 20, 24, 28, 35, 178, 181, 200, 202. Mastache and Crespo, "La ocupación prehispánica," p. 76; Sanders, Parsons, and Santley, *Basin*, pp. 179, 213.

aries according to a new vision of the natural order.[77] A total of thirty-five *encomiendas* were granted in the early 1520s, of which twenty-three survived in whole or in part into the seventeenth century.[78] Starting in 1531 *corregimientos* (Spanish administrative districts based on *cabeceras*) replaced certain of the *encomiendas* through escheatment to the crown on the death of the *encomendero,* or as a result of the New Laws, as in the case of Diego de Albornoz, the royal accountant who had to give up his *encomienda* in Tula.[79] Spanish officials entered the region as *corregidores* (officials in charge of *corregimientos*), lieutenants and constables, and as justices to investigate disputes, check boundaries, to oversee the *repartimiento* (government-controlled work gangs), or to direct the *congregaciones* (reduction of Indian communities to one town). Whenever information or adjudication of some sort was needed, someone would be sent "with the wand of justice" (*con vara de justicia*) to investigate a complaint or arrange a compromise. The Franciscans were the first religious order to enter the area. The Augustinians followed in the 1550s and set up monasteries, parishes and *doctrinas,* and by the 1560s secular priests were resident in certain towns.[80]

Other Spaniards followed rapidly on the heels of the *encomenderos,* the clerics and royal officials. Merchants came to the region to buy charcoal, wool and rope, to carry wine to the taverns in the mining areas, to cut wood to mend their carts, and to buy wheat to carry to Zacatecas. Innkeepers applied for licenses to open inns and taverns.[81] With the opening of the silver mines in Zacatecas in the far north,

---

[77] See Licate, *Creation of a Mexican Landscape,* especially Chapter 3.
[78] See Melville, "Pastoral Economy," Appendix D, for a table listing the changing status and government of the *cabeceras.*
[79] AGIC, leg. 665.
[80] In 1529 the Franciscans set up a *doctrina* in San Pedro and San Pablo Xilotepec, a parish in San José Tula from where they also visited TetpangoHueypostla, and in 1531 a *doctrina* in San Mateo Huichiapan. Later, they set up *doctrinas* in Tepexi (1552), Alfaxayuca (1559), and Tepetitlan (1571). The Augustinians set up a monastary in Actopan from where they also visited Tetepango-Hueypustla, Ixmiquilpan (1550), which had been secular, and Chapantongo (1566), which was a priorate (1569). Secular priests were resident in Hueypostla, Atitalaquia, Mizquiaguala (including Tepeitic), Axacuba (later Augustinian), Tezcatepec, Tlacotlapilco, Chiapa and Tequixquiac; Gerhard, *Guide,* pp. 45, 155, 298, 333, 384.
[81] AGNC, vol. 77, exp. 11, fol. 81v. AGNG, vol. 5, exp. 667, fol 145v; exp. 1,000, fol 209. AGNT, vol. 2337, exp. 1, fol. 390v; vol. 2813, exp. 4, fols. 1r–v. AGNI, vol. 2, exp. 46, fol 11r; vol. 4, exp. 293, fol. 88r; vol. 5, exp. 601, fol. 166v. AGNM, vol. 3, fol. 323r; vol. 8, fol. 191r, 208r; vol. 9, fols. 151r–v, 155v; vol. 11 fols. 206v–207r; vol. 17, fols. 63v–64r. AGIM, leg. 111, ramo 2, doc. 12, fol. 67v. AGIE, leg. 161-C, fol. 208r. Mendizábal, *Obras,* pp. 119–20.

increasing numbers of mule trains carrying provisions passed through the Valle del Mezquital, putting an almost intolerable pressure on the Indian communities along the route from the Valley of Mexico to San Juan del Río. Hundreds of mules needed fodder, and travelers needed food and lodging. The travelers often came into bitter conflict with the Indian communities, who tried to stop the theft of their supplies and the assaults on their persons by applying for licenses to sell supplies and to open inns; these to be supplied with beds (complete with matresses, pillows, and sheets), corrals for pack animals, and food.[82]

Spaniards did not settle in the Valle del Mezquital at first. The ideal of the Spanish government was to maintain the Indian villages free of contamination by the undesirable influence of "españoles, negros, mulatos o mestizos" (Spaniards, blacks, mulattoes or meztizos). But the *cédula* (proclamation) proclaiming this order and others following it had little effect[83] and the ethnic makeup of the region changed gradually as increasing numbers of landowners lived on their holdings. A 1588 census of the Spanish holdings in the Huichiapan and Alfaxayuca Valleys lists 22 Spanish owners and their families, together with one Spanish station administrator who lived on the land, out of a total of 101 holdings.[84] Throughout court cases Spanish witnesses give Indian towns as their place of residence. *Mestizaje,* the development of a group of people of mixed parentage (Indian and white), was undoubtedly a continuing process but there are very few references to it.

Interestingly, the largest group of foreigners in the early period was composed of African slaves. Africans first came as slaves to work on the local sheep stations, and with the opening of mines in Ixmiquilpan and Pachuca increasing numbers of Spanish miners and their black slaves appeared in the region. By 1555 groups of escaped slaves lived in the forests surrounding the mines of Tornacustla, and the *encomendero* of Tlacotlapilco commented in the 1590s that the person

---

[82] AGNI, vol. 5, exp. 601, fol. 166. AGNM, vol. 4, fols. 291, 292; vol. 5, fols. 3r–v; vol. 8, fols. 191r, 255r–v; vol. 9, fols. 155v–156r; vol. 11, fols. 206v–207r; vol. 13, fols. 1r–v; vol. 19, fols. 171v, 186v. AGNT, vol. 2729, exp. 10, fols. 152r–156.

[83] Gibson writes that "the Spanish state sought to eliminate or control . . . assaults upon Indian society by three official methods. One was to punish offenders under the Spanish law. A second was to grant permission to Indian communities to arrest intruders and deliver them to Spanish authorities. A third and most drastic technique was to prohibit the residence of non-Indians in native communities. . . . But all efforts at separation failed. . . . and no effective measures for isolating the communities from Spanish pressures were ever devised"; *Aztecs,* p. 147.

[84] AGIM, leg. 111, ramo 2, doc. 12.

who took up a grant for a sheep station near that *cabecera* deserved a prize because clearing the dense secondary growth for grazing was the only way to rid the region of sheep stealers and bandits.[85] Free blacks and mulattoes appear on the tribute rolls later in the century, mainly in the mining areas of Tornacustla and Ixmiquilpan, although small numbers also appear in the *corregimientos* of Atitalaquia, Tula, Mizquiaguala, Atengo, Xilotepec, and Chapantongo after 1580. Mulattoes were present in small numbers, and were, with the mestizo, an anomaly in the Spanish government's classification of the population as either Spaniard or Indian. They could evidently hold land, however, and one mulatto, Miguel Hernández, owned a sheep station in Xilotepec in 1590.[86]

Despite the obstacles posed to settlement in the early decades by the dense Indian population and the extent of their agricultural lands, Spaniards began to import elements of European agriculture into areas that conformed to their ideas of lands with economic potential. Beginning in the 1530s (and perhaps as early as the 1520s) they added Old World plants and animals to the agricultural products grown by the Indians, to form a kind of mixed farming. Wheat was grown for tribute in the more humid south by order of the royal officials and *encomenderos;* barley was grown in the arid northeast. Old World fruit trees such as pears, peaches, nectarines, apples, quinces, pomegranates, oranges, limes, dates, figs, *togodos*, and walnuts, as well as roses and grapes, were grown wherever climate and water resources allowed.[87] Grazing animals were pastured within the Indian agricultural lands, thereby putting in motion the processes by which herbivores and plant communities adjust to one another.

Students of ungulate irruptions have broken the process of mutual adjustment of the plant and animal communities down into four stages:

> During stage 1, there is a progressive increase in numbers in response to the discrepancy between the carrying capacity of the habitat and the numbers of ungulates present. The death rate is low and as new generations reproduce, the population curve increases rapidly. Eventually preferred species in plant communities become overutilised.

[85] AGNM, vol. 5, fol. 70r. AGNT, vol. 2717, exp. 9, fol. 7r.
[86] AGIC, legs. 661–9, 671, 675, 677–91, 693–701: Cargo de tributos de mulatos y negros libres; Cargo de servicio real de mulatos y negros libres. AGNM, vol. 16, fol. 129r. AGNI, vol. 3, exp. 150, fol. 35r.
[87] PNE vol. 1, nos. 112, 235, 293, 498, 538, 547, 548, 550, 554, 771, 781. PNE vol. 6, pp. 30, 33. AGNT, vol. 154, no. 3, vol. 269; vol. 154, no. 3, 4 pte., fol. 161; vol. 1525, exp. 1, fol. 63; vol. 1640, exp. 2, fol. 25v. AGNM, vol. 1, exp. 37, fol. 20r.

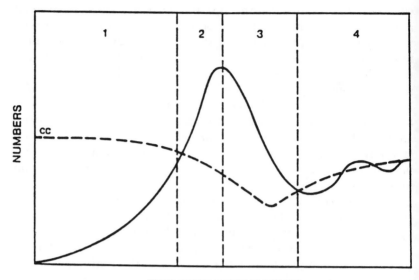

TIME AFTER INTRODUCTION

Figure 2.1. The stages of an irruptive oscillation after the introduction of ungulates to a new area. Stages 1–4 of the oscillation explained in the text. CC - Carrying Capacity. (N. Leader-Williams, *Reindeer on South Georgia*)

During stage 2, the population exceeds its carrying capacity as more extensive areas of vegetation are overutilised. Physical condition at the critical season drops noticeably; as juvenile death rate increases the population starts to level off in number. In stage 3, the population begins to decline, especially when an element of the environment such as climate becomes critical. Latterly, some plant species less susceptible to browsing or grazing pressure may begin to recover as the animal density declines to a level more nearly compatible with the current carrying capacity of the habitat. Stage 4 commences when a degree of stability has developed between numbers of ungulates and the new carrying capacity of the habitat. Population density at this stage remains lower than peak density, because plant communities have a lower cover of preferred species than when the population was first introduced. Once this complete adjustment has taken place, the introduced population, ecologically, is the same as any established population... Further irruptions of a dampened nature may occur only after creation of another discrepancy between carrying capacity and numbers present.[88] (See Fig. 2:1)

[88] Leader-Williams, *Reindeer*, p. 20.

How was this process of mutual adjustment between the introduced animal populations and the native plant communities played out in the case of the Valle del Mezquital? What were the consequences for the indigenous populations – themselves undergoing radical change? Perhaps the best way to follow these processes is to order the events according to the four stages just outlined:

Stage 1: The increase "is a predictable demographic response of populations presented with more food than needed to ensure their replacement in the next generation."[89]

In the Valle del Mezquital, stage 1 of the irruption of Old World grazing animals began with the introduction of sheep, along with cattle, horses, pigs and goats.[90] During the first twenty-five to thirty years the number of animals introduced was small: thirty-four flocks of around a thousand head were introduced in the 1530s, forty-one in the 1540s, and thirty-three in the 1550s.[91] Although the animals were at a relatively low density at this point, however, that they were maintained within the densely populated, intensively worked agricultural lands meant that they caused more damage than their low numbers imply. The legalization of squatters' rights, boundary descriptions and disputes, complaints filed by the Indians of stations encroaching on their village lands, damage done to crops, and the violent behavior of the herders, make it clear that the introduced

---

[89] Caughley, "Overpopulation," p. 10. The speed with which sheep increase their numbers on encountering new ecosystems can be extraordinary. Sixteenth-century observers reported that "herds of sheep doubled in a year or less," Gibson *Aztecs*, p. 280. Three thousand sheep introduced in 1901 and 1902 on Campbell Island (New Zealand) increased to just over eight thousand by 1907; Wilson and Orwin, "The Sheep Population of Campbell Island," pp. 462–4. The mechanism underlying the increase is fertility: the number of live births increases when there is an overabundance of food. The rapid increase of the Soay sheep on the island of St. Kilda (Scotland) following a population crash is dependent on the ability of the lambs to reproduce in their first year of life; Grenfell, Price, Albon, and Clutton-Brock, "Overcompensation and population cycles in an ungulate," pp. 825–6.

[90] Sheep seem to have been the preferred species for this region in the sixteenth century; in the seventeenth century exploitation shifted from sheep to cattle and goats. See Chapter 5, note 127.

[91] See Chapter 5 for a detailed discussion of the development of grazing enterprises and Appendix C for sources. Evidence for changes in the flock size and later the stocking rates (the number of head maintained in a specific landholding), was obtained from documentation for court cases, wills, complaints lodged by Indians, and censuses. The evidence of a flock size of around a thousand head for the first two-and-a-half decades is based in a complaint lodged by Indians, who said that thirty-one pastoralists were grazing twenty to thirty thousand head of sheep in the Xilotepec province in 1551; AGIM, leg. 1841, fols. 1r–8r. See also PNE vol. 1, p. 219.

animals were a menace by the middle of the sixteenth century.[92] Cattle and horses were considered the greater threat, their sheer size making them a more obvious target for Indian complaints about the destruction of crops, although anyone who has to deal with pigs in their garden will know the remarkably short period of time needed for just one pig to wreak havoc.

Government policy at this time was still concerned with the maintenance of Indian rights to and use of the land, and efforts were made in the 1550s to relieve the pressure on Indian croplands. As noted above, cattle and horses were outlawed from the densely populated

[92] These sources also tell us where stations were placed; see Table 5:4 for placement of stations. Complaints filed by the Indians of problems with animals:

1542 Xilotepec	AGNM, vol. 1, exp. 488, fol. 210.
Alfaxayuca:	AGNM, vol. 1, fols. 209r–210r.
1543 Xilotepec:	AGNM, vol. 2, fol. 29r.
Tlapanaloya:	AGNM, vol. 2, fols. 86r, 95v–96r.
Tezcatepec:	AGNM, vol. 2, fols. 111v–112r.
1550 Actopan:	AGNM, vol. 3, fols. 81r–v.
Alfaxayuca:	AGNM, vol. 3, fols. 112r—114v.
Xilotepec:	AGNM, vol. 3, fols. 283v–284v.
1551 Xilotepec:	AGIM, leg. 96, ramo 1.
	AGNM, vol. 3, fols. 283v–284r.
1555 Xilotepec:	AGNM, vol. 4, fols. 330v–332r.
1556 Atengo:	AGNM, vol. 4, fol. 354r.
Chapantongo:	AGNM, vol. 4, fols. 370r–v.
1557 Xilotepec:	AGIM, leg. 1841, fols. 1r–8r.
1561 Alfaxayuca:	AGNM, vol. 5, fols. 208r–v.
Otlazpa:	AGNM, vol. 5, fols. 262r–v.
Axacuba:	AGNM, vol. 5, fols. 254v–255r.
1563 Tlacotlapilco:	AGNM, vol. 6, fols. 391v–392r.
Tlapanaloya:	AGNM, vol. 7, fol. 87r.
Tlapanaloya:	AGNT, vol. 1525, exp. 1, fols. 55r, 74v.
Tepexi:	AGNT, vol. 1697, exp. 1, 2 a pte., fols. 1r–2r.
Tepexi:	AGNM, vol. 6, fol. 515r.
1564 Tula:	AGNM, vol. 7, fol. 349r.
Axacuba:	AGNM, vol. 7, fol. 295v–296r.
1565 Tequixquiac:	AGNM, vol. 8, fol. 185r.
Izcuinquitlapilco:	AGNM, vol. 8, fol. 42r.
Ixmiquilpan:	AGNM, vol. 8, fol. 64v.
1576 Tuzantlalpa:	AGNG, vol. 1, exp. 970, fol. 181r.
Ixmiquilpan:	AGNG, vol. 1, exp. 964, fols. 179r–v.
1578 Chiapa/Otlaspa:	AGNT, vol. 2686, exp. 14, fols. 1r–8r.
1580 Tepetitlan:	AGNG, vol. 2, exp. 1228, fol. 264v.
Otlaspa:	AGNT, vol. 45, exp. 1, fols. 10r–11r.
1587 Axacuba/Tlaxcoapan:	AGNT, vol. 2672, exp. 15, fol. 22.
1589 Atengo:	AGNI, vol. 4, exp. 62, fols. 18v–19r.
1590 Atitalaquia:	AGNI, vol. 4, exp. 868, fol. 224.
Xilotepec:	AGNI, vol. 5, exp. 9, fol. 2v–3v.

(continued)

central regions. The smaller animals (sheep, goats, and pigs) were not expelled, in part because they were considered to be less of a menace, but also because Spanish interests could not be ignored entirely in favor of the Indians.[93] Some stock owners rebelled against the order to move their beasts, yet the clearance seems to have been generally successful, at least in the Valle del Mezquital.[94] When cattle and horses were expelled from the Valle del Mezquital, the competition for forage was reduced and the sheep population irrupted. Flock size increased fourfold to around 3,900 head during the 1550s,[95] and to an estimated 7,500 head in the early 1560s.[96] Between 1560 and 1565 the number of flocks in the region also increased dramatically, with 168 stations taken up in this five-year period alone, so that the total number of animals jumped from and estimated total of 421,200 in the late 1550s to an estimated two million in 1565 (see Tables 5.3,6 and 4.4).

The mid-1560s were a turning point for the indigenous populations. Before this, the land was still populated by enough Indians to make the government policy of the protection of Indian land rights both necessary and feasible. After 1565, however, the advantage the

1591 Tequixquiac:	AGNT, vol. 1521, exp. 3, fol. 9.
Xilotepec:	AGNI, vol. 5, exp. 9, fols. 2v–3v.
Otlaspa	AGNT, vol. 3517, exp. 1, fol. 8r.
Tequixquiac:	AGNI, vol. 5, exp. 762, fols. 203r–v.
Tequixquiac:	AGNI, vol. 5, exp. 940, fols. 241v–242r.
Tlahuelilpa:	AGNI, vol. 6 pte. 2, exp. 192, fol. 44r.
Atitalaquia:	AGNI, vol. 6 pte. 2, exp. 231, fol. 51r–v.
1592 Ixmiquilpan:	AGNI, vol. 6 pte. 2, exp. 532, fol. 117r.
Tequixquiac:	AGNT, vol. 1748, exp. 1, fols. 19r–22r.
1594 Xilotepec:	AGNI, vol. 6 pte. 1, exp. 863, fol. 268r.
1597 Hueypustla:	AGNI, vol. 6 pte. 2, exp. 998, fols. 260r–v.
1599 Tlilcuautla:	AGNT, vol. 64, exp. 1, fols. 5r–9r.

See Table 5:12.

[93] See Chevalier, *La formación,* pp. 133, 135, for a discussion of the problems facing the viceroy in his efforts to protect Indian lands.

[94] AGIM, leg. 1841, fols. 1r–8r, case against Rodrigo de Castañeda, 1557.

[95] AGIJ, leg. 143 no. 2; leg. 154 no. 3, 3a pte., fol. 460v. AGIM, leg. 1841, fols. 3r, 7v. AGIC, leg. 671. AGNM, fols. 77r–v. AGNT, vol. 1527, exp. 1, fol. 3r; vol. 71, exp. 6, fol. 523v; vol. 1640, exp. 2, fol. 25r.

[96] Because the stocking rates recorded for the period 1560–5 vary, a rate of 7,500 per station has been used to calculate grazing rates for this period. This rate is intermediate between the average rate for the 1550s of 3,900 per station, and that for the period between 1566 and 1579 of 10,000 head per station; AGIC, leg. 671-B (10,000 head); AGNT, vol. 1525, exp. 1, fols. 50r–v (could graze 8–10,000 head); vol. 1792, exp. 1, fol. 64r (2,000 head); vol. 1640, exp. 2, fol. 25r (8,200 head on two Indian-owned stations).

Indian agriculturalists held before – of their greater numbers and the extent of the lands cultivated by them – was lost. The critical point was passed, and from this time sheep gained the ascendancy both in the lands they utilized and in their numbers. The identification of this critical point in the affairs of the Indians of the Valle del Mezquital is evident only by hindsight. In the sixteenth century, the 1576–81 epidemic known as the Great Cocolistle was considered to be the death of hopes for a healthy and productive peasantry. If we look at the shift in regional production that occurred between the mid-1560s and the mid-1570s, however, we see that the mid-1560s were the beginning of the takeover of regional production by sheep grazing, and that the 1576–81 epidemic was the final blow to Indian regional predominance both in population density and production.

Stage 2: The overshoot "results from an animal's supply of food being reduced by the grazing and browsing of the *previous* generation."[97]

In the Valle del Mezquital, the period from the mid-1560s to the end of the 1570s was marked by high densities of animals – the product of natural increase combined with the artificial maintenance of high densities and the introduction of new flocks into the region – and rapid reduction of the height and density of the vegetative cover. The overshoot lasted about five years in any one place, the timing and duration depending on the original status of the vegetation and its capacity to withstand heavy grazing.

This period saw the takeover of regional production by pastoralism and the displacement of humans by sheep. In the mid-1560s regional production was still dominated by agriculture, and although flocks of sheep grazed the grasslands, hills, and fallow fields, the landscape remained represented by numerous villages with their cultivated fields. By the mid-1570s, however, prior to the dramatic decline in the indigenous human populations, small-scale intensive pastoralism, characterized by small holdings (the *estancia*, or station, of 7.8 square kilometers), very high stocking rates, and grazing in common, dominated regional production and landscapes.

Stocking rates in the region were, by all accounts, extremely high: flock size in the 1570s in the Huichiapan and Alfaxayuca Valleys ran as high as fifteen thousand per station. Rates documented for other parts of the region were also high; the extreme was recorded for

---

[97] Caughley, "Overpopulation," p. 10. Ewes will reproduce according to the food available at the time of conception. If the population has reached its optimum density at the time of conception, then the increase represented by the lambs pushes the population beyond the carrying capacity of the plant base, and an overshoot occurs.

Tezontlalpa in the Southern Plain where, according to Indian plain-tiffs, a Spaniard was corralling more than twenty thousand head of sheep on one station.[98] As a rather conservative estimate for the entire region, a stocking rate of ten thousand head per station has been taken to represent flock size during the period 1566–79.[99]

As the waves of animals flooded over the land they transformed the vegetative cover, and by the end of the 1570s the vegetation of the region was reduced in height and density. In some places it had been removed altogether and only bare soil remained. Former agricultural lands were converted to grasslands, and the hills were deforested and grazed by thousands upon thousands of sheep. Pasture was exhausted early in the season, and some flocks were moved west each year to Michoacan for the dry season pasture.[100] The Indian villages and their surrounding croplands were reduced in size. Nevertheless, they still provided the bulk of agricultural produce, not only for their own subsistence but also for tribute and trade; the Spaniards took very little interest in developing agriculture until they were forced to do so by the dramatic depopulation of the Indian communities in the 1576–81 epidemic.

Stage 3: The crash "is a consequence of a[n ungulate] population being stranded at high density in the face of a now greatly reduced standing crop of edible vegetation."[101]

During the last quarter of the sixteenth century the plants com-posing the vegetative cover of the region shifted toward such arid-zone species as lechuguilla maguey, nopal cactus, yucca, thorn scrub, mesquite, and cardón. Both the extensive fallow lands of the deci-mated and congregated Indian villages and the grazing lands of the pastoralists were covered in a secondary growth of mesquites (now growing as *matorral* rather than as large individual trees), thorn

---

[98] AGNG, vol. 1, fol. 181r.

[99] This rate is based on the average stocking rate on the Spanish holdings in the Huichiapan and Alfaxayuca Valleys for the mid-1570s of 10,000 per station; there are also records of 15,000 head; AGIM, leg. 111, ramo 2, doc. 12. "Stocking rate" in this context is taken to mean the number of animals corralled on a station.

[100] AGIM, leg. 111, ramo 2, doc. 12. Chevalier, *La formación*, p. 139. Simpson, *Exploitation of Land*, p. 3. Transhumance is discussed in this volume, Chapter 6.

[101] Caughley, "Introduction," p. 5. Mortality increases in conditions of low food supply and is "caused primarily by starvation when high sheep population densities deplete the standing crop." The death rate can be very high and the period of the crash short: for example, up to seventy percent of the Soay sheep population on St. Kilda die over one year during population crashes. Grenfell, Price, Albon, and Clutton-Brock, "Overcompensation and population cycles in an ungulate," p. 824.

bushes, wild maguey, and thistles. (See Chapter 4 for a detailed description of the environmental changes recorded for each sub-area.) As the pasture declined in quality and quantity during the 1570s, the flock size in the Valle del Mezquital dropped sharply.[102] According to the station owners in Huichiapan and Alfaxayuca, flocks were halved by the late 1580s. The actual numbers recorded in the census of these two sub-areas, however, indicate that the stocking rate had not declined as much as the Spanish landowners claimed and was around 7,500 head; although there is evidence of a very sharp decline from other sources.[103] The flocks further declined in numbers and quality during the 1590s. Ewes were so underweight that they were beginning their reproduction cycle later, and the animals slaughtered for meat were smaller and weighed less.[104] Whereas there are records of larger flocks[105] the stocking rate for the last decade of the sixteenth century is estimated at 3,700 head per station. This estimate reflects the stocking rate of the three entailed estates (*mayorazgos*) belonging to the *encomendero* Gerónimo López. When López made his will in 1603 he formed the *mayorazgos* out of twenty-seven sheep stations he held in the Southern Plain, the southern end of the North–South Plain, and the Central Valley. These stations were stocked with 70,000 ewes; Mendizábal calculated a total population of 100,000 head (ewes and lambs), which gives an average stocking rate of 3,703 per station.[106]

Stage 4: Equilibrium "occurs because introduced mammals reduce, and then reach a balance with, their food supply."[107]

---

[102] AGNT, vol. 1106, quad. 2, fols. 1–9; vol. 1697, exp. 1, fol. 3r; vol. 1521, exp. 2, fol. 124; vol. 1527, exp. 1, fol. 3r; vol. 2762, exp. 13, fol. 5r. AGNG, vol. 1, fols. 115r, 206r; vol. 2, fol. 43.

[103] AGIM, leg. 111, ramo 2, doc. 12; AGNT, exp. 1, fol. 1r–12r. The Spanish dramatized the decline in flock size because they were arguing that the lack of workers was the cause of the decline; i.e. the more dramatic the decline, the better their argument for *repartimiento* workers. Evidence of dropping flock size from other sources: AGNT, vol. 1103, exp. 1, fol. sn (2,000 head); vol. 1791, exp. 1, fol. 135r (2,000 head); vol. 1748, exp. 1, fol. 1 (2,000 head); vol. 1728, exp. 2, fol. 15v (2,000 head).

[104] Chevalier, *La formación*, pp. 138–41

[105] For example, of 10,000 head on a station in Tequixquiac in 1592. AGNT, 1748, exp. 1, fol. sn.

[106] Mendizábal, *Obras*, vol. 6, p. 114–18.

[107] Leader-Williams, *Reindeer*, p. 258. The equilibrium between herbivores and plants is not stable, even in conditions of long-standing association. The much-studied Soay sheep population on St. Kilda, for example, "has been monitored in detail between 1959 and 1968, and from 1985 to the present [1992]. Over these periods, the population has shown a repeated pattern of crashes." Grenfell, Price, Albon,

The decline in animal numbers slowed down by the early seventeenth century and the flocks seem to have achieved an accommodation with a much-reduced and transformed vegetative cover.

The basic model of an irruptive oscillation has been modified to take into account that ungulates introduced into large islands or continents disperse from the area in which they are released. The same sequence of events described here occurs whenever a new area is occupied, with the following result:

> At the newest dispersal front, and furthest from the point of liberation, density starts to increase (stage 1); further back in the range density is at its peak (stage 2); nearest the point of liberation the population attains relative stability at a lower density (stage 4). The sequence of stages following liberation could thus be observed either spatially or temporally, at one place over a period of time, or at one time over a range of distance.[108]

A temporal and spatial sequence of stages can be discerned in the Valle del Mezquital. All parts of the Valle del Mezquital were not settled by the Spanish at the same time, nor were they subjected to the same intensity of exploitation during the sixteenth century. Pastoralists shunned areas of poor resources and introduced their flocks into lands that exhibited the best resources (water and pasture), that is, the densely populated and highly productive agricultural areas on the northern border of the Valley of Mexico. As the density of flocks increased, pastoralists expanded their operations into the less attractive areas with fewer water resources, lower rainfall, and poor pasture. The same process of environmental change was repeated in the arid sub-areas after fewer years of intensive grazing than had been the case in the more humid southern areas. This had the effect of producing a similar level of change all over the region at much the same time until, by the end of the sixteenth century, it had been transformed into a homogenous mesquite-dominated desert.

The introduction of grazing and the transformation of the vegetative cover was not the only environmental change recorded in the Valle del Mezquital during the sixteenth century, however. The Spaniards also opened mines in Ixmiquilpan and on its borders with Pachuca to the east and Cimapan to the north, and accelerated lime

---

and Clutton-Brock, "Overcompensation and population cycles in an ungulate," p. 824.
[108] Leader-Williams, *Reindeer*, p. 21.

production for the rebuilding of Tenochtitlán.[109] Both of these activities involved tree cutting, and by the late 1570s the forests disappeared in many areas; Spaniards and Indians fought over trees that were now limited to *quebradas* in areas that had been heavily forested thirty years before.[110] By 1600 sheet erosion scarred the hillsides and covered the flat and sloping lands with slope-wash debris. Gullies were cutting down through all layers.[111] In a final blow to irrigation agri-

---

[109] For Spanish lime manufacture, see AGNM, vol. 6, fols. 455–6; vol. 7, fol. 87r; vol. 8, fols. 227–8; vol. 13, fols. 41r-v, 71, 176; vol. 14, fol. 292v; vol. 16, fols. 201–2. AGNI, vol. 6, pte 2, exp. 998. AGNT, vol. 1519 exp. 4; vol. 2692, exp. 12; vol. 2697, exp. 10–11; vol. 2713, exp. 18, fol. 1r. AGIJ, leg. 154, no. 3, fol. 257v, AGNG, vol. 3, exp. 495.

[110] AGN, Tierras, vol. 2674, exp. 18, fol. 307r.

[111] See Chapter 4, notes 18–20, 23, 28, 41, 44, 49, 71–3, 75, 78, 79, 89, 96, 106, 123, and 125. In much-quoted studies of erosion in the Central Highlands published in 1949, including a study of the southeastern sector of the Valle del Mezquital, Sherburne F. Cook put forward the thesis that sheet erosion was already underway when the Spaniards arrived (Cook, *Historical Demography, Soil Erosion*). In his view, Spaniards simply exacerbated processes already underway – "finishing what the red man had already begun" (*Soil Erosion*, p. 86).

In a later work Cook appears to have modified his position, writing that "a definite change in the environment of [Santa María Ixcatlán] since the time of the conquest may be predicated" (Cook, *Santa María Ixcatlán*, p. 17). Cook demonstrated a dense agricultural population around this town up to the middle of the sixteenth century; and reported that the population migrated out of the region during the last half of that century because of hunger and lack of water – "wholly legitimate reasons in view of the land exhaustion and erosion taking place at that time" (p. 22). He then argues, however, that the extensive erosion present in the 1950s was caused by the prehispanic populations (p. 25). If this was so, one wonders why people waited until the end of the sixteenth century to migrate – a time when their population was declining rapidly and presumably lessening the pressure on the land.

I have two problems with Cook's earlier work: the first has to do with his attempts to fine-tune geological evidence beyond the level to which this sort of data lends itself; the second is with his understanding of the timing of livestock introduction and apparent disregard for well-documented livestock increase. Cook argued that extensive sheet erosion and slope-wash deposition, apparent in the stratigraphy of road cuts, gullies, and stream beds, resulted from the pressure of the dense pre-contact populations (Cook, *Historical Demography*, p. 58–9). This is a perfectly logical conclusion to draw. But I did not find any documentary evidence of the severe sheet erosion Cook supposes to have been present in the Teotlalpan at the time of the conquest. On the other hand, I did find reports of just this type of erosion associated with high densities of sheep in the 1570s and 1580s (see Chapter 4). That is, the geological evidence would seem to apply to a period about fifty years after the arrival of the Spaniards, at a time when the human population was dropping rapidly, but when the impact of the increasing animal populations could be expected. It is instructive that Cook himself had difficulties accounting for evidence of vastly accelerated environmental change between 1548 and 1580 – precisely when

culture, springs were drying out in many parts of the region. By the end of the sixteenth century the landscape was the eroded and gullied mesquite desert traditionally associated with the Valle del Mezquital. (See Chapter 4 for a description of environmental changes in each of the sub-areas of the Valle del Mezquital.)

the human populations were declining (Cook, *Historical Demography*, pp. 33–41, 52–4). Nor was he consistent in the dates he assigned to the cycle of sheet erosion and slope-wash deposition; for example, on pp. 50, 53, 54, and 57, the end of the cycle is placed at or around 1519, but on p. 51 it is put at 1600. He attempted to resolve these problems by making rather awkward statements about the destiny of the Teotlalpan. For example, he wrote that by 1519 the Teotlalpan was *"in any case ecologically doomed to destruction"* (emphasis in original) and that "the Spanish accounts, some of which have already been quoted, lead to the supposition that agriculture in the Teotlalpan had undergone a sharp decline in the sixteenth century [i.e. between 1548–1580]. *If it is assumed that such a decline had already been initiated under the last Aztec rulers, or at least was on the point of becoming manifest,* then the influence of the Spaniards was simply to induce acceleration of the process" (ibid., p. 54; emphasis added).

It may well be that sheet erosion was present when the Spaniards arrived, but it wasn't reported. In order to reconcile the geological evidence of sheet erosion with the documentary record, which indicates that the cycle of sheet erosion and slope-wash deposition did not begin before the last two decades of the sixteenth century, I have suggested that Cook's timetable of erosion events be modified (Melville, "Environmental and Social," p. 50). According to these changes the process of accelerated deterioration between 1548 and 1580 was initiated by the postconquest acceleration of deforestation for mining, lime manufacture, and grazing; overgrazing during the 1560s and 1570s intensified the pressure on the environment and resulted in a rapid process of degradation during the last two decades of the sixteenth century that was marked by sheet erosion and slope-wash deposition. These modifications have the added bonus of fitting very well with the events predicted by the model of ungulate irruptions complicated by the presence of humans. Recent attempts to retain Cook's original model are marred by the same defects as Cook's arguments: they do not really address the well-documented problem of the impact of the introduced grazing animals; and they rely too heavily on negative evidence to bolster a thesis of the impact of the pre-Hispanic populations; as well as on excessive fine-tuning of geological sequences (see for example, Butzer, "Ethno-Agriculture").

Cook treats the impact of livestock as a "subsidiary problem" in the degradation of the Teotlalpan (*Historical Demography*, p. 55). This assumption is based on his understanding that the seventeenth rather than the sixteenth century was the era of livestock exploitation of the region. Following Mendizábal, and according to his own reading of the status of the environment at the end of the sixteenth century, Cook argued that exploitation by livestock was a result of poor natural resources (ibid., p. 56). He seems to ascribe to the common notion that pastoralists naturally and inevitably take their animals where the resources are poorest, leaving the best resources for the agriculturalists. This assumes an altruism among pastoralists in their relations with agriculturalists that is not borne out by history. Indeed, the evidence from the Valle del Mezquital indicates that the pastoralists grazed their

This was not a pristine environment in 1519. The indigenous populations did not live in a "natural" world unmarked by human activity. On the contrary, it is clear that humans had been tinkering with their physical environment for millenia – and not always with happy results. Deforestation, manipulation of the hydrological regimes, modification of landforms, and transformation of the vegetative cover by agricultural practices that included domestication of plants, were all underway when the Spaniards arrived; furthermore, there is ample evidence that this sort of environmental manipulation had led in certain cases to erosion and other environmental ills.[112] This was a dynamic world,

animals in the richest, most fertile, and most densely populated agricultural regions first, only moving to the worst when their was no other choice (see this volume, Chapter 4).

These two quite different interpretations of the status of the environment at conquest and the role of the introduced livestock in the appearance of sheet erosion can be explained by looking at the documentation available to Cook and other students of the region. For example, while environmental deterioration evident by 1580 (primarily deforestation) was recorded in the *Relaciones Geográficas*, sheet erosion, which followed deforestation and occurred in the 1580s and 1590s, is recorded primarily in the documents of AGN, Tierras. Because Cook did not use Tierras for investigating environmental change in the sixteenth century, he did not realize that sheet erosion was widely recorded in the last two decades of the century but not before. [Cook used Tierras almost exclusively for the seventeenth and eighteenth centuries; ibid., p. 18.] Because the region was lightly populated by both humans and grazing animals in the seventeenth century, he correlated his evidence of slope-wash deposition with the high population densities of the preconquest era in accordance with his hypothesis. In the same way he missed the increase in density and areal extent of the semidesert species during the last quarter of the century, which is also recorded extensively in Tierras. Further, he proposed that the density and extent of these plants had not increased (ibid., p. 56). As well, by not using AGN, Mercedes, he missed the extraordinary increase in livestock raising in the sixteenth century. This may explain why, although he was clearly interested in the competition between the invading and indigenous populations, he did not really address the impact of invading grazing animals. It is significant that he was unable to find any documents pertaining to Santa María Ixcatlán in Tierras (*Santa María Ixcatlán*, p. 14); it may explain his continuing reliance on the pre-Hispanic population as an explanation of erosion in that region as well.

[112] See, for example, Joyce and Mueller, "The Social Impact of Anthropogenic Landscape Modification in the Río Verde Drainage Basin, Oaxaca, Mexico," for evidence of erosion in the pre-Hispanic period. However, Charles Frederick finds that "occupation by sedentary prehistoric populations widely believed to have had profound environmental impact appear to have had little effect in the Río Laja Basin [northwest of San Miguel de Allenda, Gto.], which lies on the northern periphery of Mesoamerica," "Abstract." It is possible that the location of this region meant that it was lightly populated. It is, however, interesting that he finds that historic settlement was "accompanied by widespread abandonment of preexisting floodplains and channel incision in excess of four meters."

continuously changing. That being said, however, the Spaniards did not simply augment processes underway; rather, they changed the relationship between humans and their physical environment. By adding a completely new element to the dynamics of ecological and social change they triggered an ecological revolution.[113] It remains to describe the nature of this revolution – to trace the reciprocal ecological and social processes by which pastoralism expanded into this New World region and to demonstrate the consequences for both Spanish pastoralists and Indian communities.

[113] The idea that the introduction of the Old World grazing animals and their human minders triggered an ecological revolution in Mexico was first put forward by Simpson in *Exploitation of Land*, p. 2.

3

THE AUSTRALIAN EXPERIENCE

What happens when pastoralism is introduced into a world that knows neither domesticated grazing animals nor the systems of resource exploitation peculiar to pastoralism? In Chapters 1 and 2 we discussed the consequences of the introduction of ungulates into new ecosystems; let us now look more closely at what happens when humans accompany these animals and manipulate the environment for profit.

There is a large and growing body of studies dealing with the relationship between pastoralism and environmental change, but they rarely tell us of the initial onslaught and, until recently, they did not allow for irreversible change. The majority of these studies, including those of the nineteenth-century American Southwest, are concerned with regions that were grazed in the past by Old World domesticates.[1] The relationship between the grazing animals and the physical environment is that of a resident population and its subsistence base; the current population of grazing animals represents a phase in a cycle of resource exploitation.[2] These studies use the ecosystem concept to order evidence of change according to an ideal of equilibrium: an ecosystem is seen as the consequence of interaction between climatic change (gradual, catastrophic, or cyclical), the physical structure of the landscape (rocks, soils, and vegetation), and the actions of the resident populations (human and faunal as well as floral). The possibilities for change are multiplied when the ecosystem is invaded by alien species. For example, invasion by grazing animals affects vegetation, soils, and the resident faunal communities, and resulting modifications in the environment stimulate changes in the invading population (e.g. increase, decrease, extinction). Despite the potential

---

[1] A significant exception is Henry Dobyns's study of the desertification of the Sonoran desert riverine oases. He discusses the different ecological impact of Indian, Mexican, and Anglo-American herding practices as but one aspect of changing modes of land use over time. See Dobyns, *From Fire to Flood.*

[2] See for example, Johannessen's study of cattle grazing and grasslands in Honduras, *Savannas.*

60

for almost endless complexities inherent in each ecosystem, however, and the nearly limitless possibilities for change provided by the shifting interfaces between these elements, change is interpreted as a movement toward homeostasis.[3] We are concerned here, however, with an environment that was clearly not moving in that direction, but rather that was profoundly disturbed by an alien invasion. The introduction of ungulates into new ecosystems results in a radically changed biological regime, and where domestic grazing animals are introduced, the process of environmental change associated with the irruption of herbivores into new environments is complicated by other variables that include land clearance methods, systems of range management, stocking rates, patterns of land tenure, and land use. Accommodation between the environment and the new species is eventually achieved but the initial onslaught causes, in Simpson's words, "an ecological revolution of truly vast proportions."[4]

In Australia the experience of colonization and the onset of exploitation of the natural resources by Old World grazing animals occurred relatively recently. Environmental transformation associated with the introduction of domestic grazing animals into the native environment has taken place in some areas within living memory.[5] Because the initiation of this process is recent, and the documentation of associated environmental changes more plentiful and somewhat more scientific than for sixteenth century Mexico, the study of the ecological consequences of the introduction of intensive pastoralism into Australia clarifies the Mexican case. There are other advantages to using Australia as a comparative case study. For one thing, sheep grazing was the initial mode of land use and the main reason for settlement in the highlands and tablelands of New South Wales, which has been chosen as the specific region for study because of similarities with the Mexican landscape and climate. For another, soil conservation, flood control, and the maintenance or improvement of the catchment value in areas earmarked for increased production to supply overseas markets, especially after World War II, formed the basis for research that has clarified the relationship between grazing and erosion and the deterioration of the water regime.[6] Australian soil sci-

[3] See Worster's discussion of the ecosystem model in "Ecology of Order and Chaos."
[4] Simpson, *Exploitation of Land*, p. 2.
[5] Or at least within the memory of people interviewed in the late 1940s and 1950s.
[6] In 1981 Geoffrey Bolton published a fascinating overview of the ecological consequences of the British settlement of Australia that provides a preliminary answer to J. M. Powell's call for "a thorough evaluation of the profits and losses to the Australian environment which were registered in the years of pastoral expansion and in the

entists have used controlled experiments and observations in their study of these related problems, and in their search for the antecedents of erosion they have also examined the historical record. Whereas most investigators seem to have accepted the landscape at the end of the nineteenth century as representative of the "natural" or precontact environment, occasional references to a survey carried out in the 1840s indicate that environmental degradation was evident at an early date, and was probably related to the introduction of Old World grazing animals.[7]

In this chapter we follow them in their search. Primary documents from the first fifty years of grazing have been searched for information about the dates of the introduction of sheep into the highlands and tablelands of New South Wales, stocking and grazing rates, environmental changes observed in these areas between 1803 and 1854, and the time lapse between the introduction of sheep and the onset of deterioration in vegetation, soils, and water resources. The results of this historical investigation are combined with the conclusions reached by Australian soil scientists about the relationship between grazing and environmental change, to provide a comparative model of the changes associated with the initial introduction of pastoralism.[8] A brief preliminary description of sheep raising as it was practiced in New South Wales in the first half of the nineteenth century provides a context for the following discussion of ecological change; similarities with Mexico are indicated.

The First Fifty Years

The areas in which sheep stations were established in New South Wales and the southern extremity of Queensland in the early period

confusion of mining activity during the [eighteen-]fifties ... Hasten the day when biogeographers, geomorphologists and historical geographers combine to interpret and communicate the ecological impact of both the 'Squatting Age' and the 'Golden Age.' " Powell, "Conservation and Resource Management," p. 41; see *Spoils and Spoilers*.

[7] Whalley, Robinson and Taylor, "General Effects," p. 174.

[8] The simultaneous study of historical and scientific material turned out to be remarkably useful as a learning process. Not only did I end up with a comparative historical sequence and an idea of the type of ecological changes associated (or at least coterminous) with the expansion of grazing, I also gained an entry into the study of grazing ecology. When I returned to the Mexican material I found that it contained remarkable amounts of ecological data, and the analysis of this data can (with the learning processes carefully concealed) stand on its own. But it is doubtful whether I would have known what to look for in the Mexican documents, let alone known how to interpret the material I collected, if I had not attempted the Australian study first.

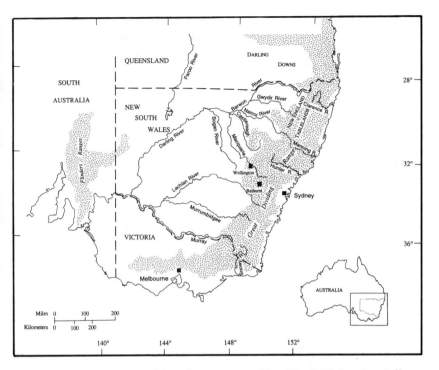

Map 3.1. Geographic reference map: New South Wales, Australia

are in many ways similar to the Valle del Mezquital. The Great Dividing Range and the undulating tablelands lying between the coastal margin and the western slopes consist in great part of old volcanic outcroppings (mostly granite) covered with thin soils, and intervening valleys with richer alluvial soils. Conglomerate rocks underlie the alluvial valley soils and abut the volcanic rocks of the mountains and hills.[9] Rainfall in the tablelands of New South Wales declines from 1000mm to 600mm east to west, a similar range to that found in the Valle del Mezquital. Climatic variability, with the ever-present risk of drought, is also similar to that found in the Mexican region.

In Australia, as in Mexico, sheep raising quickly came to be associated with legally defined areas of land and exclusive access. In both regions, too, there was a fixed core to the enterprise composed of huts and corrals: the *estancia* in Mexico and the station in Australia,

[9] Strzelecki *Physical Description*, p. 359. Australian Capital territory, *Soil Conservation Council*, pp. 7–10. There is, however, a marked difference in the topography, which can be traced to the great age of the Australian continent and the relative youth of the Mexican highlands.

and these terms have been used interchangeably in this study. In Australia the head station was placed at the center of a sheep run with outstations at every point on the compass; supplying these stations with their weekly rations was, according to a contemporary observer, "a startling nuisance."[10] The system of flock management in Australia, before the runs were fenced in the 1880s, was also very similar to sixteenth-century Mexico. Shepherds had charge of around six hundred sheep, which they corralled at night in sheep folds next to crude huts in the station area. The sheep were taken out to pasture an hour before sunrise and herded back into the folds no later than sundown. The watchmen watched the flocks at night from a watchbox and moved the folds each day. The number of sheep a man could control on foot with dogs appears to have been the same as in Mexico, where individual Indian commoners were given licenses to take herds of five or six hundred sheep to the hills to graze.[11]

In order to control the inveterate wandering of the Australian shepherds, who would stay for a short time and then move on, shepherds' contracts were drawn up stating the time of service and the number of sheep under each shepherd's care. The shepherd was held responsible for these sheep and they were counted weekly by the squatter and his overseer together, losses being discounted from the shepherd's wages.[12] The men who became shepherds in Australia very often had no prior knowledge of flock management or breeding, and none about pasture management; nor, for that matter, had the station

---

[10] Gardner, *Production and Resources*, vol. 1, p. 50.
[11] Strzelecki, *Physical Description*, p. 365. Gardner, *Production and Resources*, vol. 1, pp. 48, 72, 80. Dogs are not mentioned in the text but appear in the illustrations. For references to licenses to graze between five hundred and six hundred head of sheep in the Valle del Mezquital: AGN, General de Parte, vol. 1, exp. 74, fol. 141r; exp. 1087, fol. 206r; vol. 2, exp. 214, fo. 43r. AGN, Indios, vol. 6, pte. 1, exp. 1001, fol. 269r; vol. 6, pte. 2, exp. 207, fol. 46v; exp. 469, fol. 104v. AGN, Tierras, vol. 1697, exp. 1, fol. 3r. Konrad found that the man-to-sheep ratio varied significantly (one man per 600 sheep, 1:400, 1:200). Where pasture was excellent and there was competition, more guards were needed. Sheep were also closely guarded when moved from one place to another. He notes also that sheep dogs were reported for the sixteenth century only (*Jesuit Hacienda*, p. 182). I found no references to sheep dogs.
[12] Gardner, *Production and Resources*, vol. 1, p. 72. Strzelecki, *Physical Description*, pp. 365–6. John Dargavel, of the Centre for Resource and Environment Studies, Australian National University, pointed out that the wages were far from being free and were often tied to the convict system on ticket-of-leave conditions; ex-convicts were blocked from being landowners by many regulations; and because of the low ratio of women, ex-convicts very often remained single and the supply of itinerant, isolated stock keepers was kept up by constant recruitment of ex-convicts. Personal correspondence, December, 1984.

owners, who were mostly ex-soldiers, sailors, or businessmen.[13] In this respect they differed from their counterparts in Mexico, where the African slaves generally did have experience as herdsmen either in Africa or Spain, and the Spaniards had been stock owners.

Pasturelands were acquired by land grant or squatting. When the market opened up for Australian wools in Great Britain in the 1820s, would-be graziers flooded in waves across the land, spreading out from Sydney to the west, and then to the north, as soon as the barrier of the Great Dividing Range had been broached.[14]

The most obvious difference between the two colonies is found in the indigenous populations. The Australian Aborigines were nomadic people with no recognizable territorial rights – at least, according to European understanding of land ownership.[15] The Spanish, on the other hand, found large indigenous populations practicing intensive agriculture, although the presence of large agricultural populations did little to prevent the spectacular increase of the invading animals and the eventual conversion of Indian lands into grazing land.

Another difference is in native grazing animals. The lands that the sheep invaded in Australia already had a grazing animal: the kangaroo. In Mexico, the first lands to be grazed were agricultural lands rather than the woodlands grazed by deer. In Australia, the introduction of hard-hoofed animals into ecosystems formerly grazed by the soft-footed kangaroos resulted in marked soil deterioration. Kangaroos were quickly pushed westward out of the eastern coastal lands where they had been in ecological equilibrium for millennia, and great efforts were made to exterminate them; in fact, kangaroos were classified as vermin and hunted as so-called noxious animals. Before a relatively recent ban on the killing of the kangaroo it was in danger of extermination, and several subspecies have in fact been lost. The rabbit, which caused further destruction of the grasslands of Australia, was not introduced until 1859, after the period covered by this study.[16]

The Deterioration of the Australian Environment

The increase of the populations of introduced grazing animals was as spectacular as that recorded in the Americas. Sheep took around

---

[13] Strzelecki, *Physical Description*, p. 368. King, "Outline of Closer Settlement," p. 12.
[14] King, "Outline of Closer Settlement," pp. 15–16: "Official limits were set aside as squatters occupied half a continent within a short space of ten years." Strzelecki, *Physical Description*, p. 366.
[15] Gardner noted that each tribe had its own hunting and fishing territory, but that these rights were ignored in the rush for land; *Production and Resources*, vol. 1, p. 257.
[16] *The Australian Encyclopedia*, Vol. 7, p. 341.

eleven years to acclimatize to the Australian environment, from 1792, when they were first introduced, to around 1803, when their populations began to increase in size. Between 1803 and 1845 the sheep population of New South Wales grew to nine million head, and by 1854 it was over twelve million.[17] The expansion of the flocks was associated with a rapid spread of settlement. Following a drought experienced in the eastern coastal lands in 1813, settlers moved west and a little later north in search of new pastures. One of the early areas of expansion to the north was the Hunter Valley, first settled in 1820 with a few flocks of sheep. The Liverpool plains north-northwest of the Hunter River Valley were settled in 1826. From here settlers moved into the New England tablelands in 1832, then into the drier area of the Darling Downs to the north in 1840, and completely filled the Barwan River region with stations between 1842 and 1847. Between 1830 and 1840 half of the continent was settled by squatters.[18] The settlers repeated the same process wherever they went: they moved into new areas, acquired squatters' licenses, and began to graze their animals. In a very few years the valley or plain would be given over to grazing, primarily by sheep, but by cattle as well.[19] But the rapid growth of the invading populations was matched by the speed with which the grasses were exhausted and the numbers declined. By 1847, only seven years after settlement, the Darling Downs were showing signs of deterioration. By 1854 the pasture, though good, was reportedly "failing fast" in another newly settled area, Burnett and Wide Bay to the north. Produce in wool and tallow per head of sheep deteriorated with the declining carrying capacity.[20]

A contemporary account of the effects on the native Australian environment of the first thirty years of grazing in New South Wales is given by Sir Paul Edmund Strzelecki, a British geologist who carried out geological and botanical studies in New South Wales and Van Diemen's Land (Tasmania) in the 1840s. He wrote:

> Carpe Diem seems to have been the motto generally acted upon by the graziers: so long as the herbage thus singularly adapted for sheep promoted their increase, the evil workings of the system, or rather

[17] Strzelecki, *Physical Description*, p. 366. Gardner, *Production and Resources*, vol. 1, pp. 1, 95.

[18] Gardner, vol. 1, pp. 1, 10, 11, 15, 18c, 48, 112; King, "Outline," pp. 15–16.

[19] Gardner, *Production and Resources*, vol. 1, pp. 1–2, 6, 11, 15, 95, 112. The tablelands and the western slopes of the Great Dividing Range that were settled before 1850 were used primarily to graze sheep; Donald, "The Progress of Australian Agriculture," p. 188.

[20] Gardner, *Production and Resources*, vol. 1, p. 18c, 23.

the absence of all systems, and its consequences were lost sight of in the immediate profitable result which such an increase realized. But when that increase began to act on the pasture – when the grass of the granted lands began to disappear and the nakedness of the soils to be exposed – then had not fresh grounds with fresh pastures been at hand, the sheep owner would have paid dearly for this misman-agement of the pastoral lands. Fortunately, however, room was not wanting. The dividing range, which in the early period of coloni-zation limited the grazing operations, was soon passed over; and new pastures as luxuriant as the first ones had been were discovered. Bathurst, Liverpool Plains, Manning, Moneiro, and Murrumbidgee were soon overrun and covered with flocks and pastoral pursuits again became replete with life and promise. The pasture, however, here as in the foreground of the colony began to diminish: the occasional burnings which were from time to time resorted to in order to ame-liorate the pasture, or to produce new growth from the roots of the grasses, did but accelerate the slowly but evidently approaching evils. Dews began to be scarce, and rain still more so: one year of drought followed another; and in the summer of 1838, the whole country of New South Wales between Sydney and Wellington, the upper and lower Hunter River, Liverpool Plains, Argylshire, etc., presented with very few exceptions a naked surface without any perceptible pasture upon it for the numerous half-starved flocks.[21]

In 1854 William Gardner wrote up his survey of northern and western New South Wales for the period 1842–52. He also noted the speed with which the native pastures failed under grazing, and the rapid movement of the settlers in search of new grasslands. Writing ten years after the Hunter Valley had been abandoned by the first wave of settlers – after twenty years of heavy grazing – Gardner described the process of settlement and speculated on the causes of abandonment:

> The early settlers of the great Valley of the Hunter were never ceasing in their praises of that country, the herbage of grass were in abundance even to profusion, and the crops were never failing. Occupation for the short period of less than fifteen years, [however] informed the settlers of the pastoral character of that country which has long since been abandoned as unprofitable as a grazing district.[22] The countries under the range in the Hunter District have long ceased to be a grazing country, the few sheep or cattle kept by the Proprietors of estates or renters of Government Sections being only enabled to graze a limited number of either. In former years this

[21] Strzelecki, *Physical Description*, pp. 366–77.
[22] Gardner, *Production and Resources*, vol. 1, p. 111.

country was overstocked and has been worn out, the natural herbage of grass which appears in such abandon when first inhabited has long since disappeared, this was with the exception of a few runs which may be instanced as not having been under a regular cropping by the nibblers – the overstocking and long continued grazing of this country has finished it as far as sheep farming is concerned, it has therefore been abandoned by the sheep farmer. The few cattle remaining in these countries being in such a condition as to be unable to compete in any market, with the cattle sent from the runs of the mountain interior.[23]

Gardner considered that the loss of native pasture in the early settled areas of the colony, and later in the areas of expansion to the north and west, was directly attributable to overstocking and overgrazing.[24] He quotes an article published in the *Sydney Atlas* on 13 November 1847, which, in somewhat turgid prose, expresses his feelings about the apathy of the settlers toward the need for the protection of the pasture as well as the improvement of pasture types:

Australia being an eminently pastoral country, men should naturally suppose that no small share of attention must of course be directed to the improvement of her pastures, for the benefit of stock. No such thing.... The native tribes are unanimous on the position the seasons are altered to "the dry way" in comparison with what they were antecedent to that eventful period [introduction of grazing]. Without stopping to enquire about these changes Mr. Colonial Experience must admit that sheep runs have affected alterations on the face of Mother Earth, and pretty nearly swept the grass clean out of sight, in the space of twenty years, from many a luxuriant and lovely spot – Nature exterted her utmost till overpowered by the multitude of nibblers her grasses never allowed to rise into seed stalks for purposes of reproduction the very roots torn out and eaten, at last she retired exhausted from the conquest, crying I can do no more now man must suffer by his rapacity and negligence.[25]

Gardner listed several species of grasses that could have been used for the improvement of the native pastures and went on to say that experiments should be carried out to determine the best types for Australian needs, following the model experiments carried out on the Duke of Bedford's estates in England.[26] This type of experiment was not made until the 1880s.

[23] Ibid., vol. 1, p. 2.
[24] Ibid., vol. 1, pp. 1, 2, 3, 7, 18c, 114, 115.
[25] Ibid., vol. 1, p. 7.
[26] Ibid., vol. 1, p. 7.

Although stock raising had acquired a relatively scientific status in Europe by the beginning of the nineteenth century, the mirage of seemingly limitless pastures, combined with the extraordinary increase of the newly introduced species, led to indiscriminate grazing and overstocking.[27] The vegetation was considered in bulk and the total amount of foliage was the factor used by the stockmen to calculate the stocking rates, not the annual growth increment.[28] As a result, stocking rates were very high and the pasture deteriorated; for example, stocking rates of 205 head per square kilometer in the New England tablelands caused severe damage. As the pasture deteriorated, the stocking rates dropped: in the Darling Downs in the 1850s, the far lower rate of 77.2 head per square kilometer was considered ideal.[29] The sequence of events and the rationale behind overgrazing in the past is summed up by Hanmer:

> The native grasses can be very prolific growers in the spring and the tendency was to bring in more stock at that time. Unfortunately when these quick maturing grasses were past their best, everyone was attempting to dispose of his stock. The consequent depression in market values often led landholders to attempt to carry the increased stock numbers over. Destruction of the vegetable cover was the end result.[30]

When the "nibblers," as Gardner called them, had eaten out the native grasses and palatable shrubs, and burning no longer stimulated regrowth, the livestock owner would generally give up his lease and move on – leaving denuded and burnt soils behind. Some regeneration occurred, of course, but the original diversity of plant species was diminished and the balance of the plant communities shifted toward more arid-land types. Then the land was grazed again – but with lower densities of sheep on shorter-stemmed grasses, so that the overall vegetative cover was reduced.[31] Nothing was done to improve the pastures by applying fertilizer, to introduce grasses more resistant

[27] Strzelecki, *Physical Description*, p. 368. Butler, "Agriculture in Southern New South Wales," p. 281. King, "Outline of Closer Settlement," p. 13.

[28] Donald, "Progress of Australian Agriculture," p. 188.

[29] Gardner, *Production and Resources*, pp. 27, 50, 118. Flock size diminished by 25 percent between 1839 and 1849.

[30] Hanmer, "Land Use and Erosion," p. 281.

[31] Beadle, *Vegetation and Pastures*, pp. 11–16; Bryant, "Grazing and Burning," p. 29; Butler, "Agriculture," pp. 281–2; Costin, Wimbush, Kerr and Gray, "Catchment Hydrology," pp. 12–14; Donald, "Australian Agriculture," p. 188; Moore, "Effects of the Sheep Industry," p. 170; Moore and Biddiscombe, "Effects of Grazing," pp. 223–5; Whalley, Robinson and Taylor, "General Effects," p. 174.

to grazing, or even to regulate the intensity or duration of grazing. Indeed, virtually the only measure taken by the graziers to improve the pasture was to fire the grasslands. The time taken to graze an area to the point of destroying its immediate usefulness to the graziers was from seven to twenty years.[32]

Increasing aridity was reported in the early years of settlement. The Liverpool Plains, for example, exhibited parched and dry conditions with sunbaked soils: "The long grasses and herbage formerly protected the moisture in the ground, now cattle and sheep lay the ground bare, and the moisture is open for evaporation by the atmosphere and hot winds."[33] And in the Hunter Valley:

> The seasons have been reversed in this district and dry parched seasons have succeeded the drooping [plentifull] seasons, extending into the interior as far as the table lands of New England . . . The first settlers on [the] Hunter River remarked at their early settlement the heavy dews which fell at night, the herbage and grasses which at that time protected the ground and kept it in a cool moist state is now become by being overstocked heated during the day by the searching rays of the sun, and instead of as formerly an attractive for the moisture it is a repelative.[34]

One hundred years after Strzelecki and Gardner made their surveys, soil erosion and the conservation of soils and pastures came to be studied in earnest. Earlier suspicions regarding the effects of overgrazing by sheep were confirmed. Light grazing does not necessarily have the effect of retarding the growth and replacement of the vegetative cover; but areas which are heavily grazed, because they are attractive to sheep or because grazing is not controlled, do show deterioration under grazing.[35] The microenvironment of the vegetation is affected by overgrazing and extensive removal of the vegetative cover in the following way:

> Close grazing reduces the insulating effect of vegetation and its buffering effect on temperature changes at the soil surface, thereby increasing the chances of stem and leaf meristems being exposed to extremes of temperature. In this respect it is interesting to note that the commonly used pasture species have wide climatic tolerance ranges. Reduction of mulch or surface litter through complete or

---

[32] Gardner, *Production and Resources*, vol. 1, pp. 1, 7, 18, 62, 114, 115.
[33] Ibid., vol. 1, p. 3.
[34] Ibid., vol. 1, pp. 1–2.
[35] Hilder, "Rate of Turn-over," pp. 11, 15; Bryant, "Grazing and Burning," pp. 41–2. Moore and Biddiscombe, "Effects of Grazing," p. 225.

near complete consumption of herbage by grazing animals may also widen amplitudes of soil temperatures and reduce the infiltration of water into soils. It has also been shown that moisture infiltration in an Andropogon grassland protected from grazing is increased and evaporation reduced by the presence of surface litter. Other consequences of reduction of plant cover by grazing are increased runoff of precipitation and liability to erosion.[36]

Where overgrazing led to the complete, or almost complete, denudation of the soil surface in semiarid regions, the soil was exposed to wide temperature ranges and species characteristic of more arid regions invaded the grasslands until the density of unpalatable shrubs impeded grazing. In areas of higher rainfall there has been a convergence of plant species as a result of grazing, and the tall warm-season native perennial grasses (especially kangaroo grass, *Themeda australis*) were quickly replaced by shorter cool-season perennial grasses.[37] In the high mountain areas the tussocky native grasses were replaced by a hard-cropped turf where sheep grazed, and the diversity of herbs and grasses was diminished or lost.[38] The native vegetation exhibited the effects of the irruption of sheep into a new ecosystem augmented by the interference of stockmen, who held the numbers at artificially high levels. These effects included the diminution of species diversity in all environmental zones; an increased competitive advantage for arid-zone species as a more arid environment replaced the earlier, wetter conditions; and the reduction of the density and height of ground cover.[39]

Judging by the presence of relic bogs and fens, and by the descriptions given by Gardner and other early explorers and observers, the tablelands and high mountain environments were a good deal wetter in the early 1800s – even up to the end of the nineteenth century in some isolated areas – than they are today.[40] Gardner noted that the tablelands of the New England area had been wet and swampy when the first settlers arrived, but when he made his survey only sixteen years later, the swamps had so dried out that only another six or seven years were needed to finish the process. He ascribed the drying out

[36] Moore and Biddiscombe," "Effects of Grazing," pp. 222–3.
[37] Ibid., pp. 223–5.
[38] Costin, "The Grazing Factor," p. 7; Costin, Wimbush, Kerr, and Gray, "Studies in Catchment Hydrology," pp. 6–7, 10, 14.
[39] Moore, "Effects of the Sheep Industry." pp. 180–2; Moore and Biddiscombe, "Effects of Grazing," pp. 223–4.
[40] Costin, "Grazing Factor," pp. 5–6; Gardner, *Production and Resources*, vol. 1, p. 23; Costin, Wimbush, Kerr, and Gray "Studies in Catchment Hydrology," p. 12.

of the swamps to the formation of cattle trails, which channeled the water to natural drainage lines. In addition, shepherds were in the habit of cutting simple canals to channel the water down natural flow lines to drain the swamps for sheep grazing; cattle and sheep accelerated the process of desiccation by grazing the vegetation in such areas down to a hard-cropped turf.[41]

The shift from tall tussocky grasses to short-stemmed pasture leads to an increase in overland flow as with a bare surface, and, although ground cover may still be present in the form of pasture, rainfall is not detained for sufficient time to allow infiltration.[42] Groundwater is not replenished, and the catchment value drops. The catchment value is further decreased by opening drainage lines, burning peat bogs, cutting trees, plowing and road-cutting (both of which remove vegetation and channel water flow), and by burning to stimulate the growth of succulent new growth. All these were carried out by pastoralists.[43]

As noted in the above quote, reduction of the ground cover can affect the water resources of an entire catchment area (i.e. the drainage system of, generally speaking, a river basin[44]) by reducing water absorption. When a catchment area is in good condition a large proportion of rainfall is absorbed into the soil, the total amount of runoff is reduced, the time for the water to reach the main stream is increased, and the underground storage water that maintains springs and permanent stream flow is replenished.[45] The infiltration rate is directly correlated with the surface detention of water, a function of surface roughness. This means that when the ground cover is removed or appreciably reduced in density, groundwater recharge and sustained stream flow are also reduced – representing a decline in the catchment value. Field studies done in the 1940s and 1950s of the catchment area of the proposed Snowy River dam showed that by reducing surface roughness and thereby water absorption, grazing significantly reduced catchment values.[46]

[41] Gardner, *Production and Resources*, vol. 1, p. 23; Tewkesbury, "Soil Erosion," p. 25; Costin, "Grazing Factor," p. 9.
[42] Costin, "Grazing Factor," p. 10.
[43] Tewkesbury, "Soil Erosion," p. 25; Costin, "Grazing Factor," pp. 5–6; Costin, Wimbush, Kerr, and Gray "Studies in Catchment Hydrology," pp. 5, 19–20; Hanmer, "Land Use and Erosion," pp. 280–1; Kaleski, "Erosion and Soil Conservation," p. 2; Australian Capital Territory, *Soil Conservation*, pp. 10–13, 18–19.
[44] Costin, "Grazing Factor," p. 11.
[45] Kaleski, "Erosion and Soil Conservation," p.2.
[46] Costin, "Grazing Factor," p. 11.

As water infiltration rates decrease, the overland flow of water increases and with it the severity of flooding. This phenomenon was noted by nineteenth-century observers. In fact, the same people who saw the increasing aridity of the soils also took note of the growing severity of floods. Gardner, for example, quoted the Aborigines of the table lands as saying that the rivers flooded more after settlement than before. This suggests that the rapid clearance of the vegetation increased the overland flow of water leading to a more rapid rise of floodwaters and more frequent flooding. But although the frequency of flooding increased, the volume of the floodwaters dropped during the early years of settlement. Gardner ascribed this to drier climatic conditions and a lowered rainfall brought on by the clearing away of the vegetative cover.[47] On the other hand, a recent study suggests that because trees take a good deal of water from the soil, more remains when they are removed. Deforestation, therefore, leads to a decline in the volume of surface water, which drops as the water table rises, bringing problems of waterlogging and salination.[48] However, this seems more characteristic of low-lying lands than of hillsides, where erosion, following tree-felling and land clearance, removes the soil and reduces water absorption and water table recharge.

Erosion is perhaps the most obvious consequence of the reduction of ground cover. Where the vegetative cover is removed, the underlying soils are exposed and become unstable from being subjected to greater temperature ranges and trampling; they are also more easily eroded by wind and water. Water-borne erosion strips the soil off slopes, deposits rubble on potentially useful soils further downslope, and provides a focus for gullying along natural flow lines.[49] Wind erosion is common in arid and semiarid areas following heavy grazing or plowing, and it affects the regeneration of native vegetation in these regions by

> providing unfavourable conditions for germination [which result] from the disappearance of perennial grasses following sheep grazing and consequent erosion of the soil surface by wind. Loss of surface soil markedly reduces levels of plant nutrients such as nitrogen and, for this reason, erosion is an important factor in the slow recovery

[47] Ibid., vol. 1, p. 3.
[48] The study is referred to in Heathcote, *Australia*, p. 122. See also D. I. Smith and B. Finlayson, "Water in Australia: Its role in environmental degradation," in *Land, Water and People*, edited by Heathcote and Mabutt, pp. 25–6.
[49] Hanmer, "Land Use and Erosion," p. 282.

of perennial vegetation in overgrazed communities of arid and semi-arid regions even in the absence of further grazing.[50]

Where exposed soils are trampled by hard-hoofed grazing animals, the probability of erosion is greatly increased. It has often been pointed out that prior to the advent of the Europeans and their grazing animals the Australian soils had never been subject to trampling by hard-hoofed animals, and that the combination of grazing and trampling exacerbated natural erosion. In their study of the hydrology of the Australian Alps, Costin and his colleagues found that erosion has become an acute problem in all areas that were described in the mid-1800s as denuded by continuous heavy grazing.[51] These researchers also reported a situation of nonparallelism between soil (erosion) and vegetation trends that helps explain why graziers will continue to graze actively eroding areas – thereby accelerating the destruction of their own land. They wrote,

> Most ecologists and conservationists favour the view that soil and vegetation change in the same direction, whether it be up or down. In most cases this is true, and if the time interval is long enough, it is always so. However, there are cases when soil and vegetation trends may move in opposing directions for considerable periods. In unfavourable environments, initially severe disturbance of the soil sets downward trends in progress. Because of the depth of the solum, however, some of the surviving plants may continue to grow for the rest of their life-span, which, in the case of shrubs, may be as long as 20–30 years. Vigorous annual and short-lived perennial herbs (e.g. sorrel) may also reproduce themselves, particularly if soil erosion is largely confined to short periods of the year, and this may continue until the soil mantle has been reduced almost to the underlying rock. An important implication of this non-parallelism of soil and vegetation trends in the same area is the relative weights which should be given to soil and vegetation condition [for the assessment of the catchment value].[52]

In an earlier study Costin noted that whereas native grasses, which propagate by seedling regeneration, were affected by the selective grazing of sheep and cattle that removed the new seedlings at the edge of the tussocks, the palatable minor herbs, characterized by free-seeding and rapid propagation, could provide grazing until erosion proceeded to the underlying rotten rock.[53] In other words, grazing

[50] Moore and Biddiscombe, "Effects of Grazing," p. 223.
[51] Costin, Wimbush, Kerr, and Gray "Studies in Catchment Hydrology," pp. 12–15.
[52] Ibid., p. 30.
[53] Costin, "Grazing Factor," p. 9.

can continue in areas with marked soil deterioration. The presence of vegetation in otherwise deteriorated areas masks the severity of the soil changes, and encourages graziers to continue grazing their animals. Continued grazing in areas where erosion is ongoing vastly accelerates the process until the damage is irreparable.[54]

Fire and drought are two elements in the Australian ecological equation that we have not yet considered. The Australian environment has clearly been subject to fire for far longer than humans have inhabited the continent; the regeneration of many species of plants is triggered by the intense heat of forest fires. Human populations have also used fire to modify the environment for their own ends. In common with many New World people, the Australian Aborigines used fire as a tool. They used it to promote the vegetation suitable for the animals they hunted – a process called fire-stick farming by Rhys Jones – and they fired the bush for fun, for signaling, and to clear the ground for traveling.[55] They are thought to have developed and maintained the open woodlands typical of the landscape at the time of European arrival by frequent light burning.[56]

The Aborigines are generally thought to have been in better ecological balance with their physical environment than that achieved by the Europeans. Nevertheless, Geoffrey Bolton warns that "those who would see the Aboriginal as a noble savage, better attuned than white Australians to the needs and moods of the environment, must reckon with the possibility that the Aborigines left an impoverished ecosystem behind them."[57] Indeed, it is possible that their fires accelerated the spread of the central Australian desert, and that their hunting practices led to the extinction of several species, thus limiting the animals to which their descendants had access. Bolton goes on, however, to note that

> the Aboriginal achievement was considerable. They were fine botanists, who learned to maximise the available resources, in an environment without cereal crops and with a poorer diversity of plant life than was accessible to most other cultures. The whole of Australia was their farm, and it was a farm which they exploited with care for the needs of later generations. It may be that the increasing aridity of the land taught them forcibly that resources could not be regarded

---

[54] Costin, Wimbush, Kerr, and Gray, "Studies in Catchment Hydrology," p. 31.

[55] Jones, "Fire Stick Farming," p. 226.

[56] For a review of the arguments for and against the role of the Aborigines in the development and/or maintenance of the open grasslands of Australia, see Nicholson, "Fire and the Australian Aborigines – an enigma."

[57] Bolton, *Spoils and Spoilers*, p. 8.

as infinite, but that they must practice disciplined nomadic habits, restriction of numbers, and conservation of sources of water and food. In addition their pattern of life was imbued with a deeply felt sense of religious tradition which identified the people with the land and its natural features. The individual was subordinated to the good of the community, and the community was subordinated to the environment. There was no scope for motives of individual profit which might tempt the venturesome to either improvement or exploitation. The concept of land as private property which might be cultivated, possessed, inherited, and transformed was unknown in Aboriginal Australia.[58]

With the arrival of the Europeans the Aboriginal fires were perceived as a threat to life and property and were outlawed. The suppression of light and regular burns accelerated scrub invasion of the grasslands and an increase in density of undergrowth in the open woodlands. As the numbers of grazing animals increased, however, more land was needed and fire was again used to clear the grasslands of secondary growth and to promote grass regrowth. Fire was also used to clear forests to extend grazing, and it was used on such a scale that the deforestation and burning carried out by the pastoralists rivaled the effects of the loggers and gold miners on the Australian environment.[59] Although they were following Aboriginal practices, the Europeans' patterns of burning were much more severe, destroying the organic matter in the soil and soil fertility, and ultimately leading to degeneration of soil structure.[60]

Drought joins fire in the environmental "noise" characteristic of the Australian climate – or, rather, as an element of the patterns in the Australian environment that we have barely begun to recognize, and which we have for so long persisted in viewing as simply chaotic. It is clear that droughts and fire exacerbated the ecological effects of deforestation and overgrazing, and conversely that deforestation and overgrazing aggravated the effects of drought and fire. In his study of fire ecology in Australia, Stephen J. Pyne writes:

> Without fire Europeans could never have opened up the Australian biota for exploration on the scale they did, but it is equally true that without fire's association with axe and hoof, it is likely that the Australian scene could have absorbed a shift in fire practices without irreversible consequences. Australian grasses, for example, were re-

[58] Ibid., pp. 8–9.
[59] Ibid., p. 42.
[60] Ibid., p. 84; and Hanmer, "Land Use and Erosion," p. 282.

silient to fire but not to grazing; Australian soil could accept fire and drought, but not compaction from hooves.[61]

The long-term consequences for the Australian climate of the ecological catastrophe that followed the arrival of the Europeans have been in dispute for some time. Some nineteenth-century observers correlated the change "to the dry way," noticed by the Aborigines on the advent of the white men and their flocks of sheep and cattle, with the removal of vegetation and exposure of the soils to the sun; others disagreed that such a climatic change had occurred, or even could occur.[62] The debate over the consequences of human action for climate change continues as increasingly severe droughts and forest fires plague the Australian farmer, but without resolution.

In the first fifty years after the arrival of the white man in Australia the highlands and tablelands of New South Wales underwent process of environmental transformation that included decreasing height and density of vegetative cover, increasing aridity of soil conditions, and gaining predominance of arid-land species. With these changes went a diminishing diversity of native plant and animal species, the deterioration of catchment values, an increase in the severity of flooding, and accelerated soil loss. The transformation of the biological regime associated with the irruptive oscillation of the introduced grazing animals accounts for the first group of changes, while deforestation, maintenance of high stocking rates, and modification of fire patterns account for the latter.[63] These processes worked in a reciprocal way with drought and its attendant fires to produce an environment that stabilizes for shorter periods of time at decreasing levels of productivity.

---

[61] Pyne, *Burning Bush*, pp. 200–1.

[62] Gardner, *Production and Resources* vol. 1, pp. 3, 7, 16; Strzelecki, *Physical Description*, p. 367; Bolton, *Spoils and Spoilers*, p. 34–5.

[63] Graeme Caughley writes of the introduction of pastoralism into the western division of New South Wales: "The injection of an exotic and husbanded herbivore into an ecosystem whose components had been selected to cope with quite different forces broke the system down into a new and more simple structure. The changes wrought by grazing were augmented by management designed to change the environment further in favour of livestock. Edaphic forest was converted to induced grassland. Wildlife that killed stock were eliminated. Indigenous species that competed with stock were controlled. Dispersal was modified by fencing and artificial watering points were created. The system was changed beyond recognition." The consequences for the native fauna were the loss of four out of five species of rodent, and fourteen out of twenty species of marsupials; "Introduction," p. 4.

4

THE MEXICAN CASE

Human action enormously complicates the picture of environmental change. Even where pastoralism alone is introduced into a lightly populated region, as in New South Wales, manipulation of the environment by humans to achieve the maximum return from their animals combines with the irruptive oscillation to bring about radical, often irreversible changes in the ecosystem. Where the recipient ecosystem already contains dense human populations, and a wide range of activities are introduced along with pastoralism, the processes put in motion are correspondingly more complex. To what extent can we ascribe the erosion events in the Valle del Mezquital to the actions of the pastoralists? If, as I argue, their actions were primary variables in this process, then it should be possible to demonstrate a close correlation between the expansion of intensive pastoralism and deterioration of the environment.

Timing and Intensity of Grazing in the Valle del Mezquital

Differences in timing and degree of exploitation by pastoralism of the sub-areas of the Valle del Mezquital can be demonstrated by two variables:

1. The area of land formally converted to pastoralism by decade.
2. The grazing rates for the total area of common pasture by decade, that is, the number of head of sheep per square kilometer on all lands available for grazing.

The changing combinations of these two variables present in schematic form the history of the exploitation (the timing of the expansion by pastoralists, and the intensity of grazing) of the sub-areas of the Valle del Mezquital between 1530 and 1600 (see Tables 4.1 and 4.2). To be able to compare sub-areas of widely different surface exten-

Table 4.1. *Area of land converted to pastoralism expressed as a percentage of the total surface area of each sub-area*

	Decade ending							
	1539	1549	1559	1565	1569	1579	1589	1599[a]
Tula 1,222km²	.6	2.5	9.5	44.0	45.9	61.2	74.0	93.6
Southern Plain 483km²	6.4	9.6	11.3	24.2	32.2	47.2	73.0	81.6
Central Valley 603km²	2.5	3.8	3.8	29.7	34.9	45.5	54.6	80.3
North–South Plain 753km²	0	1.0	2.0	14.5	16.5	33.1	63.2	76.7
Xilotepec 1,898km²	9.4	18.9	22.1	28.7	30.0	34.1	43.9	68.6
Alfaxayuca 634km²	4.9	6.1	12.3	31.9	31.9	45.5	59.0	61.1
Chiapa de Mota 694km²	0	7.8	10.1	25.8	25.8	26.9	33.7	63.3
Huichiapan 1,697km²	0	0	1.3	11.0	11.0	21.1	45.5	66.1
Northern Valley 1,017km²	0	.7	.7	1.5	2.3	5.3	16.8	18.4
Ixmiquilpan 1,028km²	0	1.5	3.0	7.5	7.5	7.5	9.8	9.8
Valle del Mezquital totals 10,029km²	2.6	5.8	8.4	21.4	22.8	31.0	45.3	61.4

[a]Estimates for the 1590s are based on totals adjusted downward by 30% to account for undocumented sales.

Source: Tables 5.1–3, 6–11.

sion, the area in square kilometers of land formally converted to pastoralism by the end of each decade is expressed as a percentage of the total surface area of each sub-area. To clearly express the differing densities of animals, a graduated scale of grazing intensity was constructed using the highest grazing rate estimated for the Valle del Mezquital during the sixteenth century, 785 head per square km, as the highest point on the scale, and setting the other five levels by dividing this rate by six:

Grazing rates per KM^2	Evaluation
0–130	very low
131–260	low
261–390	medium
391–520	high
521–650	very high
651–785	saturated[1]

Table 4.2. *Estimated number of head of sheep per square kilometer of the total surface area of each sub-area expressed as a level of grazing intensity*

	Decade ending							
	1539	1549	1559	1565	1569	1579	1589	1599[a]
Tula	v lo	v lo	v lo	hi	v hi	sat	sat	hi
Southern Plain	v lo	v lo	v lo	lo	hi	v hi	sat	med
Central Valley	v lo	v lo	v lo	med	hi	v hi	v hi	med
North–South Plain	—	v lo	v lo	lo	lo	hi	v hi	med
Xilotepec	v lo	v lo	v lo	med	med	hi	hi	med
Alfaxayuca	v lo	v lo	v lo	med	hi	v hi	v hi	med
Chiapa de Mota	—	v lo	v lo	lo	med	med	med	med
Huichiapan	—	—	v lo	v lo	lo	med	hi	med
Northern Valley	—	v lo	v lo	v lo	lo	v lo	lo	v lo
Ixmiquilpan	—	v lo	v lo	v lo	v lo	v lo	v lo	v lo
Valle del Mezquital totals	v lo	v lo	v lo	lo	med	hi	hi	med

[a]Estimates for the 1590s are based on totals adjusted downward by 30% to account for undocumented sales.
—   = Sources do not indicate sheep grazing in this decade
v lo = very low   hi   = high
lo   = low   v hi = very high
med = medium   sat = saturated

[1] The "saturation" rate may appear excessive, but it does not compare with rates recorded for other regions. For example, Simpson cites Spanish reports estimating

All calculations of lands formally converted to pastoralism and of the densities of animals present in each sub-area were made for the end of each decade. An exception was made for the decade of the 1560s, which was broken into two periods, 1560–5 and 1566–9, because I realized that the period 1560–5 represented a deviation from past practices in land granting under circumstances that were not repeated again in the future, and also because the size of the herds increased dramatically in the second half of the decade.

Calculation of the Area of Land Formally Converted to Pastoralism

The area in square kilometers of lands transferred to the Spanish system of land tenure was obtained by multiplying the number of stations present in each sub-area at the end of each decade by 7.8 square kilometers (the area of a grant for a sheep station; see Chapter 5). The total number of stations per decade is cumulative, and the area in square kilometers therefore represents the *total* area of land transferred up to the end of each decade (not that which has been converted only during that decade). These totals are expressed as percentages of the total area of land composing the sub-area. (See Tables 5.1–3, 5.6–11).

Calculation of Grazing Rates

The grazing rates for each sub-area were calculated by dividing the total number of head within a sub-area at the end of each decade by the number of square kilometers of grazing land: $G = Sn/a$; where G is the grazing rate in head per square kilometer, S is the stocking rate in head per station, n is the number of stations, and a is the surface area of the sub-area in square kilometers. (See Table 4.3). Grazing rates were calculated in three steps:

1. The average stocking rate (the number of head per station) for each decade was determined for the region as a whole.

that the Indians of Tlaxcala could run 300,000 sheep on an area of 105 km² in 1542 – which gives a grazing rate of 2,857 per km² (Simpson, *Exploitation of land*, p. 13). Based on data supplied by Richard J. Morrisey in "Colonial Agriculture in New Spain," I calculated a grazing rate equivalent to 839 head of sheep per km² for the Bajío in 1582; Melville, "Environmental and Social Change," n. 42.

Table 4.3. *Grazing rates on common pasture*[a]

	Decade ending							
	1539	1549	1559	1565	1569	1579	1589	1599
Tula	.8	3	48	423	589	785	712	440
Southern Plain	8	12	56	233	414	605	703	384
Central Valley	3	5	19	286	448	584	525	378
North–South Plain	0	1	10	139	212	425	607	361
Xilotepec	12	24	111	276	385	437	423	322
Alfaxayuca	6	8	61	307	410	583	567	288
Chiapa de Mota	0	10	50	248	331	346	324	298
Huichiapan	0	0	7	107	142	273	440	310
Northern Valley	0	.9	4	15	29	69	162	86
Ixmiquilpan	0	2	15	73	97	97	95	47

[a]Estimated number of head of sheep per square kilometer of the total surface area of each sub-area

2. The stocking rate was then multiplied by the number of stations present in each sub-area at the end of each decade (see Tables 5.1–3, 5.6–10), giving the total number of head of sheep estimated to have been present by the end of each decade in each sub-area. (See Table 4.4)

3. Finally, the number of head present in each sub-area was divided by the area of the sub-area, giving the number of head per square kilometer of common grazing land per sub-area per decade.

The grazing rate is ultimately dependent on the stocking rate. The stocking rate, in turn, depends on the state of the pasture, human population densities, and markets; it changes throughout the century according to shifts in these variables. While it would be preferable to be able to differentiate between the stocking rates of the various sub-areas, it is unfortunately not feasible given the documentation. To be able to follow the changes by decade is actually a surprisingly fine

Table 4.4. *Estimated number of sheep per decade (in thousands)*

	Decade ending							
	1539	1549	1559	1565	1569	1579	1589	1599[a]
Tula	1	4	58.5	517.5	720	960	870	542.7
Southern Plain	4	6	27.3	60	200	292.5	339.3	186.8
Central Valley	2	3	11.7	172.5	270	352.5	316.8	229.7
North-South Plain	0	1	7.8	105	160	320	457.5	274.1
Xilotepec	23	46	210.6	525	730	830	802.5	617.9
Alfaxayuca	4	5	39	195	260	370	360	183.8
Chiapa de Mota	0	7	35.1	172.5	230	240	225	208.6
Huichiapan	0	0	11.7	180	240	460	742.5	532.8
Northern Valley	0	1	3.9	15	30	70	165	88.8
Ixmiquilpan	0	2	15.6	75	100	100	97.5	48.1
Valle del Mezquital totals	34	75	421.2	2,020.5	3,090	3,995	4,376.1	2,913.0

[a]Estimates based on adjusted totals

distinction for this period. (See Chapter 2 for a discussion of changes in the stocking rates over the period 1530–1600.) The stocking rates for each decade were:

Stocking Rates	Decades
1,000/station	1530s
1,000/station	1540s
3,900/station	1550s
7,500/station	1560–5
10,000/station	1566–79
7,500/station	1580s
3,700/station	1590s

A major difficulty in calculating densities of animals in the system of common pasture then prevalent is estimating the area actually grazed. If an attempt is made to withdraw from the calculation the area occupied by town sites, croplands, forests, limeworks, and so forth – simply to take into account that not all lands were grazed equally – the resulting calculation becomes very complex. Consider some of the problems involved in making such estimates. The custom of grazing harvested fields means that even croplands have to be considered as providing seasonal grazing. The areas of town sites cannot be easily estimated owing to sixteenth-century systems of recording them. Indian nobles and commoners owned sheep and undoubtedly grazed them within the village lands, which was prohibited to Spaniards.[2]

An attempt *was* made to estimate the area taken each decade from direct Indian control as a result of the population decline. This was to account for the considerable influence exerted by the Indians over the use of the land in the early decades of the colony resulting from their numerical superiority and the extent of their cultivated fields, and the subsequent decline in their numbers (and the retraction of cultivated fields) during the course of the century. However, because the assumptions necessary to make these calculations became so tortuous, the simple estimate of the densities of sheep on the total area was finally accepted as providing an adequate indication of the situation. In any event, the total area composing each sub-area is possibly the more correct estimate of the extent of common pasture, because it can be argued that all lands provided grazing at some point in the year.

Documentation of Environmental Change

Evidence for environmental change is of two basic types: first, self-conscious description of landscapes; and second, "throw-away" data, that is, pieces of information about elements of the environment gleaned from many different documents that were not necessarily written to describe or explain that environment. The source documents for first type of evidence include the *Relaciones Geográficas* ("Geographic Relations," regional descriptions made by order of the crown or the church in ca. 1548, 1569–70, and 1579–81), descriptions

---

[2] See for example, AGNT, vol. 1640, exp. 2, fols. 15–34. See Gibson, *Aztecs*, chap. 10 for a discussion of the complexities of Indian landholding and changes during the colonial era.

of villages and their resources for *congregaciones,* and descriptions of land used as evidence in court cases. These sources are invaluable; they provide general descriptions of the landscape at specific moments and indicate broad changes over time. There are, however, problems in their use, the major one being observer bias.[3] The use to which the document was to be put shaped the way in which the observer saw and described the landscape. Take the Geographic Relations as an example. Ostensibly these documents were made to record the Indians' use of the natural resources, but they were actually used to assess the potential for Spanish exploitation. This requirement shaped the perception as to which natural resources were worth mentioning, and very often their future use. (See Chapter 2 for a discussion of the definition of lands as royal or as public lands, depending on their natural resources for mining or for pastoralism.)

The second type of data fills in the details of the processes of environmental change. The major source was the surveys carried out to clarify the boundaries of landholdings for land grants and for suits over land tenure. The status of the resources enclosed by the holding was not the primary interest of the surveyors, but elements of the environment were mentioned constantly. References to elements of the environment were collected from other documents, as well – censuses of landholdings and their exploitation, for example – and information gathered by the royal treasurers. Two examples of this sort of data refer to the Southern Plain in 1601: "It is clear from the density of the growth of scrub and trees that these unused wild lands have not been worked for fifty years" (Tlapanaloya); "The [agricultural holding] stretches from one side to the other of the salt stream that flows through the pueblo, it lies about fifteen hundred pasos from the Indians' houses and croplands . . . in stony badlands that are surrounded by many unused wild lands belonging to the said Indians of the said pueblo of Atitalaquia."[4] Literally hundreds of bits and pieces of information like this were collected and grouped chronologically

---

[3] William Cronon discusses the distorting effect of the "preconceptions and expectations" of settlers in descriptions of early New England in his book, *Changes in the Land,* p. 20.

[4] "Tierras eriazas y sylvestres de matorrales y arboles salvajes que dan a entender que a mas de cinquenta años que no se labran ni benefician segun la espesura tienen," AGNT 2721, exp. 8, fol. 5v. "Es de una parte y otra del arroyo salado que pasa por el dicho pueblo abaxo apartado de las postreras casas y sementeras de los naturales como mil quinientos pasos mas o menos . . . en un pedrisco y mal pais que a su redonda tiene muchas tierras sylvestres de los dichos yndios del dicho pueblo de Atitalaquia," AGNT, 2721, exp. 8, fol. 3r.

according to the municipality, and were used to augment knowledge about environmental change indicated by the more broadly descriptive sources. Surprisingly detailed evidence of the character of the environment at specific points in time, as well as about the processes by which the landscape changed, was obtained in this way. This method makes for tediously long notes, however; it also means that it is almost impossible to quote all the sources verbatim, and only a few representative quotes have been used.

Problems were encountered in the use of these documents. There remains the issue of observer bias, and the surveys are subject to statistical error because a large number were limited to a strip of land around the edge of the landholding. Where notes were included in the surveys about the condition of the soils and vegetation or the productivity and history of land use, they were used to complete the picture. A problem encountered in all documents was the use by the Spaniards of generic terms to describe the vegetation – for example, oaks, pines, and thorns – with the possibility that a species was assigned to an incorrect genera because it resembled an Old World plant. This problem was addressed by collecting data from different sources and comparing the results with evidence of known plant associations for this and other semiarid regions of Mexico. Plant associations can sometimes be inferred from the documents, as well. For example: "grasses, lechuguilla, maguey, mesquites, and thistles"; "wooded areas of live oaks, *olinos*, pines, oaks"; "pines and other small trees that look like alder"; "mesquite trees growing in wild scrublands of thistles and thorns"; "dense with mesquite and yucca and wild nopal cactus."[5]

The use of the term *monte* by the Spaniards poses special problems. *Monte* can mean a high place, a tree-covered place, or a place where low shrubs grow; it can mean open woodlands or scrub-covered lands, or closed forests.[6] In the documents used for this study the observers sometimes noted simply the presence of a *monte*, although most often they noted the type of *monte* they were referring to such as "oak *monte*," "live oak *monte*," "pine *monte*," or "mesquite *monte*."[7] The adjective

---

[5] "Sacatales lechuguilla mesquites y cardones" [Alfaxayuca, 1611], AGNT 1872, exp. 10, fol. 3; "Arboledas de montes como enzinos olinos pinos rrobice" [Axacuba, 1579] AGII, leg. 1529; "Pinos y otros arbolillos a manera de alisos" [Xilotepec, 1592] AGNM vol. 18, fols. 41–2; "un mesquital en tierras montuossas y sylvestres de cardones e espinos" [Mizquiaguala, 1595] AGNM, vol. 20, fols. 165r–v; "serrada de misquites y palmas y tunales sylvestres" [Izmiquilpa, 1601] AGNT, vol. 2756, exp. 7, fols. 1–16.

[6] *Diccionario de Autoridades*, originally published in 1732 by the Real Aacademia Española. Facsimile Edition, Madrid, 1976.

[7] "Montes de rrobledales; montaña grande de enzinos; montezullo de enzinos; monte

montuossa can be used to indicate either lands covered by shrub growth or trees and, depending on the context, can mean woodlands or scrubby growth, for example, *"wild scrublands of thistles and thorns"; "a wooded slope of oaks and live oaks."[8] Most often scrublands are indicated by reference to the vegetation and its height and density rather than by using the terms *monte* or *montuossa*. Even where simply *montes* are mentioned, it is possible to decide whether this refers to trees or to scrubland by the use made of the resources. For example, the fact that building timber (roof beams, boards) taken from the *montes* of Chiapa de Mota and the hills behind Tornacustla makes it clear that *monte* here refers to forests. Problems can arise here, too, however, as in the case in which the Spaniards called the shrub *tlacotl* a tree because it was used in place of wood in the production of lime.[9] All of these points were taken into account when categorizing the data. Despite these problems in categorization, it is nevertheless possible to gain a clear picture of past environments.

Comparison of Grazing Intensity and Environmental Change

The apparent omission of natural climatic or fire-induced effects in the following discussion of environmental change needs explanation. First, there is little data for either climatic change or fire. Second, existing data does not point to either fire or the climate as primary variables in the process of landscape transformation. Rather, as in the Australian case, it would seem that climate and fire exacerbated changes brought about by changes in land-use, and vice versa.

The major argument against climatic change as the primary variable in the process of environmental degradation in this region is that environmental degradation did not occur in all parts of the region to the same degree; to be precise, there is a high correlation between changes in land use and environmental change. It is conceivable that there was a shift to drier climatic conditions in that the period under study falls within the peak years of the Little Ice Age (1550–1700); indeed, such a shift would favor the arid-zone species that came to

de encinos; monte de pinos; monte de mesquitales." Examples of these terms are to be found in: PNE vol. 3, p. 20, 57; PNE vol. 6, p. 32; AGNM, vol. 13, fol. 16r; vol. 19, fol. 208r; AGNT, exp. 13, fol. 404v.

8 "Tierras montuossas y sylvestres de cardones y espinos;" "loma montuossa de arboles de encinos y de rrobles." Examples of these terms are to be found in AGNM, vol 16, fols. 25r–26r; vol. 20, fols. 165r–v.

9 AGNM, vol. 7, fol. 87r.

predominate in this region. Nevertheless, the meager amount of climatic data for this period makes it difficult to see a trend in any direction, and the climate appears to have been consistently unpredictable throughout the sixteenth century.

Stephen J. Pyne writes, "Nomadism and expansion have always favoured fire; enclosure and high-yield farming have always restricted it."[10] Indeed, the consistent use of fire as a tool in resource management appears to have been introduced into the Central Highlands by the Spaniards as part of the expansion and development of pastoralism. Beginning soon after the conquest, the *Mesta* issued licenses to burn grasslands in order to promote pasture regrowth; but we have only indirect evidence of pastoralists firing the grasslands in the Valle del Mezquital.[11] There is no evidence that the Indians of the Valle del Mezquital used fire, either to clear the agricultural land or to maintain the forest floor clear of undergrowth. It is possible that the need for domestic fuel for a large population kept the forests clear of deadfall and reduced the need for burning.[12]

One final note of clarification: I have made a distinction between environmental transformation and environmental degradation. Environmental transformation refers primarily to those changes in the biological regime associated with ungulate irruptions. Environmental degradation refers to the removal of soil by extensive sheet erosion and gullying, and to the associated deterioration of the water regime. "Environmental degradation" is clearly a subjective humanist evaluation of the state of the environment; but because we are studying reciprocal environmental and social change, the valuation of environmental change as "good" or "bad" as it affects human society is perfectly legitimate.

[10] Pyne, *Fire in America*, p. 133.

[11] AGNM, vol. 3, fols. 95–6, 113. There is evidence of a fire that got out of control in a woodland area in the Valle del Mezquital; AGNM, vol. 3, exp. 249, fols. 95–6.

[12] Jeffrey R. Parsons has not found archaeological evidence of regular burns in the Valley of Mexico for the late preconquest period (verbal communication, March 1983). It is unlikely that fire was used extensively in the Valle del Mezquital, given the presence of maguey and nopal cactus. These species are destroyed by fire; see Ahlstrand, "Response of Chihuahuan Desert Mountain Shrub vegetation to Burning."

Only small amounts of wood are needed to heat the clay pots and *comals* (the flat baked-clay griddle used to cook the maize cakes that formed the basis of the diet – the ubiquitous tortilla). Sticks are fed into the fire one at a time; calculations of the amount of firewood needed for one family should not, therefore, be based on the amount of firewood needed to maintain an open fire of the European type.

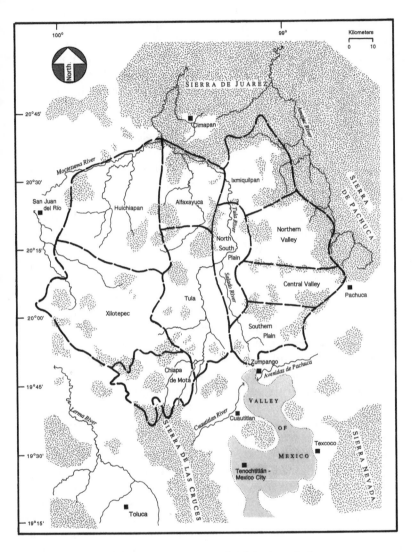

Map 4.1. Topographic map: Valle del Mezquital

Tula and the Southern Plain

Tula and the Southern Plain, lying along the northern edge of the Valley of Mexico, were two of the most densely populated and fertile areas in the Valle del Mezquital. They were the first of the sub-areas to be intensively exploited by grazing, and they were the most degraded by the end of the century. The Spaniards were attracted by the excellent resources for both agriculture and pastoralism, by the limestone hills (as sources of lime), and by the proximity to Tenochtitlán (Mexico City). The major changes in land use were conversion of lands to grazing in both areas and the accelerated exploitation of limestone quarries in the northern and western hills of the Southern Plain, as well as in the hills to the southeast of Tula. Exploitation of these rich sub-areas by grazing was especially intense; grazing rates in the 1570s reached their highest regional levels here. Although there was a sharp drop in the carrying capacity of the range during the last two decades of the century (as indicated by the drop in grazing rates between 1589 and 1599 from 711.9 to 440 per square kilometer in Tula, and from 703 to 384 per square kilometer in the Southern Plain), the rate of land takeover actually increased until by the end of the century between 81.6 percent and 93.6 percent of the total surface of these areas was formally converted to grazing. Spanish agriculture took up relatively small areas of land in the sixteenth century: 5.6 percent of the Tula sub-area (68.4 square kilometers), and 10.8 percent of the Southern Plain (52.1 square kilometers). When these areas are added to the totals of land conversion, however, the extent of land moved into the Spanish land tenure system by the end of the century becomes overwhelming. Virtually no land remained to be granted by 1600, and grants were made that were often a fraction of the legal size. However, the usual area of 7.8 square kilometers per station has been used to calculate the land converted to pastoralism and the grazing rates, because it indicates more dramatically the overexploitation of these areas – which is evident from the documentation but not always easy to convey.

These two sub-areas clearly exhibited the environmental changes associated with ungulate irruptions complicated by the maintenance of artificially high densities of animals and by burning to promote grass regrowth. During the period of rapid expansion in the 1550s and 1560s croplands and hillsides were converted to grasslands and some ground was left bare of vegetation. These grasslands and denuded soils were subsequently invaded by secondary growth consisting primarily of armed species of plants: wild maguey (*lechuguilla:* Agave lechuguilla), yucca (*palmas sylvestres:* Yucca spp.), cacti (*tunal, nopal:* prickly pear cactus: Opuntia spp.), thorn bushes (*espinos:* possibly ocotillo: Fouqueria spp.), mesquite (*mesquites:* Prosopis spp.) and *cardones* (possibly the introduced thistle Cynara cardunculus).[13] The process

---

[13] It is difficult to decide what type of plant is being referred to here. Crosby, *Columbian Exchange*, p. 112, writes that when Darwin visited Uruguay in the 1830s the savannas

of environmental change was further complicated by deforestation for lime and charcoal manufacture. By the last two decades of the sixteenth century extensive sheet erosion to hardpan (*tepetate, calichal*) was recorded for the hillsides and flatlands in both sub-areas, as were failing springs in the Southern Plain.[14]

The Tula sub-area was the most intensively grazed part of the region. By 1565, 44 percent of the land was formally converted to sheep grazing, and the estimated grazing rates were on the order of 423 per square kilometer. By the 1570s it was saturated by grazing activities, with 61.2 percent of the surface area formally converted to grazing, and estimated grazing rates of 785 per square kilometer; by contrast only 47.2 percent of the surface area of the Southern Plain was converted and the estimated grazing rates were 605 per square kilometer at the same date. By the end of the century, 93.6 percent of the Tula sub-area was formally converted to grazing; the addition of Spanish agricultural holdings brings the total to 99 percent – the most extensive takeover in the region as a whole.

The expansion of intensive pastoralism in the Tula sub-area between 1550 and 1570, and the subsequent crash, were associated first with the diminution of vegetative cover already noted and then with an increase in woody species. After 1550 the croplands became grasslands[15] and the hillsides were cleared and grazed.[16] On the high slopes of the hills surrounding Chapantongo, a thin covering of oak

were overgrown with a species of thistle: "the prickly old world cardoon (*Cynara cardunculus*)"; which could possibly be the same plant referred to as *cardón* in the documents for the Valle del Mezquital. The *Diccionario Manual e Ilustrado de la Lengua Española* of the *Real Academia Española* (Madrid, 1950) describes the *cardo* as a thistlelike plant resembling the artichoke; and the thistle is used in Mexico today to card wool, i.e., *cardar*. Ingeniero Angel Salgado Molina of the *Subsecretaria Forestal* (Mexico), however, pointed out that there is a species of the prickly pear cactus, *Opuntia streptocantha*, locally known as the *nopal cardón* which grows in the Valle del Mezquital; and the *Diccionario* lists the translation of the word *cardón* in Mexico and Peru as follows: "Planta cáctea de que existen varias especies."

[14] Here again we have problems with interpretation of sixteenth-century meaning. At times the terms *tepetate* and *calichal* are used interchangeably, but at other times a distinction is made. It turns out that a similar confusion exists today. See Barbara J. Williams, "Tepetate," for a discussion of the use of the term *tepetate* in pre-Hispanic and modern times. The term appears to have different meanings according to its use. See also Johnson, "Do as the Land Bids," p. 115.

[15] PNE vol. 6 pp. 178, 181. AGNM, vol. 6, fol. 515r; vol. 7, fol. 349r; vol. 9, fols. 132v–133r. AGNT, vol. 2735 2a pte, exp. 8, fol. 1r; vol. 2762, exp. 13, fol. 4v; vol. 2782, exp. 9, fol. 4r; vol. 3343, exp. 15, fols. 1r–11r.

[16] AGNM, vol. 3, exp. 461, fols. 169r–v; vol. 5, fols. 260r–v; vol. 13, fols. 181r–v, 182r–v. AGNT, vol. 2721, exp. 10, fol. 6r; vol. 2735 2a pte., exp. 8, fol. 1r; vol. 3670, exp. 19, fols. 1r–7v.

and live oak was reported in the 1580s, and on the lower slopes the yucca was reported for the first time in the documents for this town. During the 1590s there was a general increase in secondary growth of mesquite, thorn bushes, and thistles throughout the Tula sub-area, and in some places they grew down to the banks of the Tula River, which had been cultivated up until the 1560s. In 1603 mesquite was reported to be growing in the villages and in the lands surrounding them.[17]

Erosion was apparent in the center of the Tula sub-area by the 1570s, in the southern hills by the 1590s, and to the west and north of Tula by early 1600; prior to its appearance in the documents, soils on the high slopes were described as "sour"[18] and lower slopes and flatlands as stony.[19] The sloping lands to the west of Tula near Suchitlan and to the north near Sayula were eroded to *tepetate* by 1603. In a *visita* made in 1603 to assess the agricultural potential of the towns in the area for *congregaciones,* San Andres Suchitlan is reported to be situated on a hillside eroded to *tepetate* ("San Andres Suchitlan is situated away from the Royal Highway on a stony hillside, on *tepetate/* hardpan").[20] The villagers utilized the waters of a nearby river to irrigate maize, wheat, and beans, but the major use of the area lands was sheep grazing.[21] In Ahuehuepan, to the south of Sayula, a similar situation obtained. This town formed part of the *encomienda* assigned to Pedro de Moctezuma. In 1561, when it was described in detail along with all the other villages in the grant, there was no mention of erosion.[22] In the 1603 *visita,* however, the village is reported to be situated on *tepetate;* and it was decided that these lands would not support a more dense population, but that they were adequate for sheep ("Ahuehuepan is situated on level *tepetate* between mesquites

---

[17] AGNM, vol. 13, fols. 182r–v; vol. 17, fols. 218r–v, 224r–v; vol. 18, fols. 81r–v, 310v–311r; vol. 22, fol. 382r. AGNT vol. 71, exp. 6, fols. 521r–523v; vol. 2735 2a pte., exp. 9, fols. 1r, 7r. AGNH, vol. 410, exp. 5, fols. 77v, 79r, 84v.

[18] AGNT, vol. 3670, exp. 19, fols. 1r–7v.

[19] AGNM, vol. 17, fols. 224r–v; vol. 22, fol. 382. AGNT, vol. 45, exp. 1, fol. 7v; vol. 71, exp. 6, fols. 521v–522r, 523v; vol. 1873, exp. 12, fols. sn; 2721, exp. 10, fol. 6r; vol. 2735, 2a pte., exp. 8, fol. 1r; vol. 2735, 2a pte., exp. 19, fols. 1r, 7r; AGNH, vol. 410, exp. 5, fol. 77r. For example: "son unas lomas rrasas y pedregosas ajora ...que por su parecer parese no averse sembrado por mucho tiempo." ("they are cleared and stony flats...that look like they haven't been sown or cultivated in a long time.") AGNT, 2735, 2a pte., exp. 8, fol. 1r.

[20] "Esta [San Andres Suchitlan] ffundado ffuera del Camino Real en lo alto de una ladera pedregosa y el suelo de tepetate." AGNH, vol. 410, exp. 5, fol. 77r.

[21] AGNH, vol. 410, exp. 5, fol. 79r.

[22] AGNT, vol. 1529, exp. 1, fol. 169v.

and is not suitable for congregacion...it is suitable for sheep grazing.").[23] There are few other descriptions of the area north and west of Tula between 1561 and the end of the century. But in 1580 observers claimed that nothing but sheep were to be found in Sayula – multitudes of sheep.[24] That the flat and undulating lands to the north and west of Tula were all classified as sheep-raising areas in 1603, although supplied with water for irrigation, indicates the extent of the takeover by the pastoralists.

An illustration of the changes occurring in the southern section of Tula during the 1580s concerns an area of land on the north bank of the Tepexi River near the borders of Otlazpa and Chiapa de Mota. In 1580 two brothers asked for separate grants of arable lands in this area, next to four *caballerías de tierra* belonging to Francisco Galván.[25] In 1585 one of the brothers applied for a grant of a sheep station next to these same lands – wherever there was room.[26] In 1590 Galván asked for permission to use the four *caballerías de tierra* as a sheep station.[27] He requested the change in land use "because the land is made up of rocks, gullies, and exposed hardpan, it is not suitable for sowing crops...it is surrounded by hills and gullies of rock, tepetate and calichal...it is suitable only for sheep."[28] As it is unlikely that landowners in other areas would ask for agricultural grants in such poor lands, erosion probably occurred between 1580, when the lands were first requested, and 1585, when erosion was recorded. It is clear from this example that gullying and slope-wash originating on hillsides adversely affected the lower agricultural lands. It is probable that hillside erosion resulted from increasingly heavy grazing rather than plowing, as can be argued for the flatlands; in fact sheep stations had been granted in these hills in the 1560s, and grazing pressure increased throughout the sub-area in the 1570s and 80s.[29]

[23] "Que esta [Ahuehuepan] en un llano sobre tepetate y entre unos mesquitales no comodo por congregacion...comodo el sitio para ganado menor." AGNT, vol. 71, exp. 6, fols. 521v–522r.

[24] "No hay ni se halla en este pueblo mas de obejas y desto ay buen multiplico." PNE vol. 6, pp. 181.

[25] AGNT, vol. 2735 2a pte., exp. 8, fols. 1r–9r; vol. 2782, exp. 9, fol. 1r.

[26] "En la parte donde obiere lugar." AGNT, vol. 3433, exp. 15, fol. 1r.

[27] AGNT, vol. 2735 2a pte., exp. 9, fol. 1r. AGNM, vol. 17, fols. 224r–v.

[28] "Por ser tierra pedregosa tepetate barrancas no es por sembrarlas...esta rrodeada de cerros y barrancas y todo pedregal calichal y tepetate...no servir sino para traer en ellas ganado menor"; AGNT, vol. 2735 2a pte., exp. 9, fol. 1r.

[29] AGNM, vol. 5, fols. 167r–v, 168r, 258v–262v. AGNT, vol. 45, exp. 1, fol. 7v. See Tables 5.9–11.

Flocks of sheep accelerated the removal of the vegetative cover of the Southern Plain by trampling shrubs and eating out palatable herbs and grasses. The Indians of Tlapanaloya complained bitterly that sheep trampled the stalks of the shrub *tlacotl*, which was used as a wood substitute in the production of lime. They argued that destruction of this shrub jeopardized lime production – and therefore tributes. The Spaniards countered these charges by saying that the sheep did not eat the shrubs, and that in any case the Indians had two leagues of woodlands – which turned out to be the stands of the *tlacotl*.[30]

By the time of the geographic description of 1579, the woods that had covered the slopes surrounding Tezcatepec in the Southern Plain in 1548 had receded to the tops of the mountains between Tezcatepec and Axacuba.[31] The deforestation of these northern hills can be ascribed primarily to the activities of the lime workers, who needed fuel for their kilns. Spaniards applied for grants of limestone quarries in the limestone hills north of Tlapanaloya and east of Apasco to supply the demand for lime to rebuild the city of Tenochtitlán.[32] Deforestation of the woodlands in these hills was noticeable as early as 1562.[33] By the 1570s the woods east of Apasco and on the hills north of Tlapanaloya were also depleted by cutting and burning, and in 1576 deforestation had proceeded to the point that the Spanish lime workers were defending their sources of wood by force.[34] As the lime workers ranged farther afield to collect fuel, they were undoubtedly instrumental in maintaining this sub-area relatively free of the woody secondary growth that grew so thickly in other areas by the end of the century. The Indians also complained that sheep ate the leaves of the plants *çamal*, *cacomitle*, and *hueycamitle* so that the roots could not be harvested.[35]

By the 1560s spiny arid-zone plants began to invade this sub-area, followed by woody species. At first there were reports of abandoned

[30] AGNT, vol. 2697, exp. 11; vol. 1525, exp. 1.

[31] "En lo alto de una serrania grande." ("On the top of a high mountain.") PNE vol. 6, p. 33.

[32] AGNM, vol. 6, fols. 455v–456r; vol. 7, fol. 87r; vol. 8, fols. 227v–228r; vol. 13, fols. 41r–v. AGNT, vol. 2697, exp. 10, fols. 308r–315r; exp. 11, fol. 319r.

[33] AGNM, vol. 6, fols. 455v–456r; vol. 8, fols. 227v–228r. AGNT, vol. 2697, exp. 11, fols. 319r–329r. PNE vol. 6, 204.

[34] AGNT, vol. 2674, exp. 18, fol. 307r.

[35] AGNM, vol. 7, fol. 87r. AGNT, vol. 1525, exp. 1, fol. 74v, 91r. J. F. Schwaller suggests that "cacomitle" may be a member of the Iris family that have edible roots; personal communication, 1977.

croplands and untended magueyes,[36] then the yucca appeared;[37] this was followed by the wild maguey and the mesquite at the end of the century.[38] The fertility of the soils on the piedmont of the Southern Plain deteriorated over the same period. In 1579 the undulating lands of Tequixquiac, Tlapanaloya, and Hueypostla were reported as open, cleared, and suitable for the production of cereals.[39] During the following two decades there are increasing references to stony soils,[40] and by 1606 the lands near Hueypostla were eroded *tepetate* badlands[41] where only mesquite, yuccas, and wild magueys grew.[42] Erosion in the southern half of the sub-area was not associated with deforestation for lime production. There were no forests in this area ca. 1548,[43] and the erosion appeared forty years after the surrounding hills had last been exploited for lime manufacture.[44] Nor was erosion associated with agriculture, because erosion appeared on land that had not been used for agriculture in twenty years. Rather, these lands had been grazed by sheep at excessively high densities despite clear evidence that the range was failing.[45] The processes that led eventually to the severe erosion in this area, namely the removal of the ground cover by overgrazing – leading to increased overland flow of water – also reduced groundwater recharge. By 1595 the springs in Tequixquiac and Hueypostla, which fed the tributaries of the north-flowing stream, the Río Salado, were failing.[46]

There is no direct evidence of severe erosion in the northern section of the Southern Plain in the sixteenth century, but it is most likely that erosion did follow the deforestation of these steep hills. Erosion was primarily a problem for agriculturalists and would not usually be thought of as affecting the production of lime, wool, or meat, and unless it directly affected arable lands it was not often mentioned.

The demographic collapse of the Indian population relieved the

[36] AGNM, vol. 9, fols. 269v–270r; vol. 12, fol. 485r; vol. 18, fols. 278r–279r. AGNT, vol. 1748, exp. 1, fol. 1.
[37] AGNM, vol. 12, fols. 409v–410v; vol. 19, fol. 168; vol. 21, fols. 79v–80r.
[38] AGNT, vol. 2812, exp. 12, fols. 373–400r.
[39] "Descubierta y rrasa." ("Cleared open land.") PNE vol. 6, pp. 6, 27.
[40] AGNM, vol. 12, fol. 485; vol. 17, fols. 52r–v. AGNT, vol. 1748, exp. 1, fol. 1.
[41] "Son tierras ruinas y lomas en tepetate y tierras delgadas" ("eroded tepetate badlands with only thin soils remaining") AGNT, vol. 2812, exp. 12, fols. 373r–400r.
[42] AGNT, vol. 2812, exp. 12, fols. 373r–400r.
[43] PNE vol. 1, pp. 110, 207.
[44] PNE vol. 6, p. 30.
[45] AGNT, vol. 2812, exp. 12, fols. 373–400r.
[46] PNE vol. 1, p. 207. AGNM, vol. 21, fols. 79v–80r. AGNT, vol. 2721, exp. 8.

pressure of a dense agricultural population on the soils and vegetation of these two sub-areas during the sixteenth century. One would therefore expect to see evidence of the invasion of abandoned croplands by trees and the development of open woodlands. This is the normal sequence for this region, and sufficient forests remained at midcentury for the regeneration of woodlands.[47] Instead, the lower hillsides and the flatlands were invaded by plant species typical of arid soil conditions and well armed against grazing animals. The appearance of these spiny arid-zone plants, rather than of trees, argues for the continued disturbance of the soils by grazing animals.[48]

When gullying and sheet erosion appeared in the 1590s both areas had been intensively and increasingly exploited by sheep grazing for more than forty years, and by deforestation of the hillsides for wood to burn in the lime kilns. If erosion was present before the last decade it was not reported in any of the descriptions made specifically to assess the condition of the soils for agriculture. *Tepetate* and *calichal*, terms used interchangeably for the hardpan layer underlying the soils of highland Mexico, do not appear in earlier reports. When they do appear, they are used to describe flat or sloping lands whose potential as arable land was being investigated. In fact, when lands became eroded they lost their potential as arable lands and were thought of as being fit only for sheep. As noted above, it is most likely that hillsides were eroded, and we have clear examples of this.[49] But the evaluation of the soils per se was for their potential for crops. Steep hillsides were not potential arable lands, and erosion is indicated only by references to slope-wash debris.

The North–South Plain and the Central Valley

The densely populated southern half of the North–South Plain held the same promise as Tula and the Southern Plain for growing the imported grains.[50] The dry northern half of the North–South Plain and the Central Valley were less attractive to the Spaniards; the Central Valley had the added drawback of insufficient water for either agriculture or pastoralism because the Indians used all available water to irrigate their crops.[51] Despite these drawbacks, however, Spaniards

---

[47] Wagner, "Natural Vegetation," p. 257.
[48] Ibid., p. 257; Crosby, *Columbian Exchange*, p. 122.
[49] AGNM, vol. 17, fols. 224r–v. AGNT, vol. 2735 2a pte., exp. 9, fol. 1r.
[50] PNE vol. 1, nos. 554–6.
[51] PNE vol. 1, nos. 8, 548.

began to plant wheat and to graze their animals in the Central Valley in the 1530s, and in the North–South Plain in the next decade. By the end of the century, between 76.7 percent and 80.3 percent of the surface area of these sub-areas had been formally converted to pastoralism. As in Tula and the Southern Plain, little land was taken up by the Spaniards for agriculture in the sixteenth century: 6.1 percent (45.9 square kilometer) in the North–South Plain, and 1.3 percent (7.8 square kilometer) in the Central Valley; the total land takeover in these areas was considerably less than in the previous two areas. Furthermore the grazing pressure was lower than in Tula and the Southern Plain because there were fewer stations at the height of the era of high stocking rates (1565–79). Nevertheless, although the densities of sheep in these sub-areas did not reach the levels of saturation obtained in Tula and the Southern Plain, they represent a considerable pressure on the land, especially in the 1570s and 1580s, when they reached the estimated value of 584 head per square kilometer and 525.4 head per square kilometer in the Central Valley, and 425 head per square kilometer and 607.5 head per square kilometer in the North–South Plain.

The most striking change in the environment of these two sub-areas was the development of a dense cover of mesquite-dominated scrub on the flatlands and piedmont during the last half of the sixteenth century, associated with increasing aridity. In the fertile flatlands in the center of the North–South Plain, moist soil conditions were still present near Tlahuelilpa in 1566, as evidenced by the presence of the *agueguete* (cedar).[52] By the 1580s, however these fertile fields were being invaded by mesquite and yucca.[53] In 1595 the lands of Mizquiaguala were covered with thistles and thorn bushes;[54] in 1601 the lands north of Tlahuelilpa carried dense scrub ("[this land] is dense with thorn bushes, old cacti, and wild mesquite that is of no use to anyone").[55] By the early 1600s this same dense thorn scrub covered the flatlands between the road to Ixmiquilpan and the Tula River in the northern end of the North–South Plain between Chilcuautla and Tezcatepec, as well as the lands near Tlacotlapilco ("there is a flat area

---

[52] AGNT, vol. 1640, exp. 2, fols. 32–3.

[53] AGNM, vol. 11, fols. 242r–v; vol. 13, fols. 88r–v, 176r; vol. 14, fols. 344r–v. AGNT, vol. 1106, quad. 3, fol. 16; vol. 1728, exp. 2, fol. 15v; vol. 2777, exp. 14, fols. 2r–16r. See also Konrad, *Jesuit Hacienda*, pp. 24, 340.

[54] "Tierras montuossas y sylvestres de cardones y espinos" ("scrublands of thistles and thorns.") AGNM, vol. 20, fol. 165r–v.

[55] "Esta espeso de espinos nopales viejos mesquitales sylvestres que no son de aprovechamiento alguno"; AGNT, vol. 2721, exp. 8, fol. 9r.

thick with mesquite and maguey between Chilcuautla and Tezcatepec"; "lands thick with thorns and mesquite so dense that one can
hardly open a path" (Tlacotlapilco); "arid uncultivated scrubland full
of thistles and thick with mesquite" (Tlacotlapilco).[56] Although naturally arid, this northern area was extensively cultivated by the Indians
in 1548 and was favored by the Spanish for growing fruit trees and
date palms. By the early 1600s, however, it was considered infertile,
and the magueyes grown amongst the mesquite and thorn bushes by
the Indians of Tlacotlapilco were of little profit.[57] In the Central
Valley, mesquite, thorn bush, and yucca had begun to invade the
lower hillsides and flatlands by the 1580s.[58]

Invasion by semidesert species was not inevitable, however. In the
late 1570s and 1580s abandoned croplands in the southern half of
the North–South Plain and the western end of the Central Valley
were apparently reverting to a type of open woodland. In 1587 the
land between Atitalaquia, Tlaxcoapan, and Axacuba was covered with
live oaks ("all the land is covered with live oaks...these lands are
deserts without crops and there are no fruit trees nor anything else
to make a living by...only live oaks").[59] The process of reversion to
woodland was interrupted, however. By the 1590s these same fields
were being invaded by cacti and thorn bushes[60] until, in 1601, the
fields between Atitalaquia and Tlahuelilpa were rough and wild with
a dense scrub of thistles, thorn bushes, and mesquites.[61]

The invasion of the formerly cultivated fields in the North–South
Plain by arid-zone species of plants could be ascribed simply to the
regeneration of secondary growth on fallow lands. It is, however,
interesting that the incipient development of an open woodland of

---

[56] "Un llano de mesquites y magueyes mui espesos que estan entre los dichos pueblos
[Chilcuautla and Tezcatepec]"; AGNT, vol. 1104, quad. 22. "Lleno de espinos y
mesquitales tan espesos y juntos que apenas se podia rromper [Tlacotlapilco]; tierras
montuossas eriazas y secas lleno de cardones y mesquitales muy espesos [Tlacotlap-
ilco]"; AGNT, vol. 2717, exp. 9, fols. 3v, 4v, 5r, 6r.

[57] PNE vol. 1, nos. 112, 550. AGNT, vol. 2717, exp. 9, fol. 13r.

[58] PNE vol. 1, no. 8. PNE vol. 6, p. 17. AGNM, vol. 11, fol. 16v–17r. AGNT, vol. 2672,
exp. 15, fol. 25v.

[59] "Toda la tierra sylvestre de encinales...tierras desiertas syn cultos y que no tiene
ningunos arboles frutales ni otra cosa de aprovechamiento...sino encinales."
AGNT, vol. 2672, exp. 15, fols. 3r–33r.

[60] AGNM, vol. 13, fol. 174r; vol. 14, fols. 229v–30v; vol. 16, fol. 131r; vol. 19, fol.
228v. AGNT, vol. 69, exp. 4, fols. 1–10.

[61] "Todo parescio ser tierra sylvestre y montuossa de cardones espinos y mesquites"
("It all looks like scrubland with thistles, thorns and mesquites"). AGNT, vol. 2721,
exp. 8, fol. sn.

live oaks in the southern half of the North–South Plain was so abruptly displaced by invasion of armed species of arid-zone plants during the 1590s and after. Live oaks are the most likely form of secondary growth on fallow lands in this region if the land is not grazed. If grazing occurs and the soils are continuously disturbed, however, the secondary growth will be thorny plants of the type recorded. It is also significant that the growth pattern of the mesquite in the Valle del Mezquital underwent a change over the same period similar to that recorded for other semiarid regions where grazing has occurred: at the end of the century the mesquite no longer appeared in the documents as single large trees, but now grew in dense stands.[62]

Increasing density of woody species has been associated with grazing in other pastoral regions, including the American Southwest, the Mediterranean, Australia, and New Zealand. Research into this phenomenon has stressed the increase in numbers and density of the grazing animals. As I have argued elsewhere, however, the explanation may lie in the abrupt drop in numbers and density of grazing animals, together with changing fire regimes, rather than in increasing densities. The high densities of grazing animals reduced and weakened native grasses and thus produced conditions favorable to the invasion by arid-zone species; but the expansion of woody species occurred when the numbers of animals was dropping rapidly, not when they were increasing. Because of this, I have suggested that "the lessening of the controlling factors – i.e. the high density of grazing animals, frequent burns, and competing grasses – allowed a rapid increase in the spread of the arid-zone species in the last quarter of the sixteenth century."[63] That is, when pasture failed in the late 1570s and the numbers of grazing animals crashed, the sudden relief from intense grazing pressure, and probably from fire as well, allowed for a rapid increase of mesquite-dominated desert vegetation.[64]

The increasing predominance of mesquite-dominated desert scrub was associated with a shift in the perception of what constituted suit-

---

[62] PNE vol. 1, no. 548; PNE vol. 6, pp. 4, 17, 202. AGNT, vol. 1104, quad. 22; vol. 2717, exp. 9; vol. 2721, exp. 8, fol. 1r; vol. 2777, exp. 14, fols. 2r–16r. AGNM, vol. 11, fols. 242r–v; vol. 13, fols. 88r–v; vol. 14, fols. 344r–v; vol. 20, fols. 165r–v.
[63] Melville, "Environmental and Social Change," pp. 35–6.
[64] In order to carry, fires need fine fuel. With the removal of the grasses by overgrazing fires would no longer have the necessary fuel and we can thus postulate a decline in fires. In the Australian case, Bolton notes that "Overall it was the destruction of native grasses by intense use that interrupted the prior rhythms of fire. There was insufficient fuel to carry flame. Scrub blossomed: fire could no longer fight it back." *Spoils and Spoilers*, p. 216.

able fodder for grazing animals from grass to desert species. Around 1548 these sub-areas were considered to be unsuitable for grazing for lack of pasture, water, and room for expansion. Fodder meant grass – and the North–South Plain was lacking in this resource.[65] In 1580, however, when it had been invaded by a secondary growth of arid species, the central area of the North–South Plain (Tlahuelilpa, Mizquiaguala, and Tezontepec) was described as providing adequate fodder for grazing animals – in fact it was said to have always been grazing land.[66] The Central Valley was now also said to be good for grazing – and it too had been invaded by semidesert species.[67] By the end of the century the "good grazing lands" of the 1570s had become scrub-covered badlands.

As the quality of the forage declined, the average weight of the animals decreased. Weight loss led to a decline in the reproduction rates of the ewes, and the production of wool, tallow, and meat declined in quantity and quality. The thick secondary growth lowered the numbers of sheep that could be maintained still further. The value of these lands for the production of cereals was lost under secondary vegetation and slope-wash, and cultivated fields were reduced to Indian subsistence crops on the remaining humid bottomlands. In fact, to the considerable annoyance of the Spaniards, the Indians retained control over the best land in the North–South Plain at the end of the century.[68]

The soils underlying the heavy secondary growth in the North–South Plain, and providing the conditions necessary for the dominance of semidesert species over grasses, were thin, stony, and arid.[69] Stony soils were also reported in Izcuinquitlapilco in the Central Valley in the 1590s.[70] Although erosion is not reported for the North–South Plain during the sixteenth century, its presence can be inferred from reports of stony badlands on the lower slopes of hills that had been

---

[65] PNE vol. 1, nos. 9, 347, 555.

[66] AGNT, vol. 2777, exp. 14, fols. 2r–16r.

[67] PNE vol. 6 pp. 14, 18, 20, 24, 25, 27, 201–2. AGNT, vol. 1106, quad. 3, fol. 16; vol. 1728, exp. 2, fol. 15v; vol. 2672, exp. 15, fol. 25v; vol. 2777, exp. 14, fols. 2r–16r.

[68] For instance, three brothers (*principales* of Tlahuelilpa) inherited sheep stations and arable lands that were said to be the best in the North–South Plain, and which would have gained them a lot of money had they sold ("es notorio que son de los mejores que ay en todo este valle"), AGNT, vol. 2717, exp. 10, fols. 3v–4v.

[69] "Por ser pedriscos y tierra debil y flaca … ruin mala tierra sin agua" ("Because they are thin stony soils … badlands without water [Tlahuelilpa]"). AGN, Tierras, vol. 2721, exp. 8, fol. 1r. "Mala tierra de ningun provecho" ("useless badlands [Mizquiaguala and Tezcatapec]"). AGNT, vol. 2777, exp. 14, fols. 2r–16r.

[70] AGNM, vol. 19, fol. 138r.

grazed for many years: "[the] lands next to a high mountain range where Martín Çeron used to take his animals . . . are agricultural lands covered in grasses and stones" (Chilcuautla, 1583);[71] "lands within the boundaries of Atitalaquia that lie next to some stony hills near the road that goes to Tetepango and Axacuba" (1587);[72] "Stony badlands surrounded by a lot of unused land belonging to the Indians of the said pueblo of Tlahuelilpa . . . very stony and covered in wild mattoral" (1601).[73] The only mention I have encountered that may point directly to erosion concerns the lands where the tribute wheat was grown for the *encomendero* of Atotonilco. The *encomendero* accused the Indians of maliciously growing the tribute wheat in the worst land they had so that he got a poor harvest. Spanish witnesses agreed that the lands were poor, saying that the problem arose from salinization because the land had been irrigated for too long.[74] A witness for the *encomendero*, however, noted that these lands were characterized by ruined stony soils and *tepetate* that could mean that the topsoil had been eroded away: "where the said indigenes have planted wheat for their *encomendero* are *tepetate* and ruined stony soils."[75]

The vegetation and soil changes described thus far can be ascribed to continuous disturbance under heavy grazing; but deforestation, erosion and deteriorating catchment values in the eastern end of the Central Valley are clearly associated with mining, and deforestation of the hills behind Axacuba with lime manufacture. In 1548 the hills between Axacuba and the Southern Plain supported an extensive oak forest, but by 1580 there were signs of deforestation[76] that can prob-

---

71 "Tierras arrimado a una sierra grande donde Martin Çeron suele traer su ganado . . . que son tierras por labrar y çacatales y pedregosos [Chilcuautla, 1583]." AGNT, vol. 2692, exp. 12, fol. 4v

72 "En teminos del pueblo de Atitalaquia que este arrimada a unos çerros pedregosos junto a un camino que va dar a Tetepango y a Axacuba [1587]." AGNT, vol. 2672, 2a pte., exp. 15, fol. 335r.

73 "Un pedrisco y mal pais que a la redonda tiene muchas tierras silvestres de los dichos indios del dicho pueblo de Tlahuelilpa . . . muy espesa de piedras y matorales sylvestres [1601])." AGNT, vol. 2721, exp. 8, fol. 1r.

74 "Por la sequedad e salitral de las tierras." ("Because of the dryness and salinization of the land"). AGIE, leg. 161–c, fol. 90r.

75 "Donde ha hecho los dichos naturales sementeras a su encomendero . . . son tepetates e tierras pedregosas y rruynas". AGIE, leg. 161–C, fol. 98r.

76 In the 1579 geographic relation the oak forest of one by two leagues is no longer mentioned. Instead, the trees recorded are nopal cactus, magueyes, thorn trees, and mesquite, with some woodlands (*arboledas de montes*) containing live oaks, pines, and oaks. "Los arboles sylvestres que tienen son tunales, magueyes, espinos grandes, 'mesquites' . . . ; tienen arvoleda de montes como es enzinas, pinos, rrobres"; ("Their

ably be ascribed to the activities of the lime workers (both Spanish and Indian) of Tlahuelilpa and the Southern Plain. In the eastern end of the Central Valley, however, the mines in Pachuca were the biggest consumers of wood. The communities of Tlilcuautla and Tornacustla extensively exploited their forests to sell wood to the miners, and by 1599, while the hills behind Tlilcuautla were still forested, Tornacustla's were bare of trees.[77]

Deforestation in the eastern end of the Central Valley was associated with erosion and signs of increasing aridity. Erosion to caliche on the lower slopes was apparent around Tornacustla ("Tornacustla is situated in caliche hills where it is difficult to plant crops");[78] and even Tlilcuautla, which was still, in 1599, protected to the north by forested hills, showed some signs of erosion ("Tlilcuautla is situated on a stony slope").[79] The consequence of deforestation and erosion that most closely affected the community of Tornacustla was the deterioration of the water supply to its fields. The flatlands between Tornacustla and Tlilcuautla remained fertile and productive – but only when there was water to irrigate them.[80] In 1579 the stream carrying water from Tlilcuautla to Tornacustla flowed all year; by 1599 it carried sufficient water to reach and supply Tornacustla only during the rainy season. The rest of the year it was dry.[81]

A pattern emerges in the timing and sequence of changes in the environment during the last half of the sixteenth century in the Valle del Mezquital similar to the processes observed in New South Wales. Human activities – most notably the maintenance of very high densities of sheep, deforestation, and undoubtedly burning – amplified the process of vegetation change associated with the irruptive oscillation, and resulted in erosion and deterioration of the water regime. Rapidly increasing numbers of sheep grazed the native grasses, herbs, and shrubs during the 1560s and 1570s until the ground was left bare. Arid-zone species began to invade these grazed areas in the late 1560s,

---

wild trees are cacti, magueys, large thorn trees, mesquite . . . ; they have woodlands of wild oaks, pines, oaks.") PNE vol. 6, pp. 14, 17.

[77] AGNT, vol. 64, exp. 1, fol. 5r.

[78] "Esta [Tornacustla] en unos cerros de tierra de calichal donde ay poco dispusicion para sementeras." AGNT, vol. 64, exp. 1, fol. 4r.

[79] "Esta [Tlilcuautla] en una loma algo pedregosa." AGNT, vol. 64, exp. 1, fol. 5r.

[80] "Las tierras que el dicho pueblo de Tornacustla tiene buenas para sembrar son en un llano que esta entre los dichos pueblos de Tornacustla e Tlilcuautla en confines de ambos." ("Tornacustla's good croplands are on the flats that lie between Tornacustla and Tlilcuautla and belong to both pueblos") AGNT, vol. 64, exp. 1, fol. 4r.

[81] AGNT, vol. 64, exp. 1.

but were kept in check by the density of the grazing animals and the regular burns carried out by the herdsmen to stimulate pasture growth. In the 1570s the grasses began to fail as a result of heavy grazing and repeated burns. As the pasture failed, the flocks declined in size and quality, and the density of arid-zone species increased. With the formation of a stony pavement and exposure of the impervious hardpan (which becomes rock-hard when exposed to the sun) a microenvironment hostile to grasses developed that reinforced the shift to arid-zone species.

Xilotepec, Alfaxayuca, and Chiapa de Mota

The Spaniards were attracted to these three sub-areas because of their resources for agriculture, grazing, and lumber. As in the other fertile areas of the Valle del Mezquital, however, they did not directly exploit the sub-areas' agricultural potential, leaving farming to the Indians while concentrating on introducing grazing animals into all three areas after the conquest of Tenochtitlán. The extensive grassy *sábanas* of Xilotepec were especially attractive to graziers, and although this sub-area had a very dense agricultural population, it carried the highest density of animals in the Valle del Mezquital during the first three decades.[82] Abundant water, extensive forests, and fertile soils provided the indigenous inhabitants of Chiapa de Mota with a good living ("the indigenes live very well and do as they wish"); but sheep raising was the major Spanish use for this sub-area.[83] Similarly, whereas Alfaxayuca had water for irrigation and good soils, the Spaniards exploited it almost exclusively for grazing.[84]

Even though they were grazed from an early date, these sub-areas do not exhibit the complete conversion of land found in those already discussed. Formal conversion for grazing and agriculture was only around two-thirds of the surface area in these sub-areas, whereas it reached more than 90 percent in the Tula and Southern Plain and more than 80 percent in the North–South Plain and the Central Val-

[82] AGNM, vol. 4, fols. 291v–292r. Gerhard writes that Xilotepec was "by far the most populous private encomienda in New Spain in the late sixteenth century." *Guide*, p. 383.

[83] "Los naturales viven ricos y mucho a su plazer"; PNE vol. 1, no. 111. Chiapa de Mota appears to have been grazed later, but I think it likely that although the license recognizing squatter's rights was given to the *encomendero* in the 1540s, he had in fact stocked the sub-area much earlier than this date.

[84] See the census of Spanish holdings in the mid-1580s in AGIM, leg. 111, ramo 2, doc. 12.

ley. Nor do the records of environmental deterioration convey the same depth and extent of destruction so evident in the documents for the previously discussed sub-areas.

The huge Xilotepec province provides us with the opportunity to examine the effects of Viceroy Velasco's edicts concerning grazing animals in Indian agricultural lands. The history of responses to these edicts in this sub-area points up the problems inherent in using the entire surface area of a sub-area as the basis for estimating grazing rates. Of the fourteen complaints about damage to crops received from communities in the Valle del Mezquital during the 1540s and 1550s, Indians from Xilotepec filed six. The areas hardest hit by the invasion of grazing animals were the savannas and towns in the eastern half of the plateau. In 1551 the Indians of Xilotepec complained that twenty to thirty thousand head of sheep, and a good number of cattle and horses, were grazed in crops and woodlands as well as in the savannas, and were corralled next to the villagers' houses at night. The animals left the soils bare ("they have destroyed all the land and left it bare") and people abandoned the province because of destruction to crops.[85] In 1559, the community of San Pablo de Guantepec, which had confirmed its rights to communal lands in 1541, requested permission to move to a new place because their lands were now worthless scrublands.[86] In 1560 the lands near the town of Santa María Macua on the border between Tula and Xilotepec were reported to have been eroded by water: "a stretch of gullied land that looks as though it was eroded by water."[87]

Clearly the pastoralists were running true to form and concentrating their animals in the densely populated agricultural lands. Nevertheless, the estimated grazing rates are based on the total surface area of the Xilotepec sub-area and do not reflect the pastoralists' habit of concentrating their animals in the favored eastern half of the plateau. As a result, the grazing rates estimated for Xilotepec in the 1530s and 1540s appear too low to have stimulated the vigorous complaints made at the beginning of the 1550s, or to have caused the erosion recorded by the end of the decade. If, however, the calculations are based on a third of the surface area of the plateau, they produce estimated grazing rates that would easily account for the complaints in the 1550s: 36 head per square kilometer for the 1530s, 73 head per square kil-

---

[85] "Tienen destruida y asolada toda la tierra," AGIM, leg. 96, ramo 1. AGNM, vol. 4, fols. 330v–332r.

[86] "Montuossas y muy esteriles," ("scrub-covered and infertile") AGNT, vol. 1872, exp. 10, fol. 2r–v.

[87] "Un paisaje y quebrada que paresce ser ruina de aguas," AGNT, vol. 1588, exp. 2 bis, fols. 1–5.

ometer for the 1540s and 333 head per square kilometer for the 1550s. As the Indian population was still very high in the 1550s, a grazing rate of 333 head per square kilometer would easily account for the complaints as well as the erosion. It should be pointed out here that sheep were taken out of their corrals daily for grazing, and although the entire surface of a sub-area was theoretically available for grazing, the area grazed would be limited by proximity to the corrals and to water.

If the area actually grazed suddenly increased we would expect to see a drop in the grazing rates and an associated drop in the number of complaints. As already noted, the Valle del Mezquital was cleared of cattle in the mid-1550s. In addition, grants were made for stations located in the hills and underused areas away from villages, which meant that the southern mountains and the western half of the Xilotepec plateau were grazed, as well as the eastern half.[88] The increase in grazing area is reflected in a decline in the estimated grazing rates even though the number of sheep in the sub-area increased in the period 1559–65 (from 210,600 to 525,000); the rates changed from 333 head per square kilometer (estimate based on a third of the surface area) to 276 per suare kilometer (estimate based on the entire surface area). There are no complaints reported from Xilotepec after the 1550s until the last decade of the century.

As pastoral activities spread, environmental transformation followed, and by the 1580s most parts of the Xilotepec plateau reported changes. To the north and northeast of the *cabecera* of Xilotepec live oaks were still growing on the hillsides, but there were indications of change in the presence of yucca on the flatlands, and the hillsides were eroded.[89] In the western half of the plateau reports from the 1550s noted oak woodlands, but by the 1580s only isolated live oaks were reported growing on the flats and lower hillsides,[90] and yucca appeared in the 1590s.[91] Only the mountains to the south remained heavily forested.[92]

In the Alfaxayuca Valley, the northern half was the first to be

[88] Chevalier, *La formación*, p. 133. AGIM, leg. 1841, fols. 1r–8r.

[89] AGNM, vol. 4, fols. 291v–292r; vol. 11, 64r; vol. 13, fols. 94r–v, 210v–211r; vol. 14, fols. 84r–85r, 233v–234r; vol. 16, fols. 72r–v; vol. 17, fols. 103r–104r, 119r–v, 120r–v; vol. 18, fols. 81v–82r; vol. 19, fols. 239v–240v. AGNT, vol. 2674, exp. 32, fol. 334r.

[90] AGNM, vol. 3, fol. 766r; vol. 14, fol. 142r; vol. 17, fols. 63v–64r. AGNT, vol. 2683, exp. 2, fol. 1r; vol. 2674, exp. 22, fol. 334.

[91] AGNM, vol. 19, fols. 239v–240v.

[92] AGNT, vol. 2764, exp. 26, fol. 321; vol. 2742, exp. 10, fol. 3r. AGNM, vol. 18, fols. 266r–v, 281r; vol. 22, fol. 298v.

exploited for sheep raising. By 1570 lands near Sacachichilco that had been grazed for thirty to forty years were converted to badlands where sheep were lost in gullies and mesquite scrub.[93] And by 1611 the hereditary lands (*pagos*) of the Indians of Sacachichilco, which were located at the foot of a high hill, were stony and covered with grasses, wild maguey, thistles, and mesquite. Spanish witnesses stated that the *pago* known as Atlamani had never been farmed: "these lands have always been left unused, [they are] stony and full of grasses, wild maguey, mesquite, and thistles – they have never been prepared, sown, or cultivated."[94] *Pago* generally refers to hereditary cultivated lands, however; so either they were considered to be nonarable lands because of their current poor condition, or the Spaniards wanted to disprove Indian rights to them. In the hills to the southeast of Alfaxayuca young live oaks were reported to be growing in the 1560s.[95] Unfortunately, no documentation exists for vegetative changes in this area for later in the century, so the fate of these trees is not known.

There are no records of environmental deterioration in Chiapa de Mota until the 1590s, when erosion in the high mountain valleys is reported.[96] Possibly the heavy forests masked changes occurring on the higher slopes. It is also possible (but not probable) that the Indians, who held the majority of the sheep stations in the area, did not run as many sheep, and therefore there was less deforestation.

Thirty years elapsed between the initiation of heavy grazing and the appearance of erosion and badlands in eastern Xilotepec and northern Alfaxayuca. In Chiapa de Mota erosion appeared after fifty years of grazing. Under lighter grazing in the western half of Xilotepec the time lapse before scattered deforestation and the appearance of yucca appeared was thirty to forty years. Overall, the deterioration of the environment of these three sub-areas during the sixteenth century appears to have been less extensive or profound than that recorded for the previous four. Except for the northern end of the Alfaxayuca Valley, expanses of dense mesquite-dominated desert scrub were not reported in the sixteenth century; nor, except for the eastern end of the Xilotepec plateau, was extensive sheet erosion

[93] "Esta en unos mezquitales e tunales e barrancas donde se pierde mucho ganado." ("[The station] is in a region of mesquite, cactus scrub and gullies, where a lot of livestock are lost" AGNT, vol. 1521, exp. 2.

[94] "Que siempre han sido y al presente son tierras heriazas pedregosas llenas de za-catales lechuguilla mesquites y cardones que nunca se han harrado sembrado ni cultivado," AGNT, vol. 2678, exp. 16, fol. 288r.

[95] AGNM, vol. 8, fol. 8r.

[96] AGNM, vol. 19, fols. 203v, 210v–211r; vol. 20, fols. 998r–v.

gullying. It could be that the documentation for these sub-areas is not as complete; however, they were subjected to extensive land takeover at the end of the century, especially in Xilotepec, and many detailed boundary surveys were carried out. The documents simply do not present a picture of environmental destruction to compare with that recorded for the previous four sub-areas. I suggest that the lighter environmental deterioration evident in these sub-areas can be explained by the fact that they were not as intensively exploited; grazing rates were lower, the extent of the land converted to pastoralism was less, and there were no limestone quarries or mines to consume exorbitant amounts of wood. The absence of mining and lime manufacture may have been the deciding factor, and were mines or limestone quarries present they would undoubtedly have led to more extensive deforestation and all the problems associated with it. The two exceptions, however, eastern Xilotepec and northern Alfaxayuca, prove the rule that animals maintained at high densities result in environmental degradation. In fact, in Xilotepec we have clear evidence that high densities of animals cause environmental degradation while lower densities lead to less deterioration.

Huichiapan

Spanish settlement of the Huichiapan Plateau was slowed by the threat of invasion by the Chichimecs, and reflects, far more than the other sub-areas of the region, the interest in agriculture shown by the Spaniards when Indian agricultural output declined after the 1576–81 epidemics. Early land grants in Huichiapan were mostly for sheep stations, but starting in the 1570s grants for arable land were made for the areas around the towns, and by 1585 50 percent of all Spanish-owned holdings were agricultural.[97] This situation can be contrasted to that in other sub-areas such as Alfaxayuca, where grazing had been introduced at an early date and had dominated production; in these sub-areas there were few agricultural holdings that were not ancillary to a station.[98] Despite that agricultural holdings accounted for 50 percent of Spanish land tenure, sheep grazed an area at least five

[97] AGNM, vol. 10, fols. 46v, 82r–v; vol. 11, fols. 246r–v; vol. 12, fols. 296v–297r; vol. 13, fols. 22v–23r, 144v–145r, 404v–405r; vol. 14 fols. 70r, 230r–231r, 232v–233r; vol. 15, fols. 221v–222r; vol. 16, fols. 25r–26r, 72r–v, 112r; vol. 20, fols. 61v, 98r–v, 186v–187r; vol. 22, fols. 268v, 331v–322r. AGIM, leg. 111, ramo 2, doc. 12.

[98] In Huichiapan there were forty-six *labores:* AGIM, leg. 111, ramo 2, doc. 12. AGNM, vol. 13, fols. 144v–145r; vol. 14, fols. 232v–233v; vol. 15, fols. 256v, 286r–v; vol. 16, fol. 112; vol. 22, fols. 321v–322r.

times that used for agriculture – and they grazed the eastern hills that formed the catchment area of the plateau. The most notable change in the environment of this sub-area during the sixteenth century was the drying out of the springs that supplied the rich irrigated lands lying along the western edge of the plateau. Indeed, the history of Spanish agriculture in the Huichiapan sub-area is an excellent example of the problems facing agriculturalists in semiarid regions where the lands forming the catchment areas are overgrazed.

Spanish agricultural holdings in Huichiapan were predominantly small (85–255 hectares) intensively exploited units known as *labores*. Wheat, maize, barley, grapes, and fruit trees were grown on these units, and most were irrigated.[99] By 1600, however, the fertile western lands where the bulk of these holdings were located had problems with their water supplies. Springs were failing in San José Atlan, and the flow was insufficient to supply both the town and the four thousand grape vines belonging to Catalina Mendez. In the early 1590s, when an agreement between Mendez and the town to share the water had been made, there was enough for all; but in 1600 a new agreement was drawn up giving Mendez the sole use of the water from Saturday night to Monday morning, and to the community the rest of the time.

Tecozautla had problems with water at about the same time. Five hundred fig trees belonging to the relator Cristobal de la Cerda were not irrigated because there was not enough water for both the fig trees and the Indians' fruit trees and cotton fields. De la Cerda had been granted water rights in 1567, but in 1600 they were revoked because he no longer used the water to irrigate his trees (it was also noted that the fig trees no longer gave fruit and were located in infertile soil). De la Cerda gave as his reason for not using the water that the trees were now eight hundred *pasos* from the irrigation canal, which may indicate that the canal had been moved to accommodate a change in water table levels.[100]

Problems with the water supply did not stem from an increased number of users; indeed, the population had declined. The witnesses in the Mendez case make it clear that the problems arose because the springs were failing. "When the agreement was drawn up there was

By contrast in the Southern Plain, there were two *labores:* AGNM, vol. 14, fol. 290r–v; AGNT, vol. 2721, exp. 19, fol. 8v.

In Xilotepec there was one *labor:* AGNM, vol. 15, fols. 286r–v.

In Tula, there were two *labores:* AGNM, vol. 12, fols. 411r–v, 451r–v.

[99] For example, see the census of Spanish landholding contained in AGIM, leg. 111, ramo 2, doc. 12.

[100] AGNT, vol. 3, exp. 1, fols. 1–8.

twice as much water in the springs," they said. "Since then some of the springs have dried out and they don't give as much water as they used to. If it were necessary to irrigate [both] the hacienda and the Indians' lands today, according to the original agreement, there would not be sufficient water to do so."[101] Both San José Atlan and Tecozautla lie at the lower western edge of the Huichiapan Plateau, where the springs that supplied the irrigation system arise. The failure of springs indicates a lowered water table and most likely arose from a drop in groundwater recharge following removal of the ground cover in the higher eastern hills that form the watershed of the plateau.

Huichiapan is another huge sub-area and, as in the case of Xilotepec, problems were encountered in estimating grazing rates that adequately reflect the probable patterns of land use. The eastern hills were grazed for a longer time and more intensively than the rest of the plateau. Early grants for grazing were mostly concentrated along the southeastern and eastern borders with Xilotepec and Alfaxayuca, although some were made for the northwest around Tecozautla.[102] And even though later grants were made in all parts of the region,[103] the most favored for sheep grazing remained the eastern half.[104] The grazing rates in the eastern third of the plateau in the first three decades were probably at least twice as high as those noted in Table 4.3, if not three times as high. In the last decade of the century, despite a decline in flock size, grazing pressure in the eastern hills increased because the number of new grants made in the 1590s doubled the number of sheep stations in the area. The failure of the springs along the western edge of the plateau at the end of the century can therefore be explained by the increased grazing pressure on the vegetation and soils of the hills that formed the catchment area.

In areas that had been grazed beginning in the 1550s and 1560s, environmental deterioration followed twenty to thirty years later, in

---

[101] "Quando se hizo el concierto avia al doble mas agua en los fuentes y despues aca se an secado algunos ojos y no mana tanta cantidad como solia y si huviesen de rregar el dia de hoy la dicha hazienda y los dichos yndios por el orden y concierto que an tenido no ay bastante agua"; AGNT, vol. 3, exp. 1, fol. 3v.

[102] AGNM, vol. 3, fols. 193r–v, 193v; vol. 5, fols. 166r, 257v–258r; vol. 7, fols. 227v–228r; vol. 8, fols. 177v–178r; vol. 10, 46v–47r, 63r–v, 82r–v.

[103] See Appendix C for sources for this sub-area. Sheep stations were located within the boundaries of the following towns: Nopala, Tlaxcalilla, Acuçilapa, Amealco, San Jusepe, Tetemí, Oztoticpac, San Andres, Tlamimilulpa, Cavalçingo, Caçagualcingo, Xonacapa, and Tecozautla.

[104] In 1587 an Indian principal noted that the Spaniards pastured their sheep in the eastern half of the valley ("a la parte del oriente que es todo el balle donde pastan las obejas de los mas españoles desta comarca"). AGNT, vol. 2701, exp. 20.

the 1580s.[105] An especially clear example of such deterioration was found on the sheep station belonging to Alonso Hernandez the Elder, which had been taken up in 1555/6. By 1585 this holding was described as being completely denuded of vegetation, with possible erosion: "I saw that the said station lands were completely bare of vegetation and that it was unstocked . . . the soil is destroyed [eroded?] and [the station] is not carrying stock."[106] The vegetation around Tecozautla was characterized by mesquite and yucca, but it is unclear whether they were recent invaders or were elements of the primary vegetation of this hot, dry area. The evidence does suggest, however, that there may have been a shift from single mesquite trees to *matoral* between 1563 and the 1590s. Such a change would be in accordance with the vegetation changes associated with other heavily grazed regions.[107]

The southern hills on the border between Xilotepec and Huichiapan did not show evidence of much deterioration during the sixteenth century. Apart from the presence of a dense growth of yucca in 1582[108] the hills remained well wooded[109] and there were still extensive marshes in the 1590s.[110] To this day these hills remain one of the few areas of oak woodlands outside the Sierra de las Cruces, although the reason for this is not clear. By contrast, the lands around Xonacapa to the north are a moonscape of sheets of exposed *tepetate*. Up to the end of the sixteenth century, however, the soils of this sub-area were still in the main fertile and rich. Water shortages, either real or the result of monopolization, caused more problems for the Indian communities and the Spanish settlers than either soil infertility or erosion.

Northern Valley and Ixmiquilpan

These two sub-areas did not attract many Spanish settlers during the first sixty years of settlement. Because they lie in the rain shadow of

[105] AGNT, vol. 1867, exp. 1, fol. 6r. AGNM, vol. 13, fols. 22v–23r.

[106] "E vyo que la dicha estancia esta asolada por el suelo y despoblada . . . la qual esta por el suelo deshecho y despoblada;" AGN, Tierras, vol. 1867, exp. 1, fol. 6r.

[107] *1563:* AGNT, vol. 2092, exp. 2, fol. 1r; vol. 2718, exp. 15, fol. 11r. *1590s:* AGNM, vol. 15, fol. 221r–222r; vol. 18, fol. 264r; vol. 22, fol. 359r–v. AGNT, vol. 2701, exp. 20, fol. 1r; vol. 2703, exp. 4, fol. 1r.

[108] AGNT, vol. 3568, fol. 34r.

[109] *1580s:* AGNT, vol. 1791, exp. 1, fol. 135r–v; vol. 2762, exp. 11; vol. 2764, exp. 5, fol. 4v. AGNM, vol. 13, fol. 61r.

1590s: AGNT, vol. 3568, fol. 40; vol. 2105, exp. 1, fol. 2r; vol. 3568, fol. 42r. AGNM, vol. 16, fols. 25r–26r.

[110] AGNM, vol. 16, fols. 25r–26r; vol. 20, fols. 186v–187. AGNT, vol. 3568, fol. 42r; vol. 3672, exp. 19, fol. 6r.

the Sierra Madre Oriental they are hot and dry, and in the early years of the colony they held little promise for growing wheat or grazing animals.[111] By the end of the 1570s (when the region as a whole was dominated by intensive pastoralism) only 5.3 percent of the Northern Valley and 7.5 percent of Ixmiquilpan were formally converted to pastoralism. And although the last two decades saw an increase in the conversion of land to pastoralism in the Northern Valley, less than 10 percent of the surface area of Ixmiquilpan and 20 percent of the Northern Valley were formally converted to pastoralism by 1600. Similarly, only tiny percentages of the land surface were transferred into the Spanish land tenure system for agriculture. These arid areas did, however, have other attractions: Ixmiquilpan had silver and lead deposits, and mines were founded there in the 1540s and 1550s. Limestone hills near Tecpatepec in the Northern Plain had been exploited by the Indians since before the conquest.[112]

Because semidesert species form the primary vegetation of these two sub-areas, it is difficult to distinguish long-term trends in the environment from those associated with sixteenth-century changes in land use. For example, the appearance of dense thorn scrub by the late 1570s on the flatlands of the Northern Valley obscured earlier specialization in the cultivation of the maguey and nopal. In 1548 the flatlands around Tecpatepec and Tlanocopan were planted with prickly pear cactus, and there were few magueyes or yuccas, while in Actopan in the 1560s maguey was planted around the town and chilies were grown in a nearby marsh.[113] By 1579, however, Tecpatepec and Tlanocopan were surrounded by thorn bushes, magueyes, mesquites, wild prickly pears, and yuccas.[114] The growth was so dense by 1589 it was impossible to cultivate the land: "[these lands] are full of mesquite, prickly pear cactus, and maguey, and for that reason no one can sow or cultivate."[115] By the early seventeenth century the fallow and depopulated lands of Actopan, as well, were surrounded by fields of mesquite, yucca, and wild prickly pear: "there is a league of unused public lands all uncultivated, unpopulated, and full of mesquite, yuc-

---

[111] PNE vol. 1, no. 546–7.

[112] AGNT, vol. 1519, exp. 4, fol. 35r. PNE vol. 1, no. 546. PNE vol. 6, pp. 4, 37.

[113] PNE vol. 1, no. 548, PNE vol. 3, p. 69.

[114] "Esta poblado en un llano grande muy montuosso de [es]pinos, magueyes, tunales silvestres y otros arboles que entre ellos llamanse mesquites ... y otras palmas syluestres"; ("It is located in a large flat area very thickly covered with thorns, magueys, wild cacti, and other trees called mesquites ... and yuccas") PNE vol. 6, p. 35. Also, AGNM vol. 12, fols. 447r–448r. AGNT, vol. 2766, exp. 3, fol. 2r.

[115] "Llenas de arboles mesquite y tunales y magueyales por cuia causa no puedan sembrar ni cultivar"; AGNT, vol. 2766, exp. 3, fol. 13r.

cas, and wild prickly pear cactus."[116] Because the invasion of cultivated fields by these semidesert species coincided with the abrupt population decline of the 1576–81 epidemic, and because the grazing rates had been very low up to the end of the 1570s in this sub-area, the increase in density of semidesert species could simply reflect the normal succession on fallow lands.

A similar process of increasing density and diversity of semiarid desert species in the last half of the sixteenth century is recorded for Ixmiquilpan. In 1548 this sub-area had good woodlands (evidently mesquite) and irrigated fields,[117] but by 1601, yucca, wild prickly pear, thistle and mesquite grew densely on the lands surrounding the town.[118] Miners had been cutting the woods to the north of Ixmiquilpan since the 1540s.[119] Whereas deforestation for mines undoubtedly affected the ecology of this sub-area, however, it is not clear whether it was the actions of the miners that led to the increase in the spiny semiarid plants or, as in the Northern Plain, whether their appearance was the normal succession on fallow lands in the arid areas.

It is also difficult to distinguish long-standing soil conditions from accelerated changes. From the first, the Spaniards characterized the soils of the Northern Valley as arid and therefore unproductive.[120] Whereas the lands of Ixmiquilpan were fertile when irrigated, moreover, the rest were said to be infertile "dead lands."[121] Stony, bare hillsides reported near Tecpatepec in 1570 were mesquite-infested badlands by 1589.[122] It is possible that lime manufacture caused the deterioration in Tecpatepec, although the hills were not being worked by either Indians or Spaniards (probably for lack of wood) by the last two decades of the century, and there had been no forests there in 1548.

---

[116] "Ay una legua de tierras baldias todo eriazas y despobladas llenas de mesquites palmas y tunales sylvestres por todas partes"; AGNT, vol. 2735, 1a. pte., exp. 15, fol. 10v.

[117] PNE vol. 1, no. 293.

[118] "Una loma montuossa de mesquites y palmas y tunales sylvestres y muchos cardones"; "A wooded slope of mesquites, yuccas, and wild cacti and many thistles" AGNT, vol. 2756, exp. 7, fols. 1r–16r.

[119] PNE vol. 1, no. 293. PNE vol. 3, p. 99. PNE vol. 6, p. 4.

[120] PNE vol. 1, no. 546, 547. PNE vol. 3, p. 68. PNE vol. 6, p. 35. AGNT, vol. 2766, exp. 3, fols. 13v–14r; vol. 1519, exp. 4, fol. 35r. AGNM, vol. 12, fol. 397r; vol. 23, fols. 42r–v.

[121] "Tierra muerta," AGNM, vol. 3, fol. 323. PNE vol. 3, p. 99. PNE vol. 6, p. 6. AGNT, vol. 2756, exp. 7, fols. 11r–16r.

[122] AGNT, vol. 2766, exp. 3, fols. 2r, 3r, 13v–14r.

There is, however, clear evidence of gully formation in the eastern end of the Northern Valley beginning in the last decade of the sixteenth century. During the 1590s a stream flowing across a level meadow in the village of Tecaxique in the eastern end of the Northern Valley began to cut down its bed, and by the early 1600s had formed a deep gorge (barranca).[123] Neither deforestation nor dense agricultural populations explain this phenomenon; the community had no woods,[124] and population pressure was relieved by the demographic collapse of the village (see Appendix B, Table B.1). On the other hand, the number of flocks in the Northern Valley increased threefold during the 1580s (see Table 5.9), and it is more than likely that the removal of the vegetative cover of the hills by grazing led to an increase in the overland flow of water and the formation of the barranca of Tecaxique.[125]

Both Ixmiquilpan and the Northern Valley were grazed at very low densities until the end of the 1570s, and grazing would appear to be a complicating factor rather than the primary variable in the processes of environmental change up to about 1580. During the 1580s, however, the Northern Plain was subjected to suddenly increased grazing pressures. Although the grazing rate estimated for the Northern Valley reached only 162 head per square kilometer in this decade, a rate far lower than for the rest of the region apart from Ixmiquilpan, this does represent an abrupt increase over the 1570s, and was probably more than enough to reduce the vegetation in this arid area.

If these two sub-areas were unattractive when the Spaniards first entered the region, they appeared even less so by the 1580s. Despite the increasing density of semidesert species and the lack of surface water, however, interest in the Northern Valley as a grazing region suddenly increased during the last two decades of the sixteenth century. In the first decade of the seventeenth century Ixmiquilpan was taken over by pastoralists. The sudden interest in the arid lands reflects a lack of room in the rest of the region for continued expansion. This will be discussed in the final chapter, but it can be noted here that because there had been a generalized decline in the status of the vegetative cover of the Valle del Mezquital, with an associated drop in the carrying capacity, there was a need for more land to maintain production and profits. Further, because there had been a shift in the perception of what constituted adequate fodder for grazing ani-

[123] Cook, Historical Demography, pp. 48–50.
[124] PNE vol. 1, no. 547.
[125] See Cook, Historical Demography, for a different explanation of this phenomena.

mals,[126] the Northern Valley and Ixmiquilpan were no longer considered poor grazing lands. Rather, in a fascinating mental sleight of hand, they were now considered fit only for sheep – and for the goats that made up an increasing percentage of the flocks in the dry northeast.[127]

Pastoralism was not the only activity initiated by the Spaniards in this region, but it was the most widespread, and it had the most pervasive impact on the environment. When the sub-areas are grouped according to the timing and intensity of grazing, and evidence of the type and extent of environmental change in each grouping is compared, we find that environmental degradation was recorded in areas of high animal density and extensive land conversion, but did not appear (or was minimal) in areas of low density and limited conversion. Contrary to folk wisdom, which consigns sheep grazing to areas of poor natural resources, the better the resources in the Valle del Mezquital, the more intense the grazing and the more extensive and profound the degradation. Land *became* fit only for sheep – it was not inherently poor.

The changes in the biological regime predicted by the model of ungulate irruptions, namely diminution of height, density, and species diversity of the native vegetation; enlargement of the bare spaces between plants; and an increase in armed woody species of plants, were complicated by human activities associated with pastoralism such as the firing of grasslands and the maintenance of excessively high grazing rates, as well as by accelerated deforestation to provide timber for the mines and fuel for lime and charcoal manufacture. The result was extensive environmental degradation, including sheet erosion, gullying, and deterioration of the land's catchment value. Despite the presence of a dense indigenous population of settled agriculturalists, the landscape and environment of the Valle del Mezquital underwent a process similar to that recorded for the highlands and tablelands of New South Wales: simplification and homogenization of the vegetative

---

[126] Tecpatepec and Yetecomac were now said to have abundant pastures for grazing: PNE vol. 6, p. 20, 35. AGNM, vol. 13, fols. 176r–v.

[127] See Melville, "The Long Term Effects," for a discussion of the changes in perception of the region by the Spanish pastoralists. Goats are mentioned in: AGNT, vol. 2756, exp. 7, fol. 16r; vol. 2812, exp. 13, fol. 411; AGIM, leg. 111, ramo 2, doc. 12, fols. 29v–30r. By the mid–seventeenth century Ixmiquilpan was used for cattle; and it is an indication of the shift in vegetation that cattle were taken there to fatten before slaughter, as cattle do better than sheep on mesquite, AGNT, vol. 2943, exp. 53, fols. 1r–2v.

cover, and deterioration of the soil and water regime. In the process, pastoralism displaced intensive irrigation agriculture, thus confirming the old adage that "sheep eat men."

Environmental change "fixed" the shift in regional production from irrigation agriculture to grazing. The sixteenth-century transformation of the water regime of this region prejudiced future exploitation. The Valle del Mezquital received increasingly arid forms of land use. Sheep in the sixteenth century were followed by goats and cattle in the seventeenth, followed in turn by the cultivation of the domesticated maguey for the production of pulque, and by exploitation of the wild lechuguilla maguey for rope in the eighteenth and nineteenth centuries. The importation of water in the twentieth century confirms the continued inability of the Valle del Mezquital to internally generate springwater. The soils at the center of the wide flat valleys of the region are, even now, incredibly fertile. But the hills are bare rock and the piedmont is scarred *tepetate*. Water rushes over these surfaces in the rainy season and is not restrained long enough by the sparse vegetation to sink into the soil and replenish the water table.

Despite the temperate climate of the Valle del Mezquital, the end result of the introduction of grazing animals was not an example of the neo-Europes described by Crosby. In fact, the Valle del Mezquital was closer to the European ideal of a productive and fertile agricultural region at conquest; and it was the European invasion itself that set in motion processes that transformed it into something often perceived as archetypical of the "naturally" poor Mexican regions. The invaders did not succeed in Europeanizing this landscape, but their presence made it into something new and different. In the process the Otomí were displaced, alienated, and marginalized, their history and that of their region mystified. The Otomí are identified with the alien conquest landscape, not with the fertile, productive landscape of contact. Their skills as cultivators were forgotten, their reputation as eaters of beetles, bugs, and the fruit of the nopal cactus confirmed.

5

THE CONQUEST PROCESS

Up to this point we have taken for granted that the Spaniards introduced their animals into the New World ecosystems and that they acquired access to the pasture and water necessary to maintain their flocks; but in neither case was this a foregone conclusion arising from their presence in the New World, nor even of their defeat of the Aztec Empire. Rather, the acquisition by the Spaniards of rights, first to grass and water and later to land, was an inherent part of the conquest process.

The most obvious means by which the Spaniards acquired access to resources was force; but force in and of itself is not sufficient explanation of the process of Spanish conquest and domination. Force was used and battles were fought, but in many cases the Spanish takeover occurred without the use of organized force, and the battles were more often than not fought in the court room. To a surprising degree the Spaniards' actions in the New World were constrained (if not always restrained) by laws and customs that shaped the processes by which they acquired resources – and thus their relationships with the indigenous populations. The application of Spanish law was not straightforward, however. The New World context warped the application of the law, distorting the intent of rulings, making loopholes for opportunists. The successful application of the law required knowledge that the Indians did not have at first, and in any case there was virtually no police force. The Spaniards, quite logically, took advantage of this situation. It is in this compromised context that the Spanish conquerors and settlers were able to acquire access to water and pasture, and finally to land.

The expansion of pastoralism in the Valle del Mezquital combined legal resource exploitation, illegal land grabbing, and force; it was based on an alien perception of the natural resource base and rights to its exploitation. The natural resource base of pastoralism is grass. The Indians did not systematically exploit grass. Grass was used as needed, in making adobe for example, and it was an element of the

116

ecological niches (grasslands, forests, and edge habitats) of the wild animals such as deer and rabbits that formed part of the Indians' subsistence base. By contrast, the Spaniards had a specific use for grass and considered it a resource for the maintenance of domestic livestock wherever it grew.[1] Grazing in common, stubble grazing, and grazing on public lands were customs basic to Spanish laws governing the exploitation of grass by pastoralists and the relations between them and agriculturalists. These customs reflected the complementary roles of agriculture and pastoralism in Spanish society and were based in a strong communitarian tradition of public ownership of the soil and its fruits. Vassberg, in his study of land ownership in Golden Age Castille, writes:

> The principle that serves as the starting point for public property ownership is that no individual has the right to take for himself and monopolize those resources of Nature that are produced without the intervention of man. According to this idea, the only thing that an individual has the right to call his own is that which he has wrought from Nature through his personal efforts in the form of crops, flocks or manufactured goods. Land, therefore, cannot be privately owned, but must remain permanently at the disposition of anyone who wishes to benefit from it (Costa 1944: 370). In the purest and most primitive application of this principle, an individual could use a piece of land simply by occupying it – no external authority would be needed. The use might be for pasture or for cultivation, but possession would be dependent solely on use. When the individual no longer wished to use the piece of land, he simply abandoned it, upon which all of his claim would cease, and the land would be available for the next person who wished to use it. But it was rare to find public ownership in such a pure form. Usually the institutions of public ownership represented some form of accommodation with local conditions.[2]

Simply put, wherever and whenever land was not being used to grow crops, it could be treated as common pasture; where use could not be demonstrated, individual claims to the land lapsed. The process by which public use of Nature's fruits alternated with private rights to the land is exemplified by the custom of stubble grazing (*derrota de mieses* in Spain; *agostadero* in Mexico):[3] individual rights to the land

---

[1] Chevalier, *La formación*, p. 12. Vassberg, *Land and Society*, p. 6.

[2] Vassberg, *Land and Society*, p. 6.

[3] The *Ordenanza de Agostadero* (regulations concerning stubble grazing) reads as follows: "Por quanto en las demás partes y lugares de esta Nueva España, los indios naturales no han acabado de coger sus sementeras de maíz, agí y frijoles, y otras coasas hasta

were in effect between planting and harvest, but when crops were not growing, fields in fallow or stubble were treated as pasture and grazed in common. Grazing in common did not mean uncontrolled open access, however. On the contrary, access to pasture, whether in private lands (in fallow or after harvest) or in common pasturelands (either municipal or royal), was controlled and regulated. Local animals were kept together under the care of herdsmen selected by local authorities, and municipalities controlled the number of animals each individual was allowed to graze in the commons.[4] Grazing in common should be

fin del mes de noviembre de cada un año, y por consiguiente tiene sembradas las tales sementeras a mediado el mes de abril, y si los ganados menores salen de los sitios de sus estancias a agostar antes de estar las dichas sementeras cogidas o vuelven de los agostaderos de estar sembradas reciben los naturales grandes daños, por tanto, ordeno y mando que los dichos ganados menores puedan entrar en los dichos agostaderos desde el primero dia del mes de diciembre de cada un año en adelante y no antes, y sean obligados a salir antes del postrero dia del mes de marzo, sin estar mas en ellos, so pena de diez pesos de oro común aplicados según Ordenanzas de Mesta." *Papeles sobre la mesta de la Nueva España* vol. 16, p. 20.

Agostadero is a relative term that changes its meaning according to the context in which it is used. It derives from the verb *agostar*, which has several related meanings, including "the desiccation of plants due to excessive heat," "to plow or hoe the soil in the month of August," "to dig the soil to depth of 70 or 80 centimeters in order to plant grape vines," "to graze animals in stubble or in enclosed pasturelands," ("Agostar, tr. Secar el excessivo calor las plantas. U.t.c.r.[] Arar o cavar la tierra en el mes de Agosto.[] *And.* Cavar la tierra a una profundiad de 70 u 80 centímitros para plantar viña en ella.[] intr. Pastar el ganado en rastrojeras o en dehesas.") *Diccionario Manual.* Livestock grazing in *agostero* are livestock that, once the harvest has been lifted, enter to graze in the stubble; "dicese del ganado que, levantadas las mieses, entra a pacer en los rastrojos," ibid.

With the move to New Spain the custom of grazing livestock in harvested fields during the hottest and driest period of the year remained; but the date shifted from August, the hottest month of the year in Spain, to the peak of the hot dry months in Mexico, which falls between December and April, just prior to the period when crops are sown. In the 1550s, in response to the problems posed by the rapid increase in animal numbers, Viceroy Velasco limited the period when animals could graze in the stubble to January 1 to February 28. But in 1574, as pasture deteriorated throughout New Spain, the period during which pastoralists had access to harvested fields was expanded to December 1 through to March 31 (Chevalier, *La formación*, p. 135). In the Valle del Mezquital the majority of the Indian complaints of Spanish intrusions into their lands occurred because Spanish pastoralists did not abide by the rules, and either entered their animals before the period set aside for *agostadero*, when crops had not yet been harvested, or refused to remove their animals in time to let the Indians prepare the land for their crops; see this volume, Chapter 2, note 92.

4 Vassberg, *Land and Society*, pp. 13–18, 35. The custom of stubble grazing seems to have been associated with a fairly sedentary form of pasturage. Vassberg notes that stubble grazing provided sustenance for animals in the summer and was a very important resource because "most of Spain's animals did not participate in the pe-

contrasted with exclusive access rather than with private ownership of land. The same principle of the commonality of Nature's fruits was extended to the New World colonies: "The use of all the pasturelands, wastelands and woodlands, and water of the provinces of the Indies will be common to all citizens." The custom of stubble grazing was introduced, as well: "After harvest the lands and *heredades* that the king grants and sells in the Indies will be used as common grazing, except those [lands set aside for] milk cows and municipalities"; the community of pastures and woodlands included *tierras de señorío* (entailed estates).[5] Animals could legally graze wherever grass grew; there was, therefore, no legal hindrance to the introduction of grazing animals into even densely populated regions.[6] Furthermore, because there were no indigenous domesticated grazing animals (with the exception of in the Andes), there were no local rules governing the use of grass, and no cause for concern about superseding native cus-

riodic trans-peninsular migrations, but instead remained near the villages of their owners," (p. 14). Bishko also notes that the custom of moving animals between winter pastures near towns and villages to summer pastures in nearby mountains was "more nearly sedentary than truly transhumant"; "Castilian as Plainsman," p. 56.

This "sedentary" form of stock management was imported into the Central Highlands of New Spain and contrasts with open-range cattle ranching of northeastern New Spain (Doolittle, "Las Marismas"); animals were corralled nightly and taken out daily to their pasturelands much as they are today. Local variations of transhumance did occur, however. MacLeod has noted "a local variant of transhumance called 'agostar'" in Central America. He wrote, "Just before the beginning of the rainy season it was the practice to burn off the vegetation cover in the valley bottoms. This destroyed old, tough, and dead grasses and brush, supplied the soil with nitrogens, and provided fresh new grass for the cattle when the rains came. While the valleys were being burned and until the new grasses sprouted, the cattle were grazed at higher elevations, usually on steep slopes." MacLeod, *Spanish Central America*, p. 305. Herman Konrad discusses the acquisition by the Jesuits in the last decade of the sixteenth century and early decades of the seventeenth century of lands outside the Valley of Mexico for summer pasture in *A Jesuit Hacienda*, pp. 49–63. And transhumance did appear in the Valle del Mezquital later in the century; AGIM, leg. 111, ramo 2, doc. 12. In both the Valley of Mexico and the Valle del Mezquital transhumance seems to have been a response to the deterioration of pasture rather than a customary form of stock management in the Central Highlands. See this volume, Chapter 6 for a discussion of the appearance of transhumance in the Valle del Mezquital.

5 "El uso de todos los pastos, montes y aguas de las provincias de las Indias sea común a todos los vecinos de ellas. . . . las tierras y heredades de que el Rey hiciera merced y venta en las Indias, alzados los frutos que se sembraren, queden para pasto común, excepto las dehesas boyales y concejiles"; *Recopilación de Indias*, ley 5, tit. 17, lib. 4; ley 6, tit. 17, lib. 4; and ley 7, tit. 17, lib. 4. Quoted by Miranda, "Notas," pp. 10–11.

6 Chevalier, *La formación*, pp. 12, 119–20.

tom. From the Spanish point of view the presence of livestock did not impinge on the rights of the indigenous agriculturalists; on the contrary, it was to their benefit. In Spain, however, the actions of the pastoralists were constrained by laws and customs regulating the relations between pastoralism and agriculture – and by the fact that more often than not animal owners were also agriculturalists – whereas the situation in the New World was very different. In the New World the pastoralists were conquering Europeans and the agriculturalists were conquered New World peoples, and the rights to Nature's fruits claimed by the Spanish pastoralists often abrogated the rights of the Indians to cultivate their fields in peace.

The Spanish pastoralists treated the Central Highlands as an open commons, as they had in Spain.[7] In Spain, however, this process was restricted to a stated period each year to the lands encompassed by a municipality, and to its inhabitants: "After harvest, every possessor of a grain field or meadow was obliged to open his lands to the animals of the general public. The entire territory of a town – fields and pastures – then became a continuous commons open to all the local livestock, and perhaps to those of neighbouring towns as well, until the next sowing time, when individual rights to the cultivated plots were re-established.[8] Stubble grazing expanded the area of land to which the animals belonging to small landowners had access during a season when the natural pasture was depleted by the summer drought.[9] The functioning of an equitable system of stubble grazing depended on a community of interests and expectations, and knowledge not only of the legal system, but also of the behavior of animals. The Indians had no knowledge of pastoralism, no experience in dealing with grazing animals, and were faced with a legal system that was based in an alien culture and organized according to unfamiliar principles. The Indians' lack of knowledge and their status as conquered peoples meant that they were unable to provide an informed and effective counterbalance to the actions of the Spanish pastoralists in the early years of the colony. Trouble really began when the animals started to increase exponentially, changing the environment as they expanded across the land. Then it became clear that pastoralism did not complement agriculture as it did in Spain – it competed with it.[10]

---

[7] Gibson writes that "any lands not actually under cultivation were to be regarded as common pasture." *Aztecs*, p. 280.

[8] Vassberg, *Land and Society*, p. 13.

[9] Ibid., p. 14.

[10] Attempts made by the Cabildo of Mexico City and the Mesta to control the rapidly increasing animal populations had little effect; Miranda, "Notas," pp. 20–23.

The Indians did not, at first, own grazing animals, and were not used to fencing off their fields or defending their plantings against the depredations of them. The Spanish pastoralists ignored the rules controlling access to pasture and grazed their animals in croplands, very often on the cultivated plants themselves. The results were disastrous: crops were destroyed, pueblos abandoned, and benefits such as manuring, that the Indians might have obtained from the arrangement, were negated by the destruction. Indians were not passive in the face of this aggression; they retaliated for the destruction of their crops by killing individual animals, sometimes whole herds, and they even won court cases against Spanish pastoralists.[11]

The Spaniards viewed the introduction of domestic livestock into the agricultural lands of the indigenous population as a perfectly legal use of an unexploited resource, but they had to use force in order to establish their operations, and to gain and maintain access to pasture. Indeed, it is hard to imagine how they could have done otherwise in a densely populated agricultural region where there was no cultural or social space for them, and where there were no indigenous mechanisms to regulate the relations between agriculturalists and pastoralists. In the early decades the corrals and huts that formed the core of the grazing enterprise were simply set up in the Indians' villages – often next to their houses – and the animals were grazed in the surrounding lands. Squatting was the commonest method of acquiring stations, and many if not most of the earliest official land grants legalized squatters' rights.[12] Although illegally acquired, these small areas of land appear to have been considered negligible by the Spanish authorities and were more in the nature of a necessary adjunct to the development of pastoralism, which was actively promoted in the 1530s by Viceroy Antonio de Mendoza. The importance of animal products in Spanish culture, and the need to develop herds in New Spain to supply fresh meat, milk, cheese, wool, hides, and tallow, meant that the inconvenience the Indians experienced by having stations in their villages was a minor consideration, at least until the flocks threatened to disrupt Indian agricultural production. At such times the crown moved to protect the source of food for the colony.

Extremely violent relationships developed between the villagers and

---

[11] See for example, Gibson, *Aztecs*, pp. 280–1 and Chevalier, *La formación*, pp. 86, 130, 132, 134–7.

[12] Simpson, Gibson, and Chevalier also note that grants were often issued for lands already in the possession of the grantees; Simpson, *Exploitation of Land*, p. 6. Gibson, *Aztecs*, p. 275. Chevalier, *La formación*, p. 131.

the herdsmen (mostly black slaves), especially when the herds began to expand dramatically in the 1550s. The Indians complained bitterly of the actions of the slaves, and accused the slave owners of inciting the herdsmen to violence, or at least of acquiescing by not interfering. The slaves came in bands to rob the Indians of their women, food, and belongings, and Indians who tried to defend themselves were beaten with staffs and sometimes killed. One Indian who had gone to a station to rescue his wife was tied by his hair to the tail of a horse and dragged until he died.[13] Such stories indicate unequal power relations that were, I believe, utilized by the pastoralists for the benefit of their flocks.[14]

Pastoralists were not only able to introduce their animals into this densely populated region, they were able to expand their operations so that by the mid-1570s pastoralism dominated regional production. In part we can ascribe their success to the irruption of the sheep populations. But ultimately it depended on the fact that grass, the natural resource base of pastoralism, was not subject to ownership, and pastoralism was able to develop as a "parallel" system of resource exploitation. The best way to understand this point is to compare the expansion of pastoralism with the development of Spanish agriculture, which was embedded in the Indian systems of land use and land tenure.

Spanish agriculture was dominated by the *encomenderos* until 1551, when the *repartimiento* system of labor drafts made Indian labor available to all landowners. Up to this point, *encomenderos* had a virtual monopoly on production: they specified the tributes required, the crops they wanted grown, and used their Indian laborers for a wide range of entrepreneurial activities. They had no legal right to land within their *encomienda,* however, and were prohibited from applying for *mercedes* in their *encomienda* lands (although, as will be seen below, this proviso was ignored); and, while they did have indirect access to the land and control over production, the *encomenderos* were ultimately dependent on the Indians' labor, land use, and land tenure systems. Pastoralists, by contrast, were not restricted to the Indian communities for their source of labor, as herdsmen and shepherds were almost exclusively black slaves in the early decades.[15] Nor did they need to acquire land in order to graze their animals, because grass was a fruit

---

[13] AGNM, vol. 4, fols. 330–2.

[14] Herman Konrad has come to the same conclusion regarding the acquiescence of the slave owners in the slaves' actions (personal communication, September 1987).

[15] Ordinances against using Indian labor for sheep herding date from the 1520s; Miranda, *La función,* pp. 13–14.

of Nature and a common resource. Pastoralism was thereby able to develop unconstrained by Indian land use and land tenure rights, or by the need to draw only on Indian communities for their labor. Existence "outside" the *encomienda*/village systems of production, combined with the use or threat of force, meant that the grazing animals and their owners had all the advantages of untrammeled exploitation of new ecological and social niches, and the grazing animals expanded extremely rapidly in spite of the density of the Indian agricultural population. The formal transference of land from the Indian to the Spanish systems of land tenure followed in the wake of the conversion of land use to grazing and consolidated the shift from intensive irrigation agriculture to pastoralism; the transformation of the environment, specifically erosion and desiccation, fixed this shift. Opportunities for agricultural expansion by the Spaniards were lost in the early postconquest period, and the degradation of the fragile ecology of this semiarid region prevented the exploitation of the growing markets for agricultural products later in the century. By the time Spaniards began to take an interest in agriculture in the 1580s, sheep grazing not only dominated regional production, but large areas of the Valle del Mezquital were so degraded that the land was fit for little else.

Documentation of Landholding and Land Use

The main source for the study of both landholding and land use is the *Ramo de Mercedes* of the *Archivo General de la Nación* in Mexico City (hereafter referred to as the AGN) in which are recorded, along with instructions to government officials and licenses and permits of various kinds, land grants made by the crown to Indians and Spaniards. This source has been augmented by documentation from *Tierras, General de Parte*, and *Indios* of the AGN, and the *Justicia, Escribanía de cámara* and the *Audiencia de México* sections of the *Archivo General de Indias* in Seville, Spain (hereafter referred to as the AGI).

In 1536, Viceroy Antonio de Mendoza codified the land grants and specified the area of land to be granted according to use. The land grants that concern us here are:

> *Sitio de estancia de ganado mayor* (cattle station) area: 17.56 square kilometers
> *Sitio de estancia de ganado menor* (sheep station) area: 7.8 square kilometers
> *Caballería de tierra* (agricultural holding) area: 42.5 hectares[16]

---

[16] Taken from Gibson, *Aztecs*, p. 276.

Grants were also given for lime workings (*sitio de calera*); for water rights for mills to grind metals or flour (*herido de agua para moler metales, herido de agua para molino de pan*); and areas of land for the foundation of Indian villages or for legalization of communal lands (*tierras de fundación*).

Gibson writes, "Despite the specifications of measurement and the extreme detail of the recorded surveys, considerable real differences in size distinguished one grant from another. Estancias were not necessarily regular rectangles of the dimensions specified. Rather, they were of irregular shape, and the areas enclosed by their boundaries were only approximations of the stated sizes."[17] I have found, however, that while claims made to legitimize the very early land grants or squatters' holdings may have exceeded the legal area of land allowed, the later grants did not. The early grants were for the station site (i.e., corrals and shepherds' huts) while giving license to graze in the general area of the grant, and when the time came to apply for formal title to a station, applicants asked for areas of land that often far exceeded the area of land specified by Mendoza in 1536. As the century wore on, however, and the land filled up, space for new grants became more and more limited. The boundaries of new station sites were clearly marked, and there was less room for manipulation of space. In fact, there was so little room to maneuver at the end of the sixteenth century that grants came to be made of land remaining between earlier grants.[18]

Whether the grants were used as stated has obvious importance for this study. Simpson came to the conclusion that the *mercedes* were generally used as specified;[19] and judging by the records of court cases and investigations of various types, the specifications as to use were, in the main, complied with in the Valle del Mezquital.[20] There appears to have been a bias toward sheep raising from the beginning in this region, and after 1555, when cattle were expelled from it, applications for land grants were made only for sheep stations. At the end of the century, however, there was a higher percentage of goats in the flocks, and a few cattle stations appeared in the peripheral areas of the Northern Valley and Huichiapan.[21] Despite these difficulties, and be-

[17] Ibid., p. 276.
[18] See notes 49–53.
[19] Simpson, *Exploitation of Land*, p. 20.
[20] The order to remove cattle was evidently enforced: for example, Rodrigo de Castañeda was compelled to remove his cattle from Xilotepec in 1557, AGIM, leg. 1841, fols. 1r–8r.
[21] AGNT, vol. 2812, exp. 13, fol. 411; vol. 2756, exp. 7, fol. 16r. AGIM, leg. 111,

cause of the predominance of sheep raising, I have based my estimates of formal land takeover and shifts in land use, on the legal area of land for a sheep station of 7.8 square kilometers.

Of the 862 sheep stations documented for the Valle del Mezquital in the sixteenth century, only 407 appeared in the records as formal land grants. The remaining 455 stations were identified by references to nearby holdings (sheep or cattle stations, or agricultural holdings) that formed the boundaries of new grants, were in the vicinity of new grants, or were the subject of court cases, wills, censuses, reports (*informes*), inspections (*diligencias*), or descriptive reports (*relaciones*). Having found no formal titles for these holdings, I designated them "squatters' holdings."

In an effort to identify all the holdings in the Valle del Mezquital, references to landholdings were listed chronologically and by *cabecera*, and the descriptions of the holdings were compared and contrasted. Names of landowners and of nearby pueblos, named landmarks such as streams, dry stream beds, gorges, hills, Indian lands, and the cardinal directions (taken from the *cabecera* or from a known landmark) were all used to identify and to distinguish the separate holdings. Where duplication occurred only the earliest references were used.

As noted in Chapter 2, documentation having to do with ownership and use of land refers to the appropriate *cabecera*. The area within which a land grant was located was therefore limited; and, apart from Xilotepec, which is very large and which had only one *cabecera*, the number of land grants falling within the territorial jurisdiction of a single *cabecera* were also limited in number. The identification and differentiation of the separate landholdings was thus a more straightforward process than might be imagined.

The Process of Land Takeover

The history of the transference of land from the Indian to the Spanish systems of land tenure has been broken down into decades and grouped into eras so that the process of conversion within the different sub-areas can be compared over short periods. Because all the *mercedes* are dated, it was a simple process to assign the grants to a specific decade, and the year the *merced* was awarded was taken as the date of transference to the Spanish system of land tenure. However, a record of the year in which a squatter took possession of his land

---

ramo 2, doc. 12, fols. 29v–30r. Oxen, cows, horses and mules were found in small numbers on the agricultural grants.

is rare. In order to assign the squatters' holdings to a specific decade the date of the document in which such a holding is recorded was taken as the date of its conversion, with the following exception. As it is probable that squatters' holdings were well established when the documents recording their presence were written, the totals for each decade have been adjusted: all stations that have been identified as squatters' holdings, and that appear in the records pertaining to the first four years of a decade, are included in the totals for the previous decade. The totals for each decade therefore include all the *mercedes* awarded during the decade, plus the squatters' holdings recorded in the documents pertaining to the last six years of the decade and the first four years of the following decade. For example, the totals for the decade of the 1540s include the *mercedes* awarded between January 1, 1540, and December 31, 1549, plus the squatters' holdings recorded in documents dated January 1, 1544, to December 31, 1553.

The calculation of the area of land transferred to the Spanish system of land tenure was obtained by multiplying the total number of stations in each sub-area at the end of each decade by 7.8 square kilometers (the area of land legally encompassed by a sheep station). The resulting area in square kilometers was then expressed as a percentage of the total surface of each sub-area in order to compare the expansion of pastoralism in sub-areas of widely different surface extent.

In the original presentation of this research I noted that much of the documentation for the early years of the expansion of pastoralism was incomplete: there were gaps in the records of the land grants (*Ramo de Mercedes*), and over a thousand volumes of the land suits (*Ramo de Tierras*) had not been cataloged. I therefore adjusted the totals of the 1530s and 1540s by adding the *encomenderos* as "undocumented squatters." My reasoning was that because the *encomenderos* were active in introducing grazing animals into other areas of New Spain during the early years of the colony, as indeed they were in some parts of the Valle del Mezquital, then the addition of forty *encomenderos* as squatters to the totals for the 1530s and 40s was not excessive. This adjustment meant that "the region [could] be seen to be sprinkled with sheep stations with heavy concentrations in areas which, in fact, demonstrated the greatest strain as indicated by the number of complaints made by Indian communities."[22]

In 1986 I was shown an annotated index of the *expedientes* pertaining to the Valle del Mezquital located in AGN, *Indios, General*

---

[22] Melville, "The Pastoral Economy," p. 92.

de Parte, and *Tierras.*[23] The addition to my calculations of sixty-eight new land grants encountered in *Tierras* meant that I was able to remove the "undocumented squatters" from my calculations. This adjustment has altered my perception of the course of land takeover in some of the sub-areas, and the rate of transference now seems to have been slower than I originally proposed. The final extent and pattern of landholding in the region is much the same, however, and the heaviest concentrations of Spanish landholding still appear in the same sub-areas.

A second adjustment made in the original study has been retained, that 30 percent of the squatters' holdings documented for the 1580s and 1590s (i.e., between January 1, 1584, and December 31, 1599) has been subtracted from the totals for 1599 for all sub-areas. This adjustment takes into account the possibility of confusion with earlier holdings because the number of grants and squatters' holdings increased dramatically in the last two decades of the century. This problem applied mainly to the very large Xilotepec sub-area, where some difficulty was encountered in identifying and distinguishing all the holdings; but the adjustment was made for all sub-areas.

Tables 5.1–3, 6–11 present information about the transference of land to the Spanish systems of land tenure in each of the ten sub-areas. They include the number of stations granted during each decade or acquired by squatters and the racial category of the recipient (i.e. Indian, Spaniard, Mestizo, or Mulatto); the total number of stations present in each sub-area at the end of each decade; the area of land formally converted to pastoralism expressed as a percentage of the total surface of each sub-area. Owing to the large number of documentary references for landholding, the sources for these tables are listed chronologically and by *cabecera* in Appendix C. The text discusses the implications of political, social, and economic change for the patterns of transference outlined in the tables.

Phase 1: Expansion (1530–65)

Spanish pastoralists moved with their flocks out of the Valley of Mexico soon after the conquest of Tenochtitlán. While no direct indications exist of sheep herding in the Valle del Mezquital in the 1520s, evidence that the Spanish immediately began to develop herds in other parts of New Spain seem to indicate that they would not have ignored a

[23] Piñeda, *Catálogo.*

Table 5.1. *Land takeover, 1530–9*

	Grants	Squat.	1539	Km²	%
Landholders:	Sp	Sp			
Tula	1	0	1	7.8	0.6
Southern Plain	1	3	4	31.2	6.4
Central Valley	1	1	2	15.6	2.5
Xilotepec	2	21	23	179.4	9.4
Alfaxayuca	0	4	4	31.2	4.9
Valle del Mezquital totals	5	29	34	265.2	2.6

Grants = Documented land grants
Squat. = Land appropriated by squatters
1539 = Cumulative total of stations as of this date
Km² = Total number of stations multiplied by 7.8 square kilometers
% = Km² expressed as percentage of total surface area of each sub-area
Sp = Spaniards

Source: Appendix C.

neighboring region.[24] And, because the majority of the stock owners in the Valle del Mezquital in the 1530s were first-generation *encomenderos* it is unlikely that they lagged behind their peers in setting up herds in this region.[25] By the end of the 1530s, animals were being grazed in the richest and most densely populated sub-areas of the Valle del Mezquital.

[24] Miranda, *la función*, pp. 25–9; Matezanz, *Introducción*, p. 537; Chevalier, *La formación*, p. 118. After 1526, formal title to stations were given by the *cabildo* of Mexico City outside the actual jurisdiction of the city. The *diezmos* (tithe) which Spaniards paid in the 1520s on animals, especially sheep and pigs, in areas as far apart as Mexico City, Michoacan, Medellin, Veracruz, and Tlaxcala, demonstrate the rapidly increasing numbers of animals in the first postconquest decade (Matezanz, *Introducción*, p. 538).

[25] Of the thirty-four stock owners with herds in the region in the 1530s, twelve had been given *encomiendas* in the Valle del Mezquital in the 1520s by either Cortés or the First Audiencia, one later inherited the *encomienda*, and one was the widow of a first holder. The rest of the stock owners can be identified as holders of *encomiendas* in other regions.

Local *encomenderos* with herds in the Valle del Mezquital in the 1530s:

Technically, anyone who acquired a few animals and slaves for herding could, and did, set up as a pastoralist. *Encomenderos*, however, had a distinct edge in the development of herds and eventually in the acquisition of land grants, even though they were prohibited both from owning land within their *encomiendas* and from using their Indian tributaries as herdsmen.[26] The power and prestige of the *encomenderos* in the early decades meant that they could introduce herds into the grasslands of their own and others' *encomiendas* with relative impunity. *Encomenderos* also made successful applications for land grants within their *encomiendas;* though whether these grants fell within Indian village lands or in nominated public lands by the crown (and therefore alienable) is not stated. It is interesting to note, however, that of the twelve local *encomenderos* with herds in the Valle del Mezquital in the 1530s, only three had set up stations within the boundaries of their own *encomiendas.*[27] It was easier, it seems, to set up stations in foreign *encomiendas* than in one's own.

It is difficult to decide whether the early documents are referring to cattle or to sheep and goats, as the type of animal is rarely specified

Encomendero	Encomienda	location of station:
Francisco de Estrada*	Tuzantlalpa	Tlapanaloya
Xpobal Cabeçon*	Tuzantlalpa	Tlapanaloya
Bartolome Gomez*	Tepetitlan	Xilotepec
Xpobal Hernandez*	Apazco	Tornacustla
Gonzalo Hernandez*	Tornacustla	Tlilcuautla
Martin Lopez*	Tequixquiac	Tequixquiac
Geronimo Lopez*	Axacuba	Xilotepec
Juan de Moscoso*	Tepexi	Xilotepec
Fco. Rrodrigo*	Yeytecomac	Xilotepec
Geronimo Ruiz de la Mota*	Chiapa de Mota	Xilotepec
Lorenço Xuarez*	Tlanocopan	Xilotepec
Juan Xaramillo	Xilotepec	Xilotepec
Juan de Cuellar (heir)	Chilcuautla	Xilotepec
Beatriz de Rribera (widow of Martin Lopez)	Tequizquiac	Tequizquiac

Note: *first holders of the *encomienda*.
Sources: AGNM, vol. 1, exp. 37, fol. 20r; exp. 231, fols. 11r–v; exp. 236, fol. 112r; exp. 448, fol. 210; exp. 466, fol. 218r; vol. 2, exp. 71, fol. 29r; exp. 122, fol. 47r; exp. 125, fol. 48v; exp. 220, fol. 86r; exp. 249, fols. 95v–96r; exp. 530, fol. 217r; exp. 572, fol. 233r; vol. 4, fols. 77r–v; vol. 21, fols. 79v–80r; AGIJ, leg. 143 no. 2.

[26] The grant of an *encomienda* did not include rights to the land within the boundaries of the Indian communities making up the grant. Nor could an *encomendero* legally apply for a grant for land within his or her *encomienda*. Ordinances against using Indian labor for sheep herding data from the 1520s; Miranda, *La función*, pp. 13–14.

[27] See Note 25.

at this date. Not until the area of the grant was specified according to its function was the type of livestock stated with regularity. It is generally thought that early grants in New Spain were given mostly for sheep and goats. In the Valle del Mezquital, the bias does seem toward sheep and goats from an early date, but cattle and horses were also present.[28]

The first geographic description of New Spain (ca. 1548) does not fully describe the activities of the Spanish in the Valle del Mezquital during the 1540s. For example, only three herds in the eastern half of the region are recorded in the *Suma de Visitas* whereas there is ample evidence of many more – as can be seen in Table 5.2. The clearest evidence of the extent of Spanish pastoral activities in this decade comes from the Xilotepec sub-area, which is not included in the *Suma de Visitas*. In 1551 the Indians of Xilotepec petitioned the crown for relief from the large number of animals grazing in the savannas, stating that people were leaving their lands to escape the destruction. Thirty-one Spaniards are listed as owners of the animals that were causing the devastation. The list of livestock owners reads like a *Who's Who* of the colonial elite. Eight regional *encomenderos* figure in the list of people named, and the worst offenders include the *encomendero* of Xilotepec, Juan Jaramillo, and his second wife, Beatriz de Andrada. Although more people were involved than the thirty-one listed, those not named were probably more ordinary souls whose names were less well known (to the king at least), and whose herds were presumably smaller.[29]

Table 5.2 indicates that by the end of the 1540s the heaviest concentrations of stations were in the same general areas as in the 1530s – the headwaters of the Tula River (Tula, the Southern Plain, and Chiapa de Mota), Alfaxayuca and Xilotepec. The number of complaints made by Indian communities confirm that these sub-areas were subject to the greatest strain.

Encomenderos were still the majority of stock owners in the 1540s; and more *encomenderos* based their livestock operations within the boundaries of their own *encomiendas* than in the previous decade. For example, in 1542 Martyn López, the *encomendero* of Tequixquiac in

[28] Miranda, *La función*, p. 29; Matezanz, *Introducción*, p. 538. Sheep and pigs: Xilotepec, Tornacustla, and Tezcatepec: AGNM, vol. 1, exp. 310, fols. 143r–v; vol. 2, exp. 288, fols. 11v–12r. AGIM, leg. 1841, fols. 1r–8r. AGIJ, leg. 143 no.2.
    Mares and cows, Xilotepec and Tezcatepec: AGNM, vol. 1, exp. 37, fol. 20r; vol. 2, exp. 228, fols. 11v–12r.
[29] AGIM leg. 1841, fols. 1r–8r, petition to the crown 1551. AGNM, vol.4, fols. 77r–v, royal cédula dated 1555 replying to the petition made in 1551.

Table 5.2. *Land takeover, 1540-9*

	1539	Grants	Squat.	1549	Km²	%
Landholders:		Sp	Sp			
Tula	1	0	3	4	31.2	2.5
Southern Plain	4	1	1	6	46.8	9.6
Central Valley	2	0	1	3	23.4	3.8
North-South Plain	0	1	0	1	7.8	1.0
Xilotepec	23	1	22	46	358.8	18.9
Alfaxayuca	4	1	0	5	39.0	6.1
Chiapa de Mota	0	0	7	7	54.6	7.8
Northern Valley	0	0	1	1	7.8	0.7
Ixmiquilpan	0	1	1	2	15.6	1.5
Valle del Mezquital totals	34	5	36	75	585.0	5.8

1539　= Cumulative total of stations as of this date
Grants = Documented land grants
Squat. = Land appropriated by squatters
1549　= Cumulative total of stations as of this date
Km²　 = Total number of stations multiplied by 7.8 square kilometers
%　　 = Km² expressed as percentage of total surface area of each sub-area
Sp　　= Spaniards

Source: Appendix C.

the Southern Plain, asked for a grant of a sheep station in his own *encomienda.*[30] Pedro Valenciano and Anton Bravo, the two *encomenderos* of Hueypostla (also in the Southern Plain), were partners in a sheep station within the boundaries of their *encomienda;* although Valenciano did not declare ownership until 1553, the station dates from well before this, as Bravo died in 1548.[31] Diego de Albornoz, the royal treasurer and former *encomendero* of Tula, sold a station located within the boundaries of Tula to Juan de Jasso el mozo, the *encomendero* of

[30] AGNM, vol. 2, exp. 125, fol. 48v.
[31] AGIJ, leg. 154 no. 3, 3a pte., fol. 460v.

Table 5.3. *Land takeover, 1550–9*

	1549	Grants	Squat.		1559	Km²	%
Landholders:		Sp	In	Sp			
Tula	4	2	4	5	15	117.0	9.5
Southern Plain	6	1	0	0	7	54.6	11.3
Central Valley	3	0	0	0	3	23.4	3.8
North–South Plain	1	0	0	1	2	15.6	2.0
Xilotepec	46	3	0	5	54	421.2	22.1
Alfaxayuca	5	2	0	3	10	78.0	12.3
Chiapa de Mota	7	2	0	0	9	70.2	10.1
Huichiapan	0	3	0	0	3	23.4	1.3
Northern Valley	1	0	0	0	1	7.8	0.7
Ixmiquilpan	2	0	0	2	4	31.2	3.0
Valle del Mezquital totals	75	13	4	16	108	842.4	8.4

1549   =   Cumulative total of stations as of this date
Grants =   Documented land grants
Squat. =   Land appropriated by squatters
1559   =   Cumulative total of stations as of this date
Km²   =   Total number of stations multiplied by 7.8 square kilometers
%   =   Km² expressed as percentage of total surface area of each sub-area
In   =   Indians
Sp   =   Spaniards

Source: Appendix C.

Xipacoya, in 1546.[32] In 1550 the *encomendero* of Chiapa de Mota, Ruiz de la Mota, was noted as having seven stations within the boundaries of his *encomienda*.[33]

The documentation of the sub-areas forming the headwaters of the

[32] AGNM, vol. 3, exp. 461, fols. 169r–v. Albornoz had to give up the *encomienda* on promulgation of the New Laws in 1542, which forbade royal officials to hold *encomiendas*.

[33] AGNM, vol. 3, fol. 144.

Table 5.4. *Siting of sheep stations*

	1530s	1540s	1550s	1560s	1570s	1580s	1590s	Total
Hills/cerros	0	5	3	41	7	28	62	146
Slope/loma	0	0	0	8	1	16	32	57
Flats/llanos	1	0	2	4	3	2	12	24
Savanna/sabana	0	32	0	0	0	0	0	32
Hereditary plot/pago	0	0	0	0	1	2	9	12
Wetlands/cienaga	0	0	0	0	0	1	0	1
River/rio	0	0	0	0	1	1	3	5
Ravine/barranca	0	1	0	0	1	0	0	2
Gully/arroyo	0	0	0	8	0	7	0	15
Gorge/quebrada	0	0	0	1	1	6	0	8
Depopulated village	0	0	0	0	0	1	20	21
Croplands/sementera	0	0	0	1	0	0	0	1

Source: Appendix C.

Tula River demonstrates the attraction of these fertile areas for pastoralists. Surprisingly few stations are documented for the North–South Plain and Ixmiquilpan in this decade. I think we can take it that certainly more stations existed in the Ixmiquilpan sub-area than the two for which we have documentation, however, because mines were founded near the town of Ixmiquilpan in the 1540s, and stations would have been necessary to provide fresh meat for the workers, hides for bags to move the ore, and tallow for candles. In addition, the first *encomendero* of Ixmiquilpan, Juan Bello, left four sheep stations in this sub-area to his wife and granddaughter on his death in 1569, and it is unlikely that he waited for very many years after the conquest to set them up.[34] Nor is there evidence of stations in Huichiapan in the northwest sector of the region, where Spanish settlement was threatened by invasion by the Chichimecs. We do know,

---

[34] AGIC, leg. 671-B, will of Juan Bello.

Table 5.5. *Siting of agricultural holdings*

	1530s	1540s	1550s	1560s	1570s	1580s	1590s	Total
Hills/<u>cerros</u>	0	0	7	3.5	3	42	44	99.5
Slope/<u>loma</u>	0	0	0	19.5	5.5	58.25	49	132.25
Flats/<u>llanos</u>	0	0	0	0	4	24	26	54
Savanna/<u>sabana</u>	0	0	0	0	3	7	4	14
Hereditary Plot/<u>pago</u>	0	0	0	0	0	0	8	8
Wetlands/<u>vega</u>	0	0	0	0	0	6	2	8
River/<u>río</u>	3	0	0	0	0	2	7	12
Ravine/<u>barranca</u>	0	0	0	0	1	0	0	1
Gully/<u>arroyo</u>	0	2	0	0	0	2	2	6
Gorge/<u>quebrada</u>	0	0	0	0	0	0	6	6
Depopulated village	0	0	0	0	0	4	23	27

Source: Appendix C.

however, that the areas bordering the eastern hills of the Huichiapan plateau had sheep and cattle stations (Xilotepec, Alfaxayuca, and Chapantongo), so it is likely that there were herds grazing in this sub-area before 1549.[35]

The introduction of the (at first) tiny herds into the Indian lands was relatively peaceful; but the numerical size of a herd is not as important as the grazing rate, and small herds with restricted pasture rapidly overgraze suitable areas and begin to compete for fodder. As the numbers of animals grew, the complaints filed by Indian communities of crop destruction increased, and the relationship between the villagers and the herdsmen became increasingly violent.[36] Possibly Indians were running small flocks on their communal lands by this time; they did not receive grants, however, and do not appear in the documents as squatters.

[35] See Chapter 4.
[36] See Chapter 2, note 92, for references to complaints filed by Indian communities, and Table 5.12.

Table 5.6. *Land takeover, 1560–5*

Landholders:	1559	Grants		Squat.		1565	Km²	%
		In	Sp	In	Sp			
Tula	15	32	5	5	12	69	538.2	44.0
Southern Plain	7	3	2	0	3	15	117.0	24.2
Central Valley	3	16	2	0	2	23	179.4	29.7
North–South Plain	2	11	0	0	1	14	109.2	14.5
Xilotepec	54	8	2	0	6	70	546.0	28.7
Alfaxayuca	10	1	8	0	7	26	202.8	31.9
Chiapa de Mota	9	13	0	0	1	23	179.4	25.8
Huichiapan	3	2	5	0	14	24	187.2	11.0
Northern Valley	1	1	0	0	0	2	15.6	1.5
Ixmiquilpan	4	3	0	0	3	10	78.0	7.5
Valle del Mezquital totals	108	90	24	5	49	276	2,152.0	21.4

1559	=	Cumulative total of stations as of this date
Grants	=	Documented land grants
Squat.	=	Land appropriated by squatters
1565	=	Cumulative total of stations as of this date
Km²	=	Total number of stations multiplied by 7.8 square kilometers
%	=	Km² expressed as percentage of total surface area of each sub-area
In	=	Indians
Sp	=	Spaniards

Source: Appendix C.

Pastoralists continued to move into the region during the 1550s in the same somewhat casual fashion as before. Although contemporary witnesses reported a decline of one-half to two-thirds of the indigenous population by midcentury,[37] and a corresponding amount of agricultural land presumably was freed as a result, only thirteen *mercedes* were granted during this decade, and even more surprisingly,

[37] Motolinia, *History*, p. 302.

only twenty new squatters appear in the records. There is evidence of only 108 stations in the entire region by the end of the 1550s; in other words, only 8.4 percent of the total surface area of the region was formally transferred to the Spanish system of land tenure. It could be that although the Indian population declined, the villages managed to maintain the cultivation of extensive fields and thus retain control of the land. But when looking for an explanation of the low rate of land takeover in the 1550s, the great influence of Viceroy Velasco on Spanish–Indian relations has to be taken into account. Extensive appropriation of fallow fields may have been avoided because of Velasco's determination not only to protect the Indians' rights and relieve them of the intrusions of the Spanish-owned flocks, but also to make sure his policies were enforced.

During his term as viceroy (1550–64) Velasco enforced many old regulations and introduced new ones aimed at clearing the Indian villages of animals and preventing the use of their lands for grazing: even the customary right to communal pasture was prohibited within a radius of 3,000 pasos (one league) surrounding the villages. Grazing in harvested fields was limited to a period lasting from January 1 to February 28, and the stocking rate (number of head per station) was also limited.[38] The densely inhabited central regions of New Spain were cleared of cattle by his order, and during the 1550s Velasco made few grants for stations in heavily populated agricultural regions. Instead, he made them in the *chichimecas* and in lands thought at that time to have little or no agricultural potential.[39] It is ironic, given his good intentions, that Velasco hastened the process of takeover by making so many grants in the hills and outlying lands that he effectively opened up, or at least intensified, the exploitation of the natural grasslands and forested areas. From the descriptions contained in the *mercedes* it can be seen that there was an attempt, during the 1560s, to place stations in the hills, *quebradas*, and *arroyos* away from agricultural lands. The agricultural grants, in contrast, were given predominantly for gently sloping lands – areas suitable for ploughing but which had sufficient slope for drainage (see Tables 5.4 and 5.5). This was a distinct change from the lands favored by the early pastoralists, which had been in direct competition with Indian croplands. However, despite the move to place the stations well away from Indian

---

[38] Chevalier, *La formación*, pp. 133–5. Later, in 1574, Viceroy Martín Enríquez extended the period to December 1 to March 31; p. 135.

[39] The "chichimecs" referred to the nomadic Indians who lived north of the Central Highlands, or to the lands inhabited by them.

communities, the Spanish continued the practice of free grazing in harvested and fallow fields and ignored the regulations controlling the use of these lands. As a result, the livestock owners and Indians still regularly came into conflict. Nearly one-third of the complaints about damage to crops documented for the sixteenth century date from the period 1550–65. (See Table 5.12.)

The 1560s provide evidence of the interest shown by Indians in sheep raising: Indians received 78.9 percent of the grants made between 1560–5. The sudden increase in the number of grants during these years, and the fact that the larger percentage of them went to Indians, were undoubtedly a result of Velasco's policies, which were aimed at maintaining a strong peasant base by protecting the Indians' rights to land and encouraging their use of it in diversified ways.[40] The Indian grantees, however, were practically all nobles (variously referred to as *principales,* governors or *caciques*), and of the ninety *mercedes* granted to Indians during this six-year period, only nine communities and three commoners received grants of sheep stations; six commoners and two nobles received licenses to graze sheep in the *baldios.*[41] The Indian grants carry the same injunction limiting the number of head, generally to 2,000 head per station, as do the Spanish grants; and the rule appears to have been ignored with impunity by both Indians and Spaniards.

The problem with seeing Velasco as the primary mover in the acquisition of land by Indians through the Spanish legal system is that the Indians appear, as a result, to be lacking in initiative and to be incapable of appreciating the advantages of a formal land title. Judging by the defense of their legal rights, however, they cannot be described as either passive on their own behalf or ignorant of legal process. The concept of private ownership of land would not have

---

[40] As Gibson notes, "The viceregal order of 1558, that all useable vacant lands were to be distributed to the maceguales for cultivation, is noteworthy not because it was obeyed or enforced but because it indicates that Spaniards in the mid-century period still hoped to encourage Indian agriculture for the maintenance of Spanish society." *Aztecs,* p. 281.

[41] Nobles were generally designated *principales* in the documents, while commoners are generally noted simply as being native to a particular town. Also, the nobles are generally known by their Christian first names and hispanicized last names, with "Don" very often preceding. More often than not the commoners have Otomí or Nahuatl names.

Because the licenses were generally given for the possession of five to six hundred head of sheep, four licenses are considered to equal one station. Licenses dating from the 1590s given to nobles to brand sheep are taken to indicate that the nobles held full-size stations.

been new forty years after the conquest, and the advantages must have been apparent before this. It is likely that Velasco removed obstacles in the way of Indian grants, making possible the legal acquisition of lands for activities that formed part of the culture and society of the colonial elite. Apart from the economic and legal advantages, moreover, ownership of land within the Spanish legal system would have conferred added legitimization of the nobles within the new society, and as such would have been desirable to them.

As a general rule individual Indians and communities needed formal permission to sell or otherwise alienate the lands granted, and when permission was given to sell, the fact was called by the town crier daily for thirty days before the public auction was held.[42] Occasional marginal notations in the titles for *mercedes,* together with evidence from court cases, indicate that these lands often did stay in the original family through the sixteenth century; but wills made in the seventeenth century make it clear that the lands were alienated when there was need for money, or when sufficient pressure was placed on an individual by, for example, an *encomendero.* As Gibson writes, "The readiness with which Indian gobernadores and cabildos accepted the proposed land grants to Spaniards and formally affirmed that such grants would entail no injury to the Indian community strongly suggests collusion, coercion or bribery."[43] Gerónimo López's acquisition of two stations in the Central Valley, although it occurred later in the century, illustrates one of the ways by which Spaniards (in this case the local *encomendero*) acquired Indian lands. Two Indian *principales* were each granted a station in 1562: Don Diego de Mendoza, the governor of Axacuba, and his son, Don Pedro Garcí Hernandez. In 1607 an heir of these men donated the stations to Gerónimo López "for the many and very good things he has done and continues to do for us and for the love and good will in which we hold him." Evidently López helped Doña Angelina, the wife of Don Pedro and great-granddaughter of Don Diego, to defend Don

---

[42] The notable exception to this rule was the thirteen grants given to the Indians of Chiapa de Mota in 1560, together with permission to sell; AGNM, vol. 5, fols. 154r–156v.

[43] Gibson, *Aztecs,* p. 276. Gibson comments on the difference between the ideals of the Spanish crown regarding Indian land rights and the reality of the colonial situation: "in land sale, as in other matters where Spanish law came into conflict with the private interests of the Spaniards, the law proved impotent. Indian land sales in the Valley [of Mexico] are repeatedly recorded without formal notaries, for extremely low prices, as punishment, and in unequal trades. In effect, Indians continued to sell to Spaniards so long as there remained land to sell." Ibid., p. 281.

Pedro's station (which she had inherited from her daughter Maria) against encroachment by the nearby village of Tetepango in 1587. Her mother, Catherina de Mendoza (Don Diego's granddaughter), inherited this station, as well as the one originally granted to Don Diego, from her uncle Don Miguel. Catherina de Mendoza and her husband, Augustin Pérez, were unable to stock the two stations and they donated both holdings to López. They denied the allegation that the original *mercedes* for these stations had been acquired for the express purpose of passing them on to López.[44] (The rather convoluted inheritance pattern, by which property ascended rather than descended the generations, probably came about because of the demographic collapse and the lack of more usual heirs.)

Phase 2: Consolidation of Pastoralism (1565–80)

The period between 1565 and 1580 is chiefly remarkable for the high densities of sheep that grazed the region, and the slow rate of land takeover. By the end of the 1570s large numbers of pastoralists dominated regional production. They did not, however, dominate production by virtue of the size of their holdings, which were small, or by the total area of land they held formally, which represented less than a third of the surface of the region; rather, they dominated the exploitation of the natural resources of the region by the sheer numbers of the animals they grazed. A critical point was reached in the late 1560s when the sheep reached the apogee of their population explosion. The boom lasted for ten to twelve years at the most, yet while it lasted, individual flocks of up to twenty thousand head were corralled on one station, and ten to fifteen thousand head per station was considered normal.[45]

Although the density of animals increased the area of land converted to grazing, however, it may have actually slowed the rate of land acquisition. During the 1570s few *mercedes* were granted, and surprisingly few squatters moved into the Valle del Mezquital. Potential flock owners may have been discouraged from moving into the region in large numbers because the sheer density of the flocks already there made it difficult for new ones to find grazing.

Shifts in viceregal policies toward granting land may have slowed the rate of land takeover during this decade. Viceroy Velasco's

[44] AGNT, vol. 2354, exp. 1, fols. 1–71.
[45] The largest individual flock, of twenty thousand head of sheep, was recorded in Tezuntlalpa in 1576; AGNG, vol. 1, exp. 970, fol. 181r.

Table 5.7. *Land takeover, 1566–9*

Landholders:	1565	Grants In	Grants Sp	Squat. In	Squat. Sp	1569	Km²	%
Tula	69	0	0	0	3	72	561.6	45.9
Southern Plain	15	5	0	0	0	20	156.0	32.2
Central Valley	23	0	4	0	0	27	210.6	34.9
North–South Plain	14	0	0	0	2	16	128.4	16.5
Xilotepec	70	0	2	0	1	73	569.4	30.0
Alfaxayuca	26	0	0	0	0	26	202.8	31.9
Chiapa de Mota	23	0	0	0	0	23	179.4	25.8
Huichiapan	24	0	0	0	0	24	187.2	11.0
Northern Valley	2	0	0	0	1	3	23.4	2.3
Ixmiquilpan	10	0	0	0	0	10	78.0	7.5
Valle del Mezquital totals	276	5	6	0	7	294	2,293.0	22.8

1565   = Cumulative total of stations as of this date
Grants = Documented land grants
Squat. = Land appropriated by squatters
1569   = Cumulative total of stations as of this date
Km²   = Total number of stations multiplied by 7.8 square kilometers
%   = Km² expressed as percentage of total surface area of each sub-area
In   = Indians
Sp   = Spaniards

Source: Appendix C.

programs during the 1550s could have served to check the rate of land takeover during that decade, as I have suggested, while his policies in the 1560s accelerated the formal acquisition of land. During the fourteen years following Velasco's death the rate of formal land acquisition again decreased, and the number of *mercedes* dropped from 114 awarded by Velasco between 1560–5, to 55.5 during the period 1566–79 by viceroys Gaston de Peralta and Martín Enríquez. It is not clear, however, whether the decline in the num-

Table 5.8. *Land takeover, 1570-9*

Landholders:	1569	Grants		Squat.		1579	Km²	%
		In	Sp	In	Sp			
Tula	72	6	2	3	13	96	748.8	61.2
Southern Plain	20	3.25	0	1	5	29.25	228.1	47.2
Central Valley	27	2.25	6	0	0	35.25	274.9	45.5
North–South Plain	16	7	3	2	4	32	249.6	33.1
Xilotepec	73	3	2	0	5	83	647.4	34.1
Alfaxayuca	26	1	3	0	7	37	288.6	45.5
Chiapa de Mota	23	0	0	0	1	24	187.2	26.9
Huichiapan	24	1	2	0	19	46	358.8	21.1
Northern Valley	3	3	0	1	0	7	54.6	5.3
Ixmiquilpan	10	0	0	0	0	10	78.0	7.5
Valle del Mezquital totals	294	26.5	18	7	54	399.5	3,116.1	31.0

1569	=	Cumulative total of stations as of this date
Grants	=	Documented land grants
Squat.	=	Land appropriated by squatters
1579	=	Cumulative total of stations as of this date
Km²	=	Total number of stations multiplied by 7.8 square kilometers
%	=	Km² expressed as percentage of total surface area of each sub-area
In	=	Indians
Sp	=	Spaniards

Source: Appendix C.

bers of *mercedes* granted was due to viceregal policy or to fewer requests. Nor is it clear how viceregal policies would have affected the actions of the squatters, as they had all along shown little regard for legal niceties.

Phase 3: The Final Takeover (1580–1600)

During the last two decades of the sixteenth century the bulk of the land moved formally and finally into the Spanish system of land ten-

Table 5.9. *Land takeover, 1580–9*

Landholders:	1579	Grants			Squat.		1589	Km²	%
		In	Mz	Sp	In	Sp			
Tula	96	0	0	5	3	12	116	904.8	724.0
Southern Plain	29.25	2	0	7	4	3	45.25	352.9	73.0
Central Valley	35.25	0	0	5	1	1	42.25	329.5	54.6
North–South Plain	32	6	2	11	2	8	61	475.8	63.1
Xilotepec	83	0	0	7	0	17	107	834.6	43.9
Alfaxayuca	37	0	0	1	0	10	48	374.4	59.0
Chiapa de Mota	24	0	0	3	0	3	30	234.0	33.7
Huichiapan	46	4	0	8	0	41	99	772.2	45.5
Northern Valley	7	0	0	6	4	5	22	171.6	16.8
Ixmiquilpan	10	1	0	2	0	0	13	101.4	9.8
Valle del Mezquital totals	399.5	13	2	55	14	100	583.5	4,551.3	45.3

1579   = Cumulative total of stations as of this date
Grants = Documented land grants
Squat. = Land appropriated by squatters
1589   = Cumulative total of stations as of this date
Km²   = Total number of stations multiplied by 7.8 square kilometers
%   = Km² expressed as percentage of total surface area of each sub-area
Mz   = Mestizos
In   = Indians
Sp   = Spaniards

Source: Appendix C.

ure. More holdings were added to the regional totals during these two decades than in the previous five. Two processes underlay the acceleration of land takeover. The first was a dramatic decline in the Indian population during the 1576–81 epidemic; the second, somewhat paradoxically, was the deterioration of the environment.

The conversion of land use from intensive irrigation agriculture to intensive small-scale pastoralism between 1560 and 1580 in the Valle

Table 5.10. *Land Takeover, 1590–9*

	1589	Grants			Squat.			1599
Landholders:		In	Mz	Sp	In	Ml	Sp	
Tula	116	8.5	0	5	15	0	16	160.5
Southern Plain	45.25	3	0	3	1	0	1	53.25
Central Valley	·42.25	4	0	6	3	0	12	67.25
North–South Plain	61	8.5	1	1	3	0	5	79.5
Xilotepec	107	34	0	8	8	1	24	182.0
Alfaxayuca	48	2	0	2	1	0	0	53.0
Chiapa de Mota	30	19	0	2	4	0	5	60.0
Huichiapan	99	13	0	20.5	3	0	31	166.5
Northern Valley	22	2	0	2	0	0	1	27.0
Ixmiquilpan	13	0	0	0	0	0	0	13.0
Valle del Mezquital totals	583.5	94	1	49.5	38	1	95	862

1589 = Cumulative total of stations as of this date
Grants = Documented land grants
Squat. = Land appropriated by squatters
1599 = Cumulative total of stations as of this date
Ml   = Mulatto
Mz   = Mestizos
In   = Indians
Sp   = Spaniards

Source: Appendix C.

del Mezquital occurred independently of the demographic collapse
of the indigenous populations and was achieved by the pressure of
high densities of sheep. The sheep population reached its greatest
density in the decade before the human population was devastated
in the Great Cocolistle epidemic of the last half of the 1570s, and
declined at around the same time as the human population. The
expansion of the grazing animals depended on the amount and quality
of the pasture available rather than on the density of the human

Table 5.11. *Total area of land transferred to Spanish land tenure by 1599*

	1599	Less 30% Squatters[a]	Km²	%[b]	%[c]	%[d]
Tula	160.5	146.7	1,144.2	93.6	5.6	99.2
Southern Plain	53.25	50.5	394.2	81.6	10.8	92.4
North–South Plain	79.5	74.1	577.9	76.7	6.1	82.8
Central Valley	67.25	62.1	484.7	80.3	1.3	81.6
Xilotepec	182.0	167.0	1,302.6	68.6	3.1	71.7
Alfaxayuca	53.0	49.7	387.6	61.1	1.3	62.4
Chiapa de Mota	60.0	56.4	439.9	63.3	5.8	69.1
Huichiapan	166.5	144.0	1,123.2	66.1	7.3	73.4
Northern Valley	27.0	24.0	187.2	18.4	.5	18.9
Ixmiquilpan	13.0	13.0	101.4	9.8	.4	10.2
Valle del Mezquital	862.0	787.5	6,142.9	61.2	5.0	66.2

1599 = cumulative total of stations in 1599

[a]30% was deducted from the 1589 and 1599 totals of squatters holdings to account for undocumented sales.

[b]Area of land transferred to the Spanish system of land tenure for sheep grazing expressed as a percentage of the total surface area of each sub-area.

[c]Area of land transferred to the Spanish system of land tenure for agriculture expressed as a percentage of the total surface area of each sub-area.

[d]Total area of land transferred to the Spanish system of land tenure expressed as a percentage of the total surface area of each sub-area.

populations, and when the quantity and quality of the pasture began to deteriorate at the end of the 1570s the flocks dropped in size, even though their agricultural competitors had been reduced. The consolidation of pastoralism by formal land takeover, however, *was* closely tied to the human population decline. As Indian communities lost people there were greatly increased areas of land left fallow, and the Spanish took advantage of the situation to gain control of lands prohibited them by law. The erosion of the crown's resolve to protect the

Table 5.12. *Complaints filed by Indian communities concerning problems with animals*

	1540s	1550s	1560s	1570s	1580s	1590s
Tula	0	2	4	1	3	0
Southern Plain	3	0	4	1	0	5
North–South Plain	0	0	1	0	1	3
Central Valley	0	0	4	0	1	1
Xilotepec	2	4	0	0	0	3
Alfaxayuca	1	2	1	0	0	0
Chiapa de Mota	0	0	0	1	0	0
Northern Valley	0	1	0	0	0	0
Ixmiquilpan	0	0	1	1	0	1
Regional totals:	6	9	15	4	5	13

Source: Note 92, Chapter 2.

Indians' land rights was especially noticeable after the disastrous epidemics of the late 1570s.[46]

Most of the land transferred into the Spanish land tenure system in the Valle del Mezquital during the last two decades of the sixteenth century was for sheep raising. Nevertheless, the number of agricultural holdings increased as well because the Spanish, here as elsewhere in New Spain, were forced into taking an active interest in agriculture to make up the drop in Indian agricultural production. In this decade

---

[46] As Gibson writes, "no date can be fixed for the formal relinquishment of the policy of protection, for the policy was never formally relinquished. But events of the late sixteenth and early seventeenth centuries resulted in a relaxation of the efforts to control Spanish intrusion. The plagues, dislocations, and depopulations of the last quarter of the sixteenth century accelerated the progressive abandonment of Indian lands. Lands without Indian inhabitants could be categorised by Spaniards as vacant, unowned or unappropriated (baldías or *realengas*), and thus as lands available to Spanish intrusion 'without injury.' Actual transfers were still acomplished in standard ways, by sale transacted by Indian officials or maceguales, by forced sales coerced by Spaniards, and by formal grants." Gibson, *Aztecs*, p. 282.

alone, 366.75 new *caballerías de tierra* are documented (including 54 caballerías composing 27 *labores*); this is more than double the number documented for all the preceding decades. The great majority of these agricultural holdings were taken up by Spaniards who grew wheat, barley, maize, grape vines, and fruit trees, and who sold their produce at the nearby mines in Cimapan, Ixmiquilpan, and Pachuca as well as sending it to Zacatecas and Mexico City.[47] Despite this increase in interest in agriculture on the part of the Spaniards, however, it remained a minor element in the exploitation of the Valle del Mezquital in the sixteenth century for reasons discussed at the beginning of this chapter.

Degradation of the environment was accompanied by a drop in the carrying capacity of the range. This in turn stimulated the pastoralists of the region to acquire more land and to institute exclusive access to the pasture on their lands, in order to expand the extent of their rangeland and thus maintain their flocks. Despite the drop in carrying capacity, then, the number of stations in the region increased by 184 between 1580–9 and by a staggering 278.5 between 1590–9. In other words, the total surface area of the region formally transferred to the Spanish system for sheep raising increased by 46 percent in the 1580s and another 47.7 percent in the 1590s. At the same time, another process was initiated: the acquisition of several holdings by one landowner and the formation of latifundia (large landed estate). In the 1570s this region had been dominated by many small individual holdings, but by the early seventeenth century it was dominated by latifundia.

The final takeover of the region by the pastoralists was completed during the 1590s. By 1599 Tula, the Southern Plain, the Central Valley, and the North–South Plain were completely taken over, as were almost three-quarters of Xilotepec and Huichiapan, and nearly two-thirds of Chiapa de Mota and Alfaxayuca. Only Ixmiquilpan and the Northern Valley had less than a quarter of their land surface transferred to the Spanish land tenure system by the end of the century. As the land filled up, grants for sheep stations were made that were a fraction of the legal size (800 pasos square instead of 2,000 pasos square),[48] some were made in the leftovers between grants (*sobras*

---

[47] See Chapter 2, note 81.

[48] AGNM, vol. 13, fols. 182r–v; vol. 19, fols. 206r, 207v–208r; vol. 21, fols. 208r–209r; vol. 23, fol. 26v. AGNT, vol. 2735 2a pte., exp. 9, fol. 1r; vol. 3433, exp. 15, fol. 1r.

y demasias),[49] and stations were granted that impinged on communal lands surrounding the villages.[50] Two quotes from *mercedes* made in the early 1590s demonstrate that there was barely room for new grants in the Tula sub-area:

> [Tula, 1593:] There appears to be little land left to be able to grant the usual 2,000 pasos square; thus it seems to me that I can grant [the applicant] half a station.[51]
>
> [Tula, 1594:] I have declared and repeat that there is no room to grant a station in [Tula] to anyone else; and so I ordered it to be proclaimed.[52]

Stations now were placed all over the region in many ecological zones, and care was no longer taken to keep them well away from Indian agricultural lands and communities. By 1600 there was insufficient land left for the *ejidos* of the *cabeceras* (let alone the villages subject to the *cabeceras*) in the southeastern quarter of the region. In the Tula sub-area twelve *cabeceras* theoretically had title to 210.7 square kilometers, but only 9.7 square kilometers are estimated to have remained unconverted to the Spanish system. In the Southern Plain 36.7 km^2 remained for the six *cabeceras*, which would theoretically have required 105 km^2. There were only 129.5 km^2 in the North–South Plain, where nine *cabeceras* would have required 157 km^2, and barely sufficient land remained in the Central Valley for *ejidos*.

How did things come to this pass? In the 1550s Viceroy Velasco had moved to protect Indian agriculture because, although pastoralism was a crucial element of Spanish culture and there were strong incentives to develop ranching in the New World, Indians supplied the food that maintained the Spaniards. In addition, as subjects the Indians were entitled to the unmolested use of their lands. In the Valle del Mezquital, however, these laws did not have the desired result. In fact, the regulations of the 1550s structured relations between the Indian agriculturalists and Spanish pastoralists in such a way that Indian control over land outside the designated areas was weakened, leaving it open to Spanish usurpation.

---

[49] AGNT, vol. 3433, exp. 15, fol. 1r.

[50] AGNM, vol. 17, fols. 63v–64r, 119v–120r; vol. 18, fols. 268v–269v. AGNT, vol. 2701, exp. 20, fol. 1r; vol. 1748, exp. 1, fol. 19r.

[51] "Parece que ay poca cantidad de tierra para que se la pueda dar de los pasos que son dos mil a todas partes y asi me parece que le podia merced de medio sitio de estancia." AGNT, vol. 2721, exp. 9, fol. 1.

[52] "Y declarava y declaro no aver lugar de dar sitio de estancia en ella [*cabecera* of Tula] a otra persona y asi lo mande poner por auto." AGNM, vol. 18, fol. 156v.

The shift in viceregal practice from granting *mercedes* in densely populated areas to granting them for stations in out-of-the-way places does not seem to have relieved the density of the animals around the villages in the Valle del Mezquital, but as a result, stations were placed in the hills, and in woodlands and wastes. Transformation of woodlands and former agricultural lands into eroded badlands meant the loss to the Indian communities of traditional resources for subsistence and exchange, such as herbs and roots, animals and birds, and wood products.[53] It also had the effect of facilitating the process of land takeover. Indeed, the transformation was often so complete that indications of former modes of land use were erased, leaving only evidence of sheep grazing, such ecological changes tended to confirm Spanish claims of ownership of the land by use-right and to deny Indian claims.[54] The separation of communal rights to Nature's fruits from ownership of land became the means by which the Spaniards conquered and dominated. That is, the process of usurpation and the associated environmental transformation combined with the regulations restricting Indian control over land not under cultivation to facilitate the movement of land into the Spanish system of land use. The granting of formal legal titles simply confirmed the fact of takeover.

Whereas it is true that the laws restricting animals to specified distances from Indian communities provided a buffer, however, they also acted to further reduce effective Indian control over communally held lands, because land outside of the limits was liable to use and usurpation by the Spaniards.[55] This tendency was confirmed in 1567 when the land to which Indian communities could legally lay claim – in distinction to any holdings they may have acquired by grant – were officially restricted to the *fondo legal,* an area surrounding the village or town that measured "500 *varas* [423 meters] in each of the four cardinal directions."[56] The final blow to Indian autonomy and control of natural resources came when pastoralism shifted from common grazing to exclusive access, and from an

---

[53] For example, sheep ate the leaves of edible roots so that they could not be found for harvesting (AGNT, vol. 2697, exp. 11) and trampled stands of the shrub *tlacotl,* which was used as a wood substitute in the production of lime; AGNT, vol. 1525, exp. 1.

[54] See for example, AGNT, vol. 2678, exp. 16. Also, Gibson, *Aztecs,* p. 282.

[55] Although pre-Columbian municipal boundaries continued to be used by the Spaniards, the land within these boundaries was granted except where Indian communities had clearly established their rights.

[56] Taylor, *Landlord and Peasant,* p. 70.

abstract notion of public ownership of the soil and its fruits to private ownership of land. (These two processes will be discussed in more detail in the following chapter.)

By the 1590s Indian communal lands, theoretically protected by Spanish law, were being granted as *mercedes* for grazing, very often to Indian nobles who were able to circumvent laws prohibiting the alienation of these lands.[57] It should be noted, however, that by 1600 Indian *caciques* and communities held over one third of the sheep stations in the Valle del Mezquital. Whereas the traditional Indian resource base and systems of land use had been drastically modified and the total area of land at the disposal of the communities reduced, then, the Indian *caciques* (and to a lesser extent the villages) benefited by the Spanish legal system, which allowed them to legally hold land. Twice as many Indians received grants as did Spaniards during the 1590s, as they had in the 1560s; but greater participation by the Indians in this decade cannot be ascribed to viceregal benevolence or the desire to emulate the Spanish elite, as was the case in the 1560s. There were very different economic and social circumstances thirty years later. The viceregal government no longer actively pursued a policy of Indian land protection, and while emulation of the Spanish elite probably played a part in the decision made by some nobles to apply for sheep stations, economic necessity was surely as important a consideration.

The problems facing the Indian communities became more and more formidable. Grazing lands pressed nearer to the villages, and

---

[57] Grants made to Indian nobles of depopulated village lands (one grant per *cabecera*, unless otherwise noted):

1585 Otlaspa	AGNT, vol. 3433, exp. 15, fol. 1r
1591 Xilotepec	AGNM, vol. 17, fols. 38r–v
1593 Chiapa de Mota	AGNT, vol. 3673, exp. 15, fol. 1r
Xilotepec (five grants)	AGNM, vol. 18, fols. 266r–v, 167v–269r, 281r
Xilotepec	AGNT, vol. 2742, exp. 10, fol. 1r
Huichiapan	AGNT, vol. 3568, fol. 43r
Hueypustla	AGNM, vol. 19, fol. 121r
1594 Chiapa de Mota (six grants)	AGNM, vol. 19, fols. 202r, 203v, 206v–208r
Atitalaquia	AGNT, vol. 2674, exp. 16, fol. 288r
Atitalaquia	AGNT, vol. 69, exp. 4, fols. 1–10
1595 Xilotepec	AGNM, vol. 20, fols. 38v–39r
Chiapa de Mota (three grants)	AGNM, vol. 20, fols. 66v–69r
1596 Xilotepec	AGNM, vol. 21, fols. 121r–v
1601 Tepexi	AGNT, vol. 2754, exp. 13, fol. 3r
Ixmiquilpan	AGNT, vol. 2756, exp. 7, fol. 16v

many fertile lands were lost beneath a cover of mesquite, cactus, wild maguey, and thistles, especially in the Tula River basin and the North–South Plain.[58] See, for example, Table 5.12 for complaints made by Indians about problems with grazing animals. Irrigation waters dried up or were diverted, and court cases were fought over water rights – very often alleging lack of sufficient water for croplands, which were in any case radically reduced in extent.[59] Labor problems stemming from the decimation of the Indian population affected the communities and the nobles, as well as the Spaniards, since they were drawing on the same labor pool. The Indians faced the added problem of maintaining their own lands as well as the Spaniards – part of the labor force was removed each week to work in the *repartimiento* gangs in the mines and on local stations and *labores* – and the remaining workers were insufficient to weed and maintain already-planted lands, let alone clear those that were overgrown and fallow. In these circumstances the land grants would confer title to lands that otherwise would be lost, and since pastoralism was not labor intensive it would thus have seemed doubly attractive.

By 1600 pastoralists controlled the means of production in the Valle del Mezquital. It is true that some Indian communities managed to retain control over some of the best lands in the region, and the demographic collapse meant that they needed less land and water to irrigate it; but they had lost land for future expansion, and the degradation of the water regime meant that many communities had also lost the means to cultivate what was left.

---

[58] See Chapter 4 for a more complete description of these ecological changes.

[59] AGIE, leg. 161-C, fol. 110v. AGNM, vol. 9, fol. 3r. AGNT, vol. 3, exp. 1, fols. 1–8; vol. 64, exp. 1, fols. 1–20; vol. 1486, exp. 8, fol. 17r; vol. 2284, exp. 1, fols. 743r–744r; vol. 2813, exp. 13. AGNI, vol. 6–1, exp. 291, fol. 79r–v; vol. 6–2, exp. 532, fol. 117r.

6

THE COLONIAL REGIME

By 1600 the era of conquest was over in most parts of the Central Highlands of New Spain and a remarkably stable colonial regime was in place, typified by the rural system of production – the hacienda. Our understanding of the nature of the hacienda, its internal structure and its relations with Indian communities, towns, and evolving internal and international markets has undergone a transformation of its own as research carried out over the past twenty years produced a profusion of variants of the hacienda. It is no longer possible to sustain the traditional conceptualization of the colonial hacienda as a large, underexploited, undercapitalized estate that produced for subsistance and existed primarily for the prestige of its owner. Regional and hacienda studies have shown that while there were indeed huge haciendas in some regions, in others they were not much bigger than *labores;* that haciendas often required considerable working capital; that hacienda owners were intimately concerned with production for the market; and that rather than depending solely on debt peonage, haciendas combined a variety of methods to recruit and maintain labor such as *repartimiento,* slavery, wage labor, and sharecropping. One way out of the conceptual dilemma posed by the evidence of variability has been to shift the focus from the hacienda to its context, and analysts have, in Eric Van Young's words, come to treat the hacienda as an effect rather than a cause.[1] For example, very large, extensively exploited haciendas are now thought to have developed in regions of poor natural resources and low population densities, while regions of good natural resources and dense indigenous populations were characterized by smaller and more intensively worked estates.

The timing of Spanish settlement, and ultimately the prevalence of Spanish-owned estates, is thought to have depended on the availability of markets as well as on the character of the natural resource base.

[1] See Van Young's article, "Mexican Rural History," for a description of the various types of labor systems, p. 25.

151

Regions distant from the major markets and lacking valuable resources that would make up for the cost of transportation remained predominantly Indian in resource exploitation and land tenure until the market for their resources opened up or communications improved.[2] The labor pool, the markets, and the natural resource base are clearly crucial developmental variables in analyses of hacienda formation, but while the markets and the labor pool are treated as active variables, the natural resource base remains a passive variable throughout. Attempts by individual landowners to monopolize the increasingly scarce labor resources that resulted from the demographic collapse of the indigenous populations are considered crucial for understanding the formation of haciendas, their internal composition, and their structural relations with the regional economy. Markets also are seen to have changed, and their growth or decline is treated as an active variable in development. By contrast, the physical environment is perceived as an unchanging backdrop to human action in the eyes of most historians. Spanish perception of the usefulness of the natural resources of specific regions is seen to have changed over time, but the natural resource base *itself* more often than not is treated simply as a passive constraining or enabling variable.[3]

[2] Davies, *Landowners in Colonial Peru,* p. 158; Keith, *Conquest and Agrarian Change,* p. 136; Lockhart and Schwartz, *Early Latin America,* pp. 134–5; Lockhart, Introduction to *Provinces of Early Mexico;* Taylor, *Landlord and Peasant,* especially his Conclusion; and Van Young, *Hacienda and Market,* especially chapter 6.

[3] There are, of course, some notable exceptions: in 1952 Lesley B. Simpson proposed that the introduction of grazing animals initiated "an ecological revolution of truly vast proportions, the consequences of which permanently and profoundly affected the Mexican landscape and structure of society," *Exploitation of Land,* pp. 1–2. Enrique Florescano's study of the relationship between weather and maize prices, *Precios del Maíz,* has become a classic. Murdo MacLeod's seminal work on Central America indicated the importance of environmental change as a variable in analyses of socioeconomic change, *Spanish Central America.* Charles Gibson noted the increasing desiccation and declining soil fertility of the Valley of Mexico that resulted from the Spanish modes of resource exploitation; even so, he cautioned against exaggerating its historical significance when he wrote that "from the Indian point of view . . . lands were lost far more obviously as a result of pre-emption by Spaniards than as a result of the impoverishment of the soil," *Aztecs,* p. 306. Herman Konrad, in the conclusion to his study of the Santa Lucia Hacienda, took a different view when he described the ecological changes that had taken place within the bounds of the landholding, and noted that "the pueblos were left to cope with a deteriorated resource base, which had been savagely attacked and relentlessly exploited," *A Jesuit Hacienda* p. 340. More recent studies include Peter Bakewell's work on deforestation and mercury poisoning around Zacatecas; Robert Claxton's studies of climate and natural hazards; Herman Konrad's work in progress on the chicle trade in Yucatan; Sonya Lipsett-

The case of the Valle del Mezquital demonstrates clearly that changes in land use could lead to rapid and profound environmental change. It also demonstrates that environmental transformation could signify more than cosmetic adjustments to the landscape, such as the disappearance of milpas and trees, and the addition of sheep and desert scrub. In the Valle del Mezquital the transformation of the environment over the last quarter of the sixteenth century signified profound changes in the natural resource base. Soil erosion, invasion by desert scrub, and a fall in the water table signified a loss of productive potential. It remains to spell out the implications of the loss of productivity for the transformation of the developing colonial systems of production in this region, and ultimately for the appearance of the hacienda.

Haciendas appeared in the Valle del Mezquital after 1580, following a sequence of colonial systems of production similar to others in New Spain. Beginning in the 1530s the *encomienda* was joined by grazing enterprises and small agricultural holdings (the *labores*), and by the 1570s *estancia*-based intensive sheep grazing dominated regional production. During the last twenty years of the sixteenth century the dominant form of regional exploitation shifted from intensive to extensive pastoralism. At the same time individual landowners moved to acquire several *estancias* (usually, but not necessarily contiguous) and formed large grazing haciendas.

The primary variable in the shift from intensive pastoralism based in small holdings (*estancias*) to extensively exploited large haciendas was, I suggest, the deterioration of the carrying capacity. I suggest further that monopolization of land was a secondary variable dependent on the changing status of the range. A closer look at the relationship between the carrying capacity and changing patterns of resource exploitation in the Valle del Mezquital during the last forty years of the sixteenth century demonstrates this hypothesis.

In the late 1560s and 1570s individual pastoralists grazed incredible numbers of sheep in the Valle del Mezquital. Although he or she might own only one station, a pastoralist could profit from ownership of large numbers of animals since the flocks initially had access to lands far in excess of the area encompassed by the station, and to pasture

---

Rivera's work on water supplies in eighteenth century Puebla; Murdo MacLeod's study of drought and demography in Guadalajara; Michael Meyer's study of water on the northern frontier; Michael Murphy's work on water in the Bajío; Arij Ouweneel's study of climate and maize harvests; and Susan Swan's work on climate in the Little Ice Age.

that had never been systematically exploited by domestic grazing animals. Grazing was uncontrolled despite – or perhaps because of – common grazing. Then as today, common grazing only works when all parties agree to the rules governing the use of specified areas of land; but the Spaniards regarded all land not sown with crops as potential grazing lands, and, as conquerors, Spanish pastoralists could afford to ignore their own laws and customs when it suited them. As a result, while numbers were legally limited to 2,000 head per station, no real attempt was made to restrict stocking rates – as witness the *estancia* owner who corralled 20,000 head of sheep on one station. The spectacular growth in numbers during the period of expansion apparently indicated to the Spanish that the range had the capacity to support an infinitude of animals. The crown and its representatives did indeed recognize the legitimacy of the complaints of infractions made by the Indian communities, but the unequal power relations of the colonial situation meant that the influence of local power holders counted for more than pronouncements by a distant authority, so pastoralists continued to overstock and to overgraze.[4]

Uncontrolled grazing by vast armies of sheep degraded the range, with the result that the number of animals that could be maintained in the Valle del Mezquital (the carrying capacity) declined over the last quarter of the sixteenth century. In this situation two things could have occurred; first, flocks could have expanded into new grazing lands, or, second, they could have adjusted to the decline in their subsistence base by decreasing in numbers. In the Valle del Mezquital the problem was solved by transhumance and depopulation. Because the greater part of the region was already exploited by flocks grazing in common, expansion of the area grazed by each individual flock was not possible, and by the late 1570s some pastoralists were moving their flocks to summer pastures in Michoacan and west of Guadalajara.[5] Within the Valle del Mezquital itself the pressure on the subsistence base was

---

[4] Richard Salvucci, in his discussion of ineffective royal pronouncements concerning *obraje* labor, makes the same point: "The many exploiters – and agents of the conquest – were near at hand while the source of protection and authority was far removed." *Textiles and Capitalism*, p. 98.

[5] The number of head of sheep moved from Huichiapan seems to have been around forty thousand in 1588; AGIM, leg. 111, ramo 2, doc. 12, for names of pastoralists sending animals to Michoacan from Huichiapan. This is the only reference I have to transhumance outside the region; but see Konrad, *A Jesuit Hacienda*, pp. 49–63, for a discussion of the Jesuit managers of the Hacienda Santa Lucia, which was situated in part in the Valle del Mezquital, sending their animals to summer pasture. See also this volume, Chapter 5, notes 3 and 4 for a discussion of *agostadero* and transhumance.

reduced by decline in the sheep population in accordance with the model of ungulate irruptions; by the end of the century flock size had dropped by 63 percent, and the animal density on the ranges of this region had fallen to 72 percent of the totals in the 1570s.[6]

In order to maintain flock size and thereby profits, individual pastoralists also attempted to increase their pasturelands within the Valle del Mezquital. As a result of the decline in the carrying capacity of the range, however, much more land was needed to run one sheep in the 1590s as was in the 1570s, and pastoralists had to acquire access to more land in order to maintain flock numbers.[7] Two processes were put in motion in the 1580s to meet the demand for pastureland: rapid completion of the formal transference of land into the Spanish system of land tenure, and monopolization of land and pasture by individual pastoralists.

In those areas not initially so attractive to Spanish settlers, such as the Northern Valley and Ixmiquilpan, there was a rush to obtain *mercedes* during the last twenty years of the sixteenth century and the first decade of the seventeenth. The process of *composición de tierras*, by which land titles were legalized (and a fee paid to the Spanish crown), was put into effect in 1591, and titles to land acquired by a variety of methods were thereby standardized, completing the final step in the process of transference of land tenure from the Indian to the Spanish systems. By 1610 the greater part of the Valle del Mezquital was held formally within the Spanish system of land tenure by individual landowners, Indian communities, and institutions such as the religious orders.

In those areas where a high percentage of the land surface had already been formally taken up, however, monopolization of land at the expense of other pastoralists was the only way to increase grazing area. Starting in the 1580s, individuals such as Gerónimo López and institutions such as the Society of Jesus began a process of acquisition of large numbers of *estancias* by sale, inheritance, and donation. In order to make sure that the pasture on these large holdings benefited their own flocks, however, pastoralists not only had to acquire formal title to more extensive areas of pastureland, they also had to enforce exclusive access, in contradiction to the custom of common grazing.

---

[6] Because pastoralists continued to start new flocks in the region, the overall density remained high.

[7] Konrad found that "the accumulated impact of grazing, desiccation and deforestation had so decreased the productivity of the soil that much more land was needed per animal than a century earlier [i.e. in the sixteenth century]," *A Jesuit Hacienda*, p. 82.

In this they were assisted by the ambiguity of official attitudes toward the transition from commonage to exclusive access.[8]

By 1620 regional production was dominated by extensively grazed haciendas. The haciendas of the Valle del Mezquital were not nearly as large as the vast northern latifundia, but they were far larger than the smaller, more intensively worked haciendas that had developed in the Valley of Mexico, and for that reason I have elected to refer to them, also, as latifundia. There were still *estancias* and *labores* as well as Indian communal systems of production in the Valle del Mezquital, but latifundia represented a marked monopolization of the means of production. The Jesuits, for example, developed the huge Santa Lucia hacienda that stretched up the eastern side of the Valle del Mezquital, and Gerónimo López entailed three estates in the southeast totaling 500 square kilometers.[9]

Between 1580 and 1620 domination of regional production shifted from large numbers of animal owners who based their operations in small landholdings, to a small number of landowners with large tracts. The appearance of latifundia in the Valle del Mezquital indicated the extent to which the primary means to obtain wealth had shifted from animals to land. In a seeming paradox, land became more valuable as its value declined. Underlying this paradox was environmental change: as the productive potential deteriorated, more land with restricted access was necessary, so individual pastoralists moved to monopolize land and its value as a commodity increased.

Postconquest development was indeed constrained by the natural resource base of the Valle del Mezquital; but the environment of this region was not static. It changed rapidly and profoundly and presented shifting opportunities as well as restrictions on development. For example, by causing the means of production to shift from animals to land while at the same time making small holdings unprofitable, deterioration of the natural resource base presented opportunities to individuals for monopolization of the market. As Herman Konrad notes in his study of the hacienda Santa Lucia, "The combination of

---

[8] See Miranda, "Notas," p. 24; and Chevalier, *La formación*, p. 145.

[9] Konrad, *A Jesuit Hacienda;* Mendizábal, *Obras,* vol. 6, p. 112. Other large grazing haciendas in the Valle del Mezquital in the early seventeenth century: 421 km² (AGNT, vol. 2711, exp. 10); 293 km² (AGNT, vol. 1520, exp. 5); 180 km² (AGNT, vol. 2692, exp. 6); 124 km² (AGNT, vol. 2813, exp. 13); 104.4 km² (AGNT, vol. 2813, exp. 13); 97.8 km² (AGNT, vol. 1520, exp. 5). Ixmiquilpan was monopolized by ten goat-raising haciendas in 1617, average size 102.8 km² (AGNC, vol. 77, exp. 11, fol. 80v). Middle-size haciendas: 56 km² (AGNT, vol. 1520, exp. 5, fols. 43v–44r); 32 km² (AGNT, vol. 2284, exp. 1); 29 km² (AGNT, vol. 2692, exp. 6).

endemic misfortune and new economic opportunities placed a well-located and well-managed hacienda in fortunate circumstances."[10]

By the end of the sixteenth century the process of rapid environmental change was played out, and twenty years later, around the 1620s, the demographic collapse also drew to a halt. Labor and natural resources retreated from their preeminence as major developmental variables and became instead slowly changing factors of production in a remarkably stable colonial system. To paraphrase Eric Van Young, the hacienda system may have reflected a capability on man's part to exploit reduced environmental resources.[11]

Transformation of the Valle del Mezquital from a fertile and productive agricultural region into a mesquite-dominated badlands, the shift from common grazing to exclusive access, and the evolution of private holdings, suggest a cause-and-effect relationship between overgrazing the commons, environmental degradation, and the privatization of property rights; that is, the playing out of a "tragedy of the commons." In 1968 Garrett Hardin developed a model of the "tragedy of the commons" to argue for population control. Hardin argued that in situations of common access to resources, self-interest functions at the expense of the common good, and resources will inevitably be exploited with no thought for the future. Further, he proposed that private property is the best means to protect resources because self-interest will see to it that long-term interests are not sacrificed for short-term gain, that private property will not be over-exploited. Hardin has been criticized for his stress on self-interest as a universal motor of human behavior, and because he confused open-access commons with all types of commonly owned property. His thesis has nevertheless stimulated a number of studies demonstrating that open-access commons are the exception rather than the rule, and that where degradation of common resources occurs, the reason is to be found in the context rather than in the fact of commons per se.[12]

A closer look at the transformation of landholding and land use, and the formation of colonial systems of production in the Valle del Mezquital, indicates that grazing in common does not, by itself, sat-

---

[10] Konrad, *A Jesuit Hacienda*, p. 42.

[11] Van Young, "Rural History," p. 26.

[12] Hardin, "The Tragedy of the Commons"; McKay and Acheson, *The Question of the Commons*, write, "[i]gnoring contextual factors, many of which are assumptions built into the [tragedy of the commons] model leads to the mistake of assuming that because people are engaged in common-property activity, they are involved in a tragedy of the commons." p. 7.

In the present case the context is the conquest.

isfactorily account for developments in this region. For one thing, there were two separate systems of common use-rights, not one: First, the Indian systems of communally owned resources that were in place when the Spaniards arrived; and second, the introduced Spanish custom of common grazing. There were, as well, two processes by which common use-rights gave way to private property rights: the transition from communally owned resources to private landholdings, and the shift from open-access to exclusive-access grazing.

Furthermore, there is no evidence that the presence of indigenous commons had led to overexploitation, as degradation did not appear until the last quarter of the sixteenth century. Privatization of rights to the land was part of the generalized takeover of Indian resources, and began long before the range showed signs of stress. And although there is a clear correlation between deterioration of the range under overgrazing and the move to restrict access to pasture, this process was associated with monopolization of pasture on land already held as private property, not with privatization per se.

Open-access commons are, without doubt, problematic. They are most likely to be overexploited in the manner described by the Hardin model because there are, by definition, no rules controlling their use. In fact open-access commons are quite rare, and it is important to understand why they exist when they do. In the present case, open-access commons existed in the early years of the colony because of the unequal power relations between the conqueror and the conquered, and due to the Indians' inability to effectively counterbalance the Spanish pastoralists, but we are left with the question of what motivated the pastoralists to overexploit and thus to cause environmental degradation. Was overstocking and the resulting overgrazing motivated solely by the desire for short-term gain at the expense of long-term interests, as suggested by the Hardin model? This suggests that the pastoralists had perfect information – that they knew their actions would cause degradation, and carried on regardless. I suggest that decisions to overstock were based primarily on misperception of the ability of the range to withstand both intensive agriculture and intensive grazing. That is, degradation of the environment was caused ultimately by ignorance.

Evidence of the Spaniards' early perception of the Valle del Mezquital is contained in the geographic relation of ca. 1548. The Spaniards described a densely populated region where grains were grown in large quantities for subsistence, exchange, and tribute. It was well wooded and supplied with adequate springwater and runoff dams to maintain extensive irrigation systems. The climate was recognized as difficult, but the region was nevertheless described as fertile and very productive, with good potential for wheat growing in all but the arid northeast sector. The limited extent of native pasture and the dense agricultural populations did seem to preclude the development of pastoralism, but pastoralism was an essential element of Spanish culture, and grazing animals were added to what must have seemed an incomplete landscape. As the animals expanded into new ecological niches their population grew rapidly.

Left to themselves the original flocks would probably have reached an accommodation of some sort with the native vegetation, at a slightly lower carrying capacity than that achieved initially but without profound or lasting damage to the range. Pastoralists added more flocks during the period of initial increase and consistently held the flocks at very high densities, however, thereby amplifying the rate and degree of population growth and causing a reciprocal increase in the speed and profundity of the vegetation and soil changes. The transformation of the environment outstripped the ability of the vegetation of this semiarid region to regenerate, and even as pastoralism came to dominate regional production the pasture failed and the carrying capacity began to decline. Despite clear evidence of deterioration of the range and declining productivity, however, yet more stations were granted and more flocks developed; as we have seen, more stations were taken up in the 1580s and 1590s than in the previous five decades combined. Decisions to add yet more flocks to a region in which the carrying capacity was dropping rapidly were made by individual pastoralists responding to market forces: between about 1563 and 1580 the market for pastoral products shifted from a buyer's market, where supplies were abundant and prices low, to a seller's market, where supplies were dropping and prices rising.[13]

They were also responding to a shift in their perception of the potential of the region. Comments in the geographic relation of 1579–81 and in the records of surveys made in the last quarter of the century make it clear that the Spaniards' evaluation of the potential of the Valle del Mezquital had changed radically. It was no longer seen in terms of a wheat-growing region, but was now thought of and written about as being fit only for sheep.[14] This reevaluation of the potential of the region was clearly associated with a shift in the perception of what constituted suitable fodder for grazing animals from grass to

---

[13] Chevalier, *La formación*, pp. 139–40; Simpson, *Exploitation of Land*, p. 22; André Gunder Frank, *Mexican Agriculture*, ch. 6.

[14] AGNT, vol. 2735, 2ª pte., exp. 9, fol. 1r.

desert species. Around 1548 certain areas were considered unsuitable for grazing due to lack of pasture, water, and room for expansion; at this date pasture meant grass. By 1580, however, when these same areas had been invaded by a secondary growth of arid species, they were described as providing adequate fodder for grazing animals – in fact they were said to have always been grazing land.[15] That the desert species maintained fewer animals would only confirm the evaluation of the region as inherently poor, and thus suitable for little other than sheep grazing. It also may be that the deterioration of the range was not clear in the late 1570s. Costin's study of the effects of grazing in the Australian Alps demonstrates clearly that grazing can continue in areas with marked soil erosion because the presence of vegetation in otherwise deteriorated areas masks the severity of the soil changes.[16]

For as long as the pasture lasted and flocks increased, Spaniards persisted in thinking of this as a fertile and productive region. They made no attempt to monopolize land, and continued to graze in common; the ideal of the successful pastoralist as a *señor de ganado* (livestock owner) remained in force. There was no fund of knowledge in either the Indian or the Spanish world to indicate that this particular region could not sustain such pressures; in fact all experience up to the middle of the 1570s seemed to point to continued success.

When experience did show that the range could not provide for infinite increase, however, individual pastoralists became concerned with pasture conservation. As noted above, seasonal transhumance out of the Valle del Mezquital began in the late 1570s in response to the deterioration of the ranges, and pastoralists began to control the exploitation of pasture on their lands within the valley by enforcing exclusive access to their holdings. As a result, property boundaries were ever more clearly defined.[17] These small holdings were not suf-

---

[15] PNE vol. 1, nos. 9, 347, 555; PNE vol. 6, pp. 14, 18, 20, 24, 25, 27, 201–2; AGNT, vol. 1106, quad. 3, fol. 16; vol. 1728, exp. 2, fol. 15v; vol. 2672, exp. 15, fol. 25v; vol. 2777, exp. 14, fols. 2r–16r;

[16] A. B. Costin, *Grazing Factor*, p. 9; and Costin et. al., *Studies in Catchment Hydrology*, p. 31.

[17] Dusenberry wrote that the Mexicans became concerned with pasture conservation in the 1570s; *The Mexican Mesta*, p. 113. Seasonal transhumance from this region to Michoacan is reported in a census of Spanish holdings in the northwest sector of the region in 1585; AGIM, leg. 111, ramo 2, doc. 12. Chevalier notes the ambivalence with which viceroys and the *mesta* officials confronted the problem of pastoralists enforcing exclusive access in contradiction to the custom of common grazing; *La formación*, 145. *Mercedes* and land suits from the 1580s and 1590s show evidence of increasing concern over the precise definition of boundaries; see Appendix C.

ficient to provide grazing for the large flocks needed to maintain profits, however, nor for the prestige that came with the ownership of vast herds of animals and high profits. As a result, individual pastoralists began to monopolize land and to form latifundia. Successful pastoralists were now known as *terratenientes* (landowners).[18] More flocks were added because recent experience indicated that grazing was the only way to turn a profit in a region that was now perceived as inherently poor. Given the market context and contemporary understanding of the region's potential, this was a logical and rational response.

Pastoralists showed every sign of selfishly maximizing short-term gains at the expense of long-term interests, and the degradation of the environment clearly resulted from overexploitation. All but one of the assumptions underlying the "tragedy of the commons" model are thus verified.[19] However, the specific historical context of this process of environmental degradation challenges the model's assumptions that users of the commons have perfect information. Indeed, perfect information in the context of the conquest of the New World would have been impossible; this was, after all, a world new to the Spaniards, and pastoralism was an alien institution to the Indians. It is true that the Spaniards gained some experience of New World environments in the Caribbean, but they clearly did not understand the processes by which alien species expand into new ecosystems. The Indian nobles, who presumably did understand the nature of their environment, could not predict the consequences of the introduction of sheep into this semiarid land.

The context of these events points to quite a different explanatory model. I argue that the transformation of this region from a complex agricultural mosaic into a mesquite desert dominated by privately owned grazing latifundia was not the inevitable result of the existence of "the commons"; rather, it arose out of the fluid and unequal power relations inherent in the process of conquest, and, most importantly, out of ignorance of the nature of New World environments. It is tempting to view the degradation of the environment of the Valle del

---

[18] The shift from animals to land occurred all over New Spain and was reflected in the shift from animal owners to landowners in the composition of the *Mesta;* Dusenberry, *Mexican Mesta,* p. 59; Miranda, "Notas," p. 24.

[19] Among the assumptions built into the "tragedy of the commons" model Mckay and Acheson list the following: "common property is always of the open-access variety; ... the users are selfish, unrestricted by social norms of the community, and trying to maximize short-term gains;... the users have perfect information; and ... the resource is being used so intensively that over exploitation and depletion are possible." *Question of the Commons,* p. 7.

Mezquital as an inevitable result of conquest and settlement, and the development of latifundia in this region as the inevitable outcome of introducing sheep into a semiarid subtropical region of marked seasonal rainfall and high steep-sided hills. Environmental degradation, however, was only inevitable in the sense that ignorance of the New World environments was bound to have unexpected consequences, because nobody could predict the outcome of changing land use on the basis of past experience: neither the Spaniards, who did not know the land, nor the Indians, who did not know sheep. The ultimate causal factor in the degradation of this region was, therefore, human choice. The decision to introduce sheep into an unknown and little-understood region can be seen as the initial stimulus that set the processes of environmental transformation in motion, but the most significant factor in the way these processes developed was the decision made by the Europeans to ignore their own customs regulating grazing. The decision to disregard the regulations controlling the stocking rates for individual holdings was based in their perception of the Valle del Mezquital, first as a rich and fertile region and then, as the consequences of overexploitation became clear, as a region that was fit only for sheep. This decision was combined with the exercise of power to gain access to pasture, and individuals were thus able to benefit at the expense of the common good. At the same time, and almost incidentally, long-term interests were sacrificed for short-term gain.

Was the Valle del Mezquital an isolated case? Clearly, much research needs to be done to answer this question with confidence, but an examination of such contemporary evidence as is available indicates that it was not. This evidence, which we will examine here, points to a close correlation between a generalized process of deterioration in pastoral regions throughout New Spain and the change from a buyer's to a seller's market for pastoral products at the end of the sixteenth century. I propose as a working hypothesis that this shift in market orientation resulted from processes of environmental change similar to those that caused the decline in productivity in the Valle del Mezquital.

The strongest evidence supporting this proposition is found in the following two facts. First, as predicted by the model of ungulate irruptions, wherever grazing animals were introduced in New Spain their population history mirrored the experience of the Valle del Mezquital; that is, they increased exponentially, peaked, crashed, and finally stabilized. Indeed, the history of the introduced animals verifies the model itself. Second, contemporaries correlated the decline in the animal populations with environmental deterioration and overexploitation.

The spectacular increase in the herds of introduced animals was not peculiar to the Valle del Mezquital, but rather was a generalized phenomenon noted by many contemporary writers, and the density of animals in some regions exceeded that obtained in the Valle del Mezquital.[20] An abrupt decline in flock size was also reported for all regions, the timing of the collapse apparently depending on the period of original invasion and the type of animal introduced.[21] Pigs, sheep, cattle, and horses appear to have acclimatized and expanded in much that order. Pigs were the first to demonstrate the adaptability of Old World animals to New World environments. Even sheep that had not done well in the Caribbean Islands grew rapidly in numbers in the more temperate environment of the Central Highlands. The sudden cessation of this prodigal increase and the collapse of the herds not only meant loss to individual pastoralists, but also affected the growing economy of the colony as well. The textile industry was threatened, as was the ample supply of meat needed to sustain work in the mines.[22] Contemporary observers saw the sudden decline in animal populations as stemming from two distinct processes: first, overexploitation of the herds, and second, deterioration of the animals' subsistence base, leading to lower reproduction rates and an inability to replace the numbers lost.

Many sixteenth-century Spaniards thought that the killing of huge numbers of animals for their hides or tallow alone, excessive consumption of meat by Indians, and the depletion of herds by thieves and bands of wild dogs (themselves introduced species gone feral) explained the decline in numbers. Others were concerned with the evident inability of the herds to reproduce themselves, and blamed the deterioration of the range for the decline. Viceroy Martín Enríquez clearly correlated the decline in animal fertility with deterioration

[20] See Simpson, *Exploitation of Land*, pp. 2–6, for contemporary witness to the increase of grazing animals. See also this volume Chapter 4, note 1, for estimated densities in other regions.

[21] This collapse occurred at roughly the same time from the early 1560s to the mid-1570s in the Central Highlands, and a decade or two later in the near north as the animals made their way northward and repeated the irruptive cycle; Chevalier, *La formación*, pp. 137–40.

[22] The *obraje* system of woolen textile production, initiated in the 1530s, was dependent on the wool clip; Salvucci, *Textiles and Capitalism*. The mines were dependent primarily on leather but also on the copious supply of meat which, it was thought at the time, made it physically possible to do such heavy work; Chevalier, *La formación*, p. 141.

of the range when he wrote in 1574 that "livestock does not multiply as it used to: cows used to bear calves before two years of age – because the land was not trampled and pasture was fertile and extensive; but now that [the pasture] has failed the cows do not bear before three or four years of age."[23] Modern scholars have also concluded that the deterioration of the range and the decline in numbers was related. Chevalier, for example, thought that the deterioration of the natural resource base underlay the diminution of the herds of cattle in the north as well as the center of Mexico. Simpson wrote that because sheep and goats destroy their own subsistance base, the decline in flock size was the direct result of overgrazing. Simpson also pointed out that most of the regions exploited by sheep raising in the early colonial period are now marred by extensive erosion.[24]

Officials and individual pastoralists made several attempts to correct the problems facing the pastoral sector of the economy. As noted above, the Mexicans became concerned with pasture conservation in the 1570s, and the *Mesta* (Stockmen's association) passed several ordinances in that decade regulating the firing of grasslands and restricting the killing of female stock, the number of animals butchered, and Indian consumption of meat.[25] (Actually, it is unlikely that the rate at which animals were butchered increased significantly in the 1570s, because the Indian population declined abruptly between 1576–81, and with it went a considerable market for fresh meat.[26]) The reaction of large numbers of individual pastoralists to the deterioration of the ranges produced patterned responses. Seasonal transhumance out of the Central Highlands began around this time in response to deteriorating ranges in the regions where pastoralism was first carried out, and pastoralists began to enforce exclusive access.[27] There was a generalized shift from animals to land as the means to wealth and prestige, as well. In fact, the composition of the *mesta* changed after the 1570s from animal owners to landowners, a process that may also reflect deterioration of the pasture and a need to monopolize land in order to maintain flocks, as I have proposed for the

---

[23] Quoted in Chevalier, *La formación*, p. 138.
[24] Ibid., p. 139; Simpson, *Exploitation of Land*, p. 23.
[25] Dusenberry, *Mexican Mesta*, p. 111. Chevalier, *La formación*, p. 138.
[26] Gibson notes that the preoccupation with Indian meat eating was aimed primarily at beef rather than mutton (*Aztecs*, p. 346). Chevalier, however, writes that twenty times as much mutton was consumed than beef in the Meseta Central (*La formación*, pp. 142–3).
[27] See Chevalier's discussion of this point; *La formación*, p. 129.

Valle del Mezquital.[28] Despite these official and individual responses, however, the situation had not improved by the 1590s. As Viceroy Velasco wrote to his successor in 1595, the measures regulating the exploitation of the herds had been unsuccessful and the herds had not increased; Mexico was no longer, as it had been when he was a boy, a place where meat was plentiful and cheap.[29]

The conjunction in the late 1570s of the two processes, overexploitation of the herds and of the range, produced a no-win situation for pastoralists. Stockmen were trapped: the forces that produced the high prices also made it impossible for them to meet the demand by increasing production – indeed their productivity was declining. Rapid deterioration in the range meant that the herds were unable to replace themselves; but because the range was deteriorating so quickly, it made more sense to kill animals before they died of starvation, especially as the rise in prices meant high profits. In the 1580s stockmen were recklessly killing even their female stock in defiance of viceregal orders forbidding the practice.[30]

Whether pastoralists everywhere responded to this situation by monopolizing land and pasture as in the Valle del Mezquital is a topic for future research. That they did to some extent is evident in the formation of haciendas. But were these haciendas latifundia, that is, were they exceptionally large in size? Was the shift from high numbers of small landowners and high productivity to small numbers of large landowners and low productivity a general phenomenon? Was there, as I have suggested elsewhere, a profound structural shift in the pastoral sector of the political economy of New Spain that was based ultimately on environmental change?[31]

This study, and the questions it raises about the evolution of the political economy of New Spain, has implications for recent debates on the growth and development of the New World societies. Evidence pointing to a correlation between a shift in market orientation and environmental change has implications for this debate by providing further evidence that local variables – in this case the physical environment – played a major role at a crucial point in the development of the political economy of New Spain. It does not, however, imply that these particular variables continued to be primary. Whereas the

---

[28] See note 18.
[29] Quoted in Simpson, *Exploitation of Land*, p. 22.
[30] Chevalier, *La formación*, p. 140.
[31] Melville, "Environmental and Social Change," p. 53.

history of the Valle del Mezquital demonstrates that the environment cannot be viewed as an unchanging constraining or enabling variable on development, it is equally apparent that environmental change does not occur constantly at the same speed; nor does environmental change always imply degradation. In New Spain as a whole, as in the Valle del Mezquital, the processes put in motion by the European invasion seem to have slowed down after the sixteenth century. Humans do learn eventually, and the inhabitants of New Spain used knowledge gained in the era of rapid change to develop stable systems to exploit the land, as other less immediate influences took preeminence in social change.

The Europeans did not conquer paradise. To hold that the indigenous populations were the caretakers of paradise denies them their history and reduces them to stereotypic saintlike figures. However, the Europeans did not simply augment processes already underway, either. Rather, by adding completely new and alien elements to the dynamics of social and ecological change, they unwittingly triggered a cascade of processes that resulted in a world as alien to the indigenous peoples as it was to the Europeans themselves, and one that was, moreover, diminished.

Appendix A
SUB-AREAS

The Southern Plain. Surface Area: 483 km². *Cabeceras:* Apasco, Huey-postla, Tequixquiac, Tezcatepec and Tuzantlalpa (twin *cabeceras*), Tla-panaloya.

The Southern Plain lies at the very northern end of the Valley of Mexico and would appear to fall naturally within its boundaries, but in fact this sub-area is part of the drainage system of the Tula River and is therefore included in the Valle del Mezquital. The decision to include the Southern Plain in the Valle del Mezquital on geographic criteria was reinforced by affiliation of the *cabeceras* within this plain with the preconquest geopolitical division known as the Teotlalpan.[1]

Two subject pueblos of Hueypostla: Tlacotlapilco and Tezcatepec are located several kilometers from the *cabecera* in the North–South Plain and are not included in the Southern Plain; Tlilcuautla (subject to Tezcatepec and Tuzantlalpa),[2] which lies at the eastern end of the Central Valley, was also excluded from the Southern Plain.

The North–South Plain. Surface Area: 753 km². *Cabeceras:* Atitalaquia, Atotonilco, Chilcuautla, Mizquiaguala, Tezontepec, Tlacotlapilco, Tlahuelilpa, Tlamaco.

The main problem here was to separate the documentation for the pueblo of Tezcatepec located in the North–South Plain from that pertaining to the *cabecera* of the same name located in the Southern Plain. The documents pertaining to the northern pueblo were iden-tified by references to its boundaries with the *cabeceras* of Mizquia-guala, Tezontepec, and Chilcuautla, and to its status as a subject of Hueypostla. The documentation of the southern *cabecera* was iden-tified by references to the name of the *encomendero*, its status as a *cabecera*, and its boundaries with Tuzantlalpa. Documents for Chil-

---

[1] The Southern Plain, the Central Valley, the North–South Plain, and the Northern Valley are names given to these areas by Sherburne F. Cook; together they form the pre-Hispanic region known as the Teotlalpan. Cook, *Historical Demography.*

[2] Gerhard, *Guide,* p. 299.

cuautla (subject to Ixmiquilpan) were identified by references to common boundaries with Tlacotlapilco, and to the name of the *encomendero*.[3]

The Central Valley. Surface area: 603 km². *Cabeceras:* Axacuba, Izcuinquitlapilco, Tetepango, Tornacustla.

The pueblo of Tlilcuautla in the eastern end of the Central Valley was subject to Tezcatepec and Tuzantlalpa, twin *cabeceras* in the Southern Plain,[4] and documentation for lands falling within its boundaries was identified by reference to the name of the pueblo and common boundaries with Tornacustla.

The Northern Valley. Surface area: 1,017 km². *Cabeceras:* Actopan, Tecaxique-Chicavasco, Tecpatepec, Tlanocopan, Yetecomac.

This valley lies parallel to the Central Valley north of a range of high hills. Both the Central Valley and the Northern Valley communicate in the west with the North–South Plain, and their eastern ends terminate in the foothills of the Sierra Madre Oriental.

Ixmiquilpan. Surface area: 1,028 km². *Cabeceras:* Ixmiquilpan, Tlacintla.

Ixmiquilpan lies to the north of the North–South Plain and is separated from it by a low ridge of land. The northern boundary of this sub-area was difficult to define for the sixteenth and seventeenth centuries. Gerhard thought that the territorial jurisdiction of Ixmiquilpan extended farther north than Cimapan to approximately lat. 20° 55′ N.[5] I found no evidence that the territory extended this far north, however, and in the *Suma de Visitas* it is noted that Ixmiquilpan lay in a flat plain surrounded by hills and mountains.[6] The present-day municipalities of Ixmiquilpan and Cardonal conform more-or-less to the latter description and have therefore been used to represent the territorial extension of Ixmiquilpan. Chilcuautla, although subject to Ixmiquilpan, is included in the North–South Plain.

Alfaxayuca. Surface area: 634 km². *Cabecera:* Alfaxayuca.

The Alfaxayuca Valley runs parallel to the North–South Plain, to the west of a dividing range of high hills. Alfaxayuca was subject to Xilotepec in the sixteenth century, but documentation of the lands in

[3] Ibid., *Guide*, p. 156.
[4] Ibid., p. 299.
[5] Ibid., p. 155.
[6] *PNE* vol. 1, no. 293.

the Alfaxayuca Valley has been identified by reference to the *cabecera*, or to pueblos which fall within its boundaries.[7]

Huichiapan. Surface area: 1,697 km². *Cabecera:* Huichiapan.
　The Huichiapan Plateau starts high in the hills west of Alfaxayuca and slopes westward to merge with the hills east of San Juan del Río. The northern border is defined by the Moctezuma River and the southern edge of the plateau is bounded by low hills separating it from the Xilotepec Plateau; the hills generally fall within the jurisdiction of Hichiapan. As with Alfaxayuca, Huichiapan was a subject of Xilotepec in the sixteenth century.[8] Documentation relating to the lands in Huichiapan were identified by references to the *cabecera*, or to pueblos identified as falling within its jurisdiction.

Xilotepec. Surface Area: 1,898 km². *Cabecera:* Xilotepec.
　The Xilotepec Plateau stretches southeast to northeast (Xilotepec to Polotitlan) and is tilted along its long axis to the northeast. Physically, the Xilotepec Plateau stops short of San Juan del Río. Although the jurisdiction of the province of Xilotepec extended north to include Cimapan and Queretaro at conquest,[9] the area of study has been confined to the entity known after 1552 as the Xilotepec Province.
　Following the defeat of Tenochtitlán by the Spanish, the Xilotepec Province in its preconquest form was given in *encomienda* to four men, but in the later 1520s it was reassigned to Juan Jaramillo, husband of Marina, Cortés's interpreter. By 1552 this huge *encomienda* had been divided between Jaramillo's widow (his second wife, Beatriz de Andrada), and his daughter Maria Jaramillo (daughter of Marina). Beatriz de Andrada retained the half known from then on as the "Xilotepec half," which included the *cabeceras* Xilotepec, Alfaxayua, and Huichiapan. Maria Jaramillo kept the "Queretaro half," which included the towns from San Juan del Río north.[10]
　The documentation for Alfaxayuca and Huichiapan is quite easily distinguished from that of Xilotepec. Lands referred to as falling within "the chichimecs" did, however, cause some difficulties, which were resolved by discounting all references made simply to "the chichimecs"; only if it was clearly stated that such lands fell within the

---

[7] Gerhard, *Guide*, p. 386.
[8] Ibid., p. 386.
[9] Ibid., p. 383.
[10] AGIJ, leg. 129, exp. 5; AGIJ, leg. 148, exp. 1; leg. 168; and Gerhard, *Guide*, 383–4. See also, Melville, "Elite Formation."

chichimecs of Alfaxayuca or of Huichiapan were they retained and used. In many cases it seems that most references to "the chichimecs" refer to lands north of San Juan del Río and therefore fall outside the area of study.

Three *cabeceras*, Zayanaquilpa and Chapantongo (both included in the Tula sub-area) as well as Chiapa de Mota (separate sub-area) also were subject to Xilotepec at conquest.[11] They were granted as separate *encomiendas*, however, and their documentation is easily identified.

Chiapa de Mota. Surface area: 694 km². *Cabecera:* Chiapa de Mota.

This mountainous region blends in with the hills and mountains forming the high western boundary of the Valley of Mexico and has been included in this study by virtue of its north-facing political ties with the province of Xilotepec at conquest.[12]

Tula. Surface area: 1,222 km². *Cabeceras:* Atengo, Chapantongo, Michimaloya, Nextlalpan, Otlazpa, Sayula, Suchitlan, Tepetitlan, Tepexi, Tula, Xipacoya, Zayanaquilpa.

All the *cabeceras* except Chapantongo lie within the hills and valleys of the headwaters of the Tula River. Chapantongo lies to the north of Sayula on the ridge of land separating the eastern hills of the Huichiapan Plateau from the high hills lying between the North–South Plain and the Alfaxayuca Valley. The predominant drainage is to the southwest, and Chapantongo therefore does not, strictly speaking, fall within the headwaters of the Tula River. It is most difficult to separate the territorial jurisdictions of Chapantongo and Sayula, however, because sixteenth-century names of villages or places, apart from the two *cabeceras*, do not correspond to modern names. Apparently the territorial jurisdiction of Sayula extended up into the highlands to the north and west, and that of Chapantongo extended south, but the line of demarcation between the two is not clear. For this reason Chapantongo has been included in the Tula sub-area rather than in Xilotepec.

[11] Gerhard, *Guide,* pp. 385–6.
[12] Ibid.

Appendix B
POPULATION ESTIMATES

Table B.1. *Tributary population by* cabecera *and decade*

Cabeceras	1570s		1580s		1590s	
Actopan	1570	(7,500)	1587	4,853[a]	1596	3,818[b]
					1599	2,984
Apasco	1570	(1,210.5)	—	—	1592	2,984
					1593	331.5
Atengo	1570	456	1584	171.5	1592	171.5
	1570	463.5				
	1578	302				
Atitalaquia	1570	(1,409)	1580	834	1592	532.5
	1577	1,223	1584	633	1594	514.5
					1599	425
Subject pueblos	1570	(1,616)	—	—		included in Atitalaquia
Atotonilco	1570	(1,810)	—	—	1592	363.5
Axacuba	1570	(4,284)	—	—	1592	1,003.5
					1594	747
					1599	604.5
Chiapa de Mota	1570	(3,320)	—	—	1592	975
					1599	644
Chapantongo	1570	(1,578)	1581	660	1592	540.5
	1577	1,253			1592	374.5
	1578	828				
Chilguautla	1570	(1,218)	—	—	1592	150
					1597	346.5
					1599	228.5
Hueypostla	1570	(1,815.5)	—	—	1592	928.5
					1598	789.5[b]

171

Table B.1. (cont.) *Tributary population by* cabecera *and decade*

Cabeceras	1570s		1580s		1590s	
Ixmiquilpan	1570	(2,697)	1583	2,609	1590	2,332
					1592	2,202
					1595	1,727
					1599	1,597
Minas de Ixmiquilpan	1570	(52)	—	—		included in Ixmiquilpan
Izquincuitlapilco	1570	(4,000)	1584	1,322	1592	1,111.5
	1578	1,983			1599	669
Michimaloya	1570	(1,600)	—	—	1592	249.5
Mizquiaguala	1570	(806)	1581	315.5	1592	315.5
	1578	538.5				
La mitad en Encomienda	—	—	—	—	1598	438.5[b]
Nextlalpan	1570	(600)	—	—	1592	253.5
					1599	188
Otlaspa		included in Tepexi	—	—	1599	549.5
Sayula	1570	(300)	1581	163	1592	104.5
	1577	246	1589	104.5		
Suchitlan	1570	(900)	—	—	1592	357
Tecaxique	—	—	—	—	1592	147.5
Tecpatepec/ Tlanocopan	1570	(588)	—	—	1592	234.5
						88.5
Tepetitlan	1570	(900)	—	—	1592	324

Table B.1. (cont.) *Tributary population by* cabecera *and decade*

Cabeceras	1570s		1580s		1590s	
Subject pueblos	1570	(1,560)	—	—	included in Tepetitlan	
Tepexi del Rio	1570	(3,500)	—	—	1592 1599	748 715
Tequixquiac	1570	(1,909.5)	—	—	1592 1598	416 226[b]
Tetepango	1570	(488)	1584	231	1592 1595 1596 1598	230.5 268.5 312 142
Tezcatepec-North	1570	(200)	—	—	included in Hueypustla	
Tezcatepec y Tuzantlalpa-South	1570	(2,365.5)	—	—	1592 1594	449 286.5
Tezontepeque	1570	(487)	—	—	1592	195.5
Tianguistongo	1570	(245.5)	—	—	1592 1597	624.5 574
Tlacintla	1570	(1,280)	1582	947.5	1590 1592 1598	711.5 659.5 425.5
Tlacotlapilco	1570	(800)	—	—	included in Hueypustla	
Tlahuelilpa	1581	419.5	1592	415.5		
Tlamaco	1570	(900)	—	—	1592	232
Tlapanaloya	1570	(345)	—	—	1592	132.5

Table B.1. (cont.) *Tributary population by* cabecera *and decade*

Cabeceras	1570s		1580s		1590s	
Tornacustla	1570	(800)	1579	400[c]	1592	200.5
					1598	147
Tula	1570	(2,800)	1580	903	1592	601
	1577	2,721	1583	767		
	1578	1,434	1589	601		
Subject pueblos	1570	(1,480)	—	—		included in Tula
Estancias de Motezuma	1576	424	—	—	1592	281
Xilotepec	1570	(6,065)	1583	5,096	1590	3,504.5
			1585	3,658.5	1592	3,414
Alfaxayuca	1570	(2,361)	1585	1,378[d]		? included in Xilotepec
Huichiapan	1570	(5,125)	1585	1,644[d]		? included in Xilotepec
Xipacoya	1570	(2,200)	—	—	1592	373.5
Yeytecomatl	1570	(380)	1581	106	1592	106
	1570	363.5				
	1577	204.5				
Zayanaquilpa	1571	803.5	1582	350.5	1592	235.5
	1578	461.5				

[a]AGNG, vol. 3, exp. 39
[b]AGII, leg. 1530
[c]AGII, leg. 1529
[d]AGIM, leg. 111, ramo 2, doc. 12

Numbers in parentheses are derived from the ecclesiastical *visita* carried out between 1569 and 1571 that formed the source for the *tasaciones* made by the *real hacienda* officials (AGIM, leg. 336A, ptes. 1 and 2). These totals have been used to provide a baseline for the whole region for 1570.

? included = No information available, possibly included in *cabecera* totals
Subject pueblos = Totals for villages subject to the following *cabecera*
— = No information available

Sources: See "Sources for Tables B.1,2." See also Melville, "The Pastoral Economy," Appendix A, for totals for ca. 1548, and for the 1550s and 1560s.

able B.2. *Changes in the tributary population in twelve* cabeceras, *1560–99*

abeceras	1560s	Trib. Pop.	1570s	Trib. Pop.	1580s	Trib. Pop.	1590s	Trib. Pop.
tengo	1567	618.5	1578	302	1584	171.5	1592	171.5
titalaquia	1569	1,409	1577	1,223	1584	633	1599	425
hapantongo	1564	1,578	1578	282	1581	660	1592	374.5
miquilpa	1566	2,713	1570	2,697	1583	2,609	1599	1,597
quinquitlapilco	1568	3,873	1578	1,983	1584	1,322	1599	669
Mizquiaguala	1564	806	1578	538.5	1581	315.5	1592	315.5
ayula	1564	352.5	1577	246	1589	104.5	1592	104.8
etepango	1564	495	1578	578	1584	231	1598	142
lacintla	1562	1,233.5	1570	1,280	1582	947.5	1598	425.5
ula	1566	3,089.5	1578	1,434	1589	601	1592	601
etecomac	1569/71	380	1577	204.5	1581	106	1592	106
ayanaquilpa	1568	803.5	1578	461.5	1582	350.5	1592	235.5
otals:		17,352.5		11,775.5		8,051.5		5,167

rib. Pop. = Tributary Population

ource: See "Sources for Tables B.1,2".

Sources for Tables B.1 and B.2

1560s:

AGIC, leg. 664, "Quenta y Averiguación (1553–69): Izcuinquitlapilco."

AGIC, leg. 665, "Relación y averiguación (1553–69): Tula, Taymeo y Yeytecomatl, Tlaçintla y Izmiquilpa."

AGIC, leg. 670.

AGIC, leg. 678, continuation of legajo 665: "Yeytecomatl, Yzmiquilpa y Tlaçintla, Ixquinquitlapilco."

AGIC, leg. 785, "Cargo: Tributos y Tasaciones, Pueblos en la real corona (1531–69): Atitalaquia, Atengo, Axacuba, Çayanaquilpa, Yzquinquitlapilco, Mesquiaguala, Yzmiquilpa, Tlaçintla, Çayula."

AGIC, legs. 786A and B, "Copias autorizadas por Yrigoyan en 1574"; "Quentas y averiguaciones (1553–69) leg. 786A: Atitalaquia, Chapatongo, Tabalilpa, Tula, Çayula; leg. 786B (burnt): Atengo, Tetavanco."

1570s:

AGIM, leg. 336A, ramo 2, 104(7), fols. 3r–28r, Ecclesiastical Visita 1569–71. Same as PNE vol. 3, with additional information in a section not published in PNE: AGIM, leg. 336A, ramo 2, 104(5), 2ª pte., fols. 3r–4v: Chiapa, Tepexi y Otlazpa, Huichiapan, Xilotepec.

AGIC, leg. 679.

AGIC, leg. 692, "Tributos y Tasaciones (1 Jan. 1573–31 Dec. 1584): Atitalaquia, Atengo, Chapantongo, Çayula, Çayanaquilpa, Yzquinquitlapilco, Yeytecomatl, Mezquiaguala, Tetabanco, Tula."

1580s:

AGIC, leg. 668, "Cargo: tributos reçagados (30 Jan. 1586–30 Apr. 1590; 1 May 1590–30 Apr. 1591): Atitalaquia, Atengo, Chapantongo, Çayula, Çayanaquilpa, Izmiquilpa, Tlaçintla, Yeytecomatl, Yzquinquitlapilco, Mizquiaguala, Tlahuilipa, Tetavanco, Tula, Xilotepeque la mitad, Atengo."

AGIC, leg. 677, "Resultas: Averiguacion que haze Juan Martinez de Fuyca de los tributos de Pueblos que estan en la rreal corona para la satisfaccion de la quenta que se va tomando a los oficiales de la real hacienda (12 Nov. 1576—1 Apr. 1577): Atengo, Atitalaquia, Çayula, Çayanaquilpa, Yzmiquilpa y Tlaçintla, Tlazintla, Yzmiquilpa, Yeytecomatl, Mezquiaguala, Tavalilpa, Tula, Tetavanco, Xilotepeque."

AGIC, leg. 692.

AGIC, leg. 785.

AGNG, vol. 3, exp. 29, fols. 15v–16r: Actopan, 1587.

AGIM, leg. 111, ramo 2, doc. 12.

GII, leg. 1529. (Same as PNE vol. 6.)

590s:

GIC, leg. 688.

GIC, leg. 692.

GIC, leg. 694, "Cargo: Servicio real, (1592–94): Pueblos en la real orona: Atitalaquia, Atengo, Chapantongo, Çayula, Çayanaquilpa, 'eytecomatl, Yzquinquitlapilco, Mizquiaguala, Izmiquilpa y Tlaçintla, 'lahuelilpa, Tetepango, Tula, Xilotepeque la mitad. Pueblos de en-omenderos: Atotonilco, Zacomulco, Asuchitlan, Chiapa, Tula, Mich-naloya, Mizquiaguala, Teçontepeque, Tequixquiac, Tecaxique, 'ornacustla, Tecpatepeque, Tianquistongo, Tlamaco, Tlapanaloya, 'uçantlalpa y Tezcatepeque, Xipacoya, Xilotepeque, Apasco, Axa-uba, Chilcuautla, Hueypustla e Tlacotlapilco y Tianguistongo."

GIC, leg. 694, "Cargo y Tributos."

GIC, leg. 695A and B, "Cargo: servicio real, tributos," (1594–5).

GIC, leg. 696, "Cargo: Servicio Real, Tributos," (1595–6).

GIC, leg. 697, "Cargo: Servicio Real, Tributos," (1596–7).

GIC, leg. 698A, "Cargo: Servicio Real, Tributos," (1597–8).

GIC, leg. 699, "Cargo: Servicio Real, Tributos," (1598–9).

GIC, leg. 700, "Cargo: Servicio Real, Tributos," (1599–1600).

GIC, leg. 701, "Cargo: Servicio Real, Tributos," (1600–1).

GII, leg. 1530, fols. 13v–19r; *encomiendas,* their *encomenderos* and ributaries ca. 1597.

Appendix C

SOURCES FOR LAND HOLDING AND LAND USE

Actopan: **AGNM,** vol. 3, fols. 81r–v; vol. 6, fols. 327v–328r. **AGNT,** vol. 1486, exp. 2, fols. 4r–8. **AGNG,** vol. 2, exp. 1341, fols. 281v–282r.

Alfaxayuca: **AGNM,** vol. 1, fols. 209r–210r; vol. 3, fols. 100v–101r, 112r–v; vol. 5, fols. 170v, 257v; vol. 6, fols. 330v–331r; vol. 7, fols. 117r, 123v, 318r–v, 353r; vol. 8, fols. 8r, 74v–75r; vol. 10, fols. 21r–v, 88r–89r; vol. 11, fols. 215r–v; vol. 13, fols. 7v–8r; vol. 18, fol. 322r; vol. 19, fols. 23v–24r, 24v; vol. 20, fols. 24v, 38v–39r. **AGNT,** vol. 1583, exp. 1, fols. 290, 291r; 294; vol. 1872, exp. 10, fol. 3r; vol. 2105, exp. 1, fol. 15r; vol. 2674, exp. 21, fol. 325r; vol. 2678, exp. 35, fols. 1r–11r; exp. 36, fols. 1r–10r; vol. 2764, exp. 4, fol. 43r; vol. 3663, exp. 3, fols. 1r. **AGNG,** vol. 1, exp. 883. **AGNI,** vol. 5, exps. 908, 1046. **AGIM,** leg. 111, ramo 2, doc. 12.

Apasco: **AGNM,** vol. 6, fols. 455r–456r; vol. 7, fols. 187v–188r; vol. 8, fols. 227v–228r; vol. 12, fols. 60v–61; vol. 13, fols. 41r–v. **AGNT,** vol. 1896, exp. 2, fols. 17r–18r; vol. 2764, exp. 18, fol. 307r.

Atengo: **AGNM,** vol. 4, fol. 345r; vol. 7, fols. 30r, 317r; vol. 12, fols. 448v–449r; vol. 14, fols. 66r–67r; vol. 18, fols. 310v–311rv; vol. 22, fol. 382r. **AGNT,** vol. 1106, quad 2, fols. 1v, 55r–56v; vol. 2337, exp. 1, fol. 394v. **AGNI,** vol. 4, exp. 62. **PNE,** vol. 1, p. 22.

Atitalaquia: **AGNM,** vol. 5, fols. 100r–v; vol. 6, fol. 452r; vol. 12, fols. 449r–450v, 295r–v; vol. 13, fols. 174v, 186v–187r; vol. 14, fols. 43v, 59r–v, 152r–153r; vol. 15, fols. 277r–v; vol. 16, fols. 86r–v; vol. 19, fol. 228v; vol. 20, fols. 60r, 61r–v. **AGNT,** vol. 69, exp. 4, fols. 1–10; vol. 1873, exp. 8, fol. 1r; vol. 2413, exp. 1, fols. 2r, 80r, 87–92; vol. 2672, exp. 15, fols. 1r, 31r; vol. 2672, exp. 16, fol. 1r; vol. 2674, exp. 16, fol. 288r. **AGNG,** vol. 1, exps. 88, 89. **AGNI,** vol. 3, exp. 789; vol. 4, exp. 868, 873; vol. 6, pte. 2, exp. 207, 231, 469, 590. **Mendizábal,** vol. 6, pp. 114–16.

Atotonilco: **AGNM,** vol. 8, fols. 84r–v, 255r–v; vol. 14, fols. 1r, 292r–v; vol. 15, fols. 28r–v; vol. 16, fols. 77v–78v; vol. 23, fols. 124r–v. **AGNT,** vol. 2735 pte. 2, exp. 8, fol. 1r. **AGNI,** vol. 2, exp. 771. **AGIE,** vol. 161 pte. C, fol. 195r.

Axacuba: **AGNM**, vol. 5, fols. 254r–255r; vol. 7, fols. 30v–31r, 31v, 295v–296r; vol. 9, fol. 35r. **AGNT**, vol. 2354, exp. 1, fols. 2r, 9v. **AGIE**, vol. 161, pte. C, fol. 195r. **Mendizábal,** vol. 6, pp. 114–16.

Chiapa de Mota: **AGNM**, vol. 3, fol. 144; vol. 5, fols. 154r–157r; vol. 7, fols. 52r–v; vol. 8, fols. 29r, 191r, 228r–v; vol. 11, fols. 1173r–v; vol. 12, fols. 303v–304r; vol. 13, fols. 210v–211r; vol. 14, fols. 26v, 27r, 77v, 249v–250r; vol. 17, fols. 103v–104r; vol. 19, fols. 103v–104r, 202r, 203r, 206r–208v, 210v–211r; vol. 20, fols. 66r–69r, 78r–79r; vol. 22, fol. 244r. **AGNT**, vol. 65, exp. 1, fol. 1; vol. 2686, exp. 14, fol. 1r; vol. 3673, exp. 15, fol. 1r.

Chapantongo: **AGNM**, vol. 4, fols. 290v, 370r–v; vol. 13, fols. 15v–16r, 182r–v; vol. 17, fol. 113. **AGNT**, vol. 1708–2, ult. quad., fol. 1; vol. 2117, exp. 1, fol. 53v; vol. 2764, exp. 11, fol. 1; vol. 3542, exp. 16, fols. 4r–v.

Chilcuautla: **AGNT** vol. 1105, quad. 10, fol. 26r; vol. 1103, fol. 1; vol. 1104, quad. 22. **PNE**, vol. 1, p. 60.

Hueypostla: **AGNM**, vol. 12, fols. 281v–282r, 333r; vol. 18, fols. 278v–279r; vol. 19, fols. 121r, 165; vol. 22, 331v–332r; vol. 23, fols. 87v–88r. **AGNI**, vol. 6 pte. 2, exp. 998, fols. 260r–v. **AGIJ,** leg. 154, no. 3, 3a pte., fol. 460v.

Huichiapan: **AGNM**, vol. 3, fols. 193r–194r; vol. 5, fols. 166r, 257v–258r; vol. 7, fols. 227v–228r; vol. 8, fols. 50v, 177v–178r; vol. 10, fols. 46v–47r, 63r–v, 82r–v, 237r–238r; vol. 11, fols. 100r–v, 238v, 245r–v; vol. 12, fols. 37r–v, 296v–297r; vol. 13, fols. 22v–23r, 38r–v, 61r, 144r–145r, 404v–405r; vol. 14, fols. 70r, 71v–72r, 230r–231r, 232v–233v; vol. 15, fols. 221v–222r, 256v; vol. 16, fols. 5r–v, 25r–26v, 70v, 72r–v, 112, 201v–202r; vol. 17, fols. 38r–v; vol. 18, fols. 97r–v, 127r–v, 247r–v, 264r, 269v, 285; vol. 19, fols. 249r; vol. 20, fols. 60v–61r, 61v, 98r–v, 186v–187r, 209v; vol. 22, fols. 268v, 299r–v, 321v–322r, 359r–v, 375r–v, 443v–444r, 447v–448v. **AGNT,** vol. 1486, exp. 8, fol. 30r; vol. 1791, exp. 1, fols. 135r–v; vol. 1867, exp. 1, fol. 1r; vol. 1872, exp. 10, fol. 1r; vol. 2092, exp. 2, fols. 1r–v, 2r, 22r; vol. 2102, exp. 1, fols. 7r, 8r; vol. 2105, exp. 1, fols. 2r, 8r; vol. 2177, exp. 1, fols. 4r; vol. 2337, exp. 1, fols. 390v, 391r; vol. 2701, exp. 20, fol. 1r; vol. 2703, exp. 4, fol. 1r; vol. 2718, exp. 15, fols. 1r–6v; vol. 2719, exp. 39, fol. 1r; vol. 2762, exp. 11, fol. 1r; vol. 2764, exp. 5, fols. 1r–10r; vol. 2777, exp. 1, fol. 2r; vol. 3541, exp. 10, fols 1r–v 14r; vol. 3568, fols. 4r, 22r, 34r, 35r, 40r, 42r, 43r. **AGNI**, vol. 2, exp. 379; vol. 6 pte 2, exp. 1086. **AGNG**, vol. 1, exp. 193; vol. 2, exps. 88, 161, 214, 674, 923; vol. 4, exp. 292. **AGIM**, leg. 111, ramo 2, doc. 12.

Ixmiquilpan: **AGNM**, vol. 3, fols. 171, 302r, 323r; vol. 6, fols. 546r–v; vol. 7, fols. 192v–193r; vol. 8, fols. 64v, 208r–v; vol. 22, fols. 258r–v.

AGNT, vol. 1527, exp. 1, fols. 3r–4r; vol. 2692, exp. 12, fol. 1r; vol. 3663, exp. 6, fol. 148r; exp. 9, fol. 156r; exp. 12, fol. 163r. **AGNI,** vol. 2, exp. 620; vol. 6, pte. 2, exp. 532. **AGNG,** vol. 2, exp. 1247; vol. 4, exp. 43.

Izcuinquitlapilco: **AGNM,** vol. 6, fols. 322v–323r; vol. 7, fol. 349r; vol. 8, fol. 42r; vol. 9, fols. 3r, 185v–186r; vol. 9, fols. 221v–222r; vol. 10, fols. 6v–8r, 100r; vol. 21, fols. 14v–15r. **AGNT,** vol. 1792, exp. 1, fol. 64r. **Mendizábal,** vol. 6, pp. 114–16.

Michimaloya: **AGNM,** vol. 6, fols. 528v; vol. 11, fols. 206r–v; vol. 13, fols. 86r–v. **AGNT,** vol. 2337, exp. 1, fol. 391r.

Mizquiaguala: **AGNM,** vol. 11, fols. 216v; vol. 12, fols. 367r; vol. 13, fols. 15r–v, 71r–v, 88r–v; vol. 14, fols. 344r–v; vol. 15, fols. 9v; vol. 16, fols. 105r–107r; vol. 20, fols. 165r–v; fols. 271v–272r. **AGNT,** vol. 1106, quad. 3, fol. 11; vol. 1519, exp. 4, fols. 1r–199r; vol. 1520, exp. 4, fol. 1r; exp. 5, fols. 48r, 49r, 51v; vol. 2777, exp. 14. **AGNI,** vol. 6 pte. 2, exp. 351. **Mendizábal,** vol. 6, pp. 114–16.

Nextlalpan: **AGNM,** vol. 12, fols. 448v–449r; vol. 17, fols. 218r–v; vol. 20, fols. 208v–209r.

Otlazpa: **AGNM,** vol. 3, fols. 176r–v; vol. 5, fols. 167r–v, 168r–v, 258v–260v, 262r–v; vol. 10, fols. 104r–v; vol. 17, fols. 224r–v. **AGNT,** vol. 45, exp. 1, fols. 2, 7v; vol. 2354, exp. 1, fol. 27; vol. 2735, pte. 2, exp. 8, fol. 1r; exp. 9, fol. 1r; vol. 2782, exp. 9, fol. 1r; vol. 3433, exp. 1, fol. 1r; vol. 3517, exp. 1, fols. 11r, 12r, 14r; vol. 3670, exp. 19, fol. 1r. **AGNG,** vol. 1, exp. 1002, 1185.

Sayula: **AGNM,** vol. 6, fols. 369r–v; vol. 7, fols. 164r–v; vol. 9, fols. 277r–v; vol. 12, fols. 411r–v, 451r–v; vol. 13, 209r–v.

Suchitlan: **AGNM,** vol. 9, fols. 132v–133r. **AGNT,** vol. 2334, exp. 1, fol. 396r; vol. 2337, exp. 1, fols. 392r–393v.

Tecaxique: **AGNM,** vol. 19, fol. 138r; vol. 23, fols. 42r–v.

Tecpatepec: **AGNM,** vol. 12, fols. 397v, 447r–448r; vol. 13, fols. 71v, 166v, 176r–v; vol. 16, fols. 201v–202r, **AGNT,** vol. 1519, exp. 4, fols. 1r–199r; vol. 2766, exp. 3, fols. 1r–22r.

Tepetitlan: **AGNM,** vol. 13, fol. 166v; vol. 16, fols. 99v–100r. **AGNG,** vol. 1, exp. 548; vol. 2, exp. 1228.

Tepexi: **AGNM,** vol. 3, fols. 101r–v, 824v; vol. 4, fols. 292v; vol. 5, fols. 167r–v; vol. 6, fols. 515r, 516r–v; vol. 7, fol. 349r; vol. 8, fol. 50r; vol. 11, fols. 254r–v; vol. 13, fols. 181r–v; vol. 18, fols. 165v–166r; vol. 21, fol. 161v; vol. 23, fol. 26v. **AGNT,** vol. 1697, exp. 1, fols. 2r, 3r, 4r, 6r; exp. 1 pte. 2, fols. 1r–2r; vol. 2284, exp. 1, fols. 744v; vol. 2721, exp. 10, fol. 6r; vol. 2721, exp. 13, fols. 1r–8r; vol. 2729, exp. 10, fol. 152r; vol. 2754, exp. 13, fols. 1r–20r; vol. 2762, exp. 12, fol. 154r; exp. 13, fols. 147r, 153r; vol. 3517, exp. 1, fol. 5r. **AGNG,** vol. 1, exp. 538, 539.

Tequixquiac: **AGNM,** vol. 2, fol. 48v; vol. 8, fol. 185r; vol. 9, fols. 269v–272v, 276r–v; vol. 12, fols. 314v–315r, 332v, 429r–v, 485; vol. 13, fols. 244v–245r; vol. 14, fols. 290r–v; vol. 17, fols. 52r–v; vol. 18, fols. 127r–228r; vol. 19, fol. 27; vol. 21, 79v–80r. **AGNT,** vol. 1748, exp. 1, fols. 1r, 19r–22r, 39r, 48r–49r. **AGNI,** vol. 5, exp. 762, 940. **AGNG,** vol. 1, exp. 255.

Tetepango: **AGNM,** vol. 10, fols. 13v–14r; vol. 11, fols. 16v–17r; vol. 19, fols. 150r–151r; vol. 22, fol. 440v. **AGNT,** vol. 1520, exp. 5, fols. 54v–55r; vol. 2742, exp. 17, fols. 2r, 7r, 8r, 19r. **AGNI,** vol. 6, pte. 1, exp. 750. **AGNG,** vol. 1, exp. 184. **Mendizábal,** vol. 6, pp. 114–16.

Tezcatepec (S): **AGNM,** vol. 2, fols. 11v–12r; vol. 8, fols. 409v–410v; vol. 23, fols. 113r–v.

Tezcatepec (N): **AGNT,** vol. 1106, quad. 2, fols. 1–9; vol. 1106, quad 3, fol. 11; vol. 1104, quad. 22.

Tezontepec: **AGNM,** vol. 1, fol. 214; vol. 5, fols. 317r–v; vol. 18, fols. 184v–185v; vol. 22, fols. 440v–441r. **AGNT,** vol. 1103, quad. 3; vol. 1106, quad. 3, fol. 16; vol. 1721, exp. 11, fol. 27r; vol. 1728, vol. 2, fols. 1r–v. **AGNG,** vol. 1, exp. 716; vol. 2, exps. 245, 246, 793.

Tianquistongo: **AGNM,** vol. 7, fol. 37r.

Tlacotlapilco: **AGNM,** vol. 6, fols. 391r–392r; vol. 12, fols. 435v–437r. **AGNT,** vol. 2717, exp. 9, fol. 3r.

Tlacintla: **AGNM,** vol. 6, fol. 468r; vol. 8, fol. 208r; vol. 12, fols. 471v–472r; vol. 23, fol. 107r.

Tlahuelilpa: **AGNM,** vol. 2, fols. 246v–248r; vol. 5, fols. 100r–v; vol. 7, fol. 164r; vol. 10, fols. 82v–83r, 164v; vol. 11, fols. 242r–v, vol. 18, fol. 180r. **AGNT,** vol. 1640, exp. 2, fols. 15, 16r, 19; vol. 2776, exp. 1, fols. 1r–11r; vol. 3, fol. 22r. **AGNI,** vol. 6, pte. 2 exp. 192.

Tlamaco: **AGNM,** vol. 5, fol. 7r; vol. 11, fols. 206v–207r; vol. 12, fol. 343r; vol. 14, fols. 229v–230v; vol. 16, fols. 4r, 73r–v, 131r; vol. 17, fol. 55r. **AGNG,** vol. 2, exp. 243; vol. 5, exp. 291. **Mendizábal,** vol. 6, pp. 114–16.

Tlanocopan: **AGNM,** vol. 13, fols. 15r–v. **PNE,** vol. 1, p. 219.

Tlapanaloya: **AGNM,** vol. 2, fols. 86r, 95v–96r; vol. 5, fols. 253r–v; vol. 7, fol. 87r; vol. 8, fols. 98r, 101v; vol. 9, fols. 151r–v, 155v–156r; vol. 15, fols. 161v–162r. **AGNT,** vol. 1525, exp. 1, fol. 1; vol. 2674, exp. 18, fol. 307r; vol. 2697, exp. 10, fols. 308r–315r, exp. 11, fol. 319r. **AGNI,** vol. 3, exps. 753, 754, 805; vol. 4, exp. 216.

Tlilcuautla: **AGNM,** vol. 2, fol. 47r; vol. 12, fol. 443r. **AGNT,** vol. 64, exp. 1, fols. 1r, 5r.

Tornacustla: **AGNM,** vol. 5, fol. 70r; vol. 19, fols. 217v–218r; vol. 20, fols. 180v–181r, 204r–v. **AGNG,** vol. 1, exp. 94; vol. 2, exp. 992. **AGIJ,** leg. 143 no. 2. **Mendizábal,** vol. 6, pp. 114–16.

Tula: **AGNM,** vol. 3, fols. 169r–v; vol. 4, fol. 30; vol. 5, fols. 36, 122r,

157v, 208r–v; vol. 6, fol. 359r; vol. 8, fols. 59r, 67r–v, 69r, 191r; vol. 18, fols. 67r–68r, 77v, 101r, 156v; vol. 19, fol. 194r. **AGNT,** vol. 71, exp. 6, fol. 523v; vol. 1527, exp. 2, fols. 4v–7r, 18r–v; vol. 2284, exp. 1, fol. 817v; vol. 2337, exp. 1, fols. 391v, 395r–396r; vol. 2721, exp. 9, fol. 1r–10v; vol. 2713, exp. 18, fol. 1r; vol. 2737, exp. 14, fols. 1r–11r; vol. 2813, exp. 13, fol. 412r; vol. 3460, exp. 1, fol. 3r. **AGNI,** vol. 2, exp. 225. **AGNG,** vol. 3, exp. 173; vol. 5, exps. 378, 478, 486, 611. **AGIE,** leg. 161, pte. *c*, fol. 195r.

Tuzantlalpa: **AGNM,** vol. 6, fol. 456r. **AGNG,** vol. 1, exp. 970.

Xilotepec: **AGNM,** vol. 1, fols. 3v–4r, 11r–v, 20r–v, 111r–112r, 113r–v, 143r–v, 168r–v, 210, 218,; vol. 2, fols. 29, 76, 207, 217r, 233r; vol. 3, fols. 85r–v, 195v–196r, 283v–284v; vol. 4, fols. 126v, 291r–292r, 293r, 330v–332r; vol. 5, fols. 164v–166v; vol. 6, fols. 404v–405r, 541r–v; vol. 8, fols. 54r, 59r, 98r, 244r; vol. 11, fols. 64r, 262v–263r, 122v–123r; vol. 12, fols. 305v–306r; vol. 13, fols. 1r–v, 13v–14r, 86v; vol. 14, fols. 84r–85r, 142v, 233v–234v; vol. 15, fols. 286r–v; vol. 16, fols. 112r, 129r, 129v–130v, 170v; vol. 17, fols. 15v–16r, 37v–40r, 63v–64r, 103r–v, 118v–120r; vol. 18, fols. 41r–42r, 81v–82r, 236r–v, 246r, 266r–269r, 281r–v, 327r; vol. 19, fols. 85v–86v, 239r–240v; vol. 21, fols. 112r, 115r, 121v–122, 133r–v, 208r–209r, 211v–212r; vol. 22, fols. 208r–209r, 297v–299r; vol. 23, fols. 45v–46r. **AGNT,** vol. 1486, exp. 8, fol. 30–36r; vol. 1538, exp. 10, fols. 1r–5v; vol. 1588, exp. 2 bis., fols. 1–5; vol. 1652, exp. 6, fols. 10r–v; vol. 1698, exp. 1, fol. 1; vol. 1794, exp. 1, fol. 8; vol. 1857, exp. 5, fol. 1r; vol. 2118, exp. 1, quad. 3, fols. 1r–9r; vol. 2177, exp. 1, fol. 2r; vol. 2337, exp. 1, fol. 390r–392v; vol. 2674, exp. 22, fols. 1, 2r, 334r; vol. 2688, exp. 2, fol. 1r; vol. 2674, exp. 21, fols. 325r–331r; vol. 2704, exp. 23, fols. 1r–4r; vol. 2757, exp. 5, fols. 1r–16v; vol. 2764, exp. 2, fol. 18r; exp. 4, fol. 46r; exp. 5, fols. 1r–10r; exp. 8, fol. 82v; exp. 22, fols. 333r–343r; exp. 26, fols. 321r, 335; vol. 3568, fols. 1r, 5r. **AGNI,** vol. 2, exps. 46, 353; vol. 3, exp. 150; vol. 5, exp. 9; vol. 6, pte. 1, exp. 863, 865, 1000, 1001. **AGNG,** vol. 1, exps. 532, 724, 964, 1087; vol. 3, exp. 426; vol. 5, exp. 116. **AGIM,** leg. 96, ramo 1; leg. 1841, fols. 1r–8r.

Xipacoya: **AGNM,** vol. 2, fols. 141v–142r. **AGNT,** vol. 1873, exp. 12, fol. 1r; vol. 2284, exp. 1, fols. 743r–744r, 798v–799r, 815r–v; vol. 2721, exp. 19, fol. 8v; vol. 2812, exp. 13, fol. 412r.

Yetecomac: **AGNM,** vol. 13, fol. 7r. **Mendizábal,** vol. 6, pp. 114–16.

Zayanaquilpa: **AGNM,** vol. 6, fols. 402r, 402v–403r; vol. 13, fols. 7v–8r; vol. 14, fol. 51r; vol. 16, fols. 89r–v; vol. 19, fols. 171v, 186v. **AGNT,** vol. 2337, exp. 1, fol. 392v; vol. 2684, exp. 12, fol. 1r.

ABBREVIATIONS

Archival Sources

Archivo General de la Nación (Mexico City)
AGNA   AGN, Archivo Histórico de Hacienda
AGNC   AGN, Ramo de Civil
AGNG   AGN, Ramo de General de Parte
AGNH   AGN, Ramo de Historia
AGNI   AGN, Ramo de Indios
AGNL   AGN, Libro de Congregaciones
AGNM   AGN, Ramo de Mercedes
AGNT   AGN, Ramo de Tierras

Archivo General de Indias (Seville)
AGIM   AGI, Audiencia de México
AGIE   AGI, Escribanía de cámara
AGIC   AGI, Contaduría
AGII   AGI, Indiferente General
AGIJ   AGI, Justicia
AGIP   AGI, Patronato

Published Primary Sources

PNE   Papeles de la Nueva España, vols. 1, 3, and 6.

Secondary Sources

HMAI   Handbook of the Middle American Indian

GLOSSARY

Agostadero	Seasonal summer pasture; stubble grazing
Alcalde	Judge and *cabildo* member
Alcalde mayor	Spanish official in charge of a district
Alcaldía	District or jurisdiction of an *alcalde mayor*
Arroyo	Small stream or stream bed
Audiencia	Court and governing body under the viceroy, or the area of its jurisdiction
Baldías	Vacant or public lands
Barranca	Ravine
Caballería de tierras	Unit of agricultural land, about 42.5 hectares
Cabecera	Head town
Cacique	Indian chief or local ruler
Calichal	*Caliche;* hardpan layer underlying soils
Cardones	Possibly the introduced *Cynara cardunculus* or the *nopal cardón* (*Opuntia streptocantha*)
Cédula	Royal (or other) order
Composición de tierras	Legalization of land title
Congregación	Congregation or concentration of scattered populations
Corregidor	Spanish officer in charge of a district
Corregimiento	Institution, office or jurisdiction of a *corregidor*
Diligencia	Inspection
Doctrina	Doctrine; parochial jurisdiction
Encomendero	Possessor of an *encomienda*
Encomienda	Grant of Indian tribute and labor; area of the Indians granted
Eriaza	Uncultivated land

184

Estancia de ganado mayor	Cattle ranch, about 1,756 hectares
Estancia de ganado menor	Sheep or goat station, about 780 hectares
Ganado mayor	Cattle, horses, mules, or donkeys
Ganado menor	Sheep, goats, or pigs
Gobernador	Governor
Hacienda	Landed estate
Informe	Report
Jaguey	Man-made depression to collect water
Labor	Farm; generally for agriculture
Legua	League
Llanos	Flatlands
Loma	Small hill
Macegual	Indian commoner
Maguey	Agave
Mayorazgo	Entailed estate
Merced	Grant, generally of land
Mesquite	Mesquite
Mesta	Stockmen's association
Mestizaje	Race mixture or mestization
Mestizo/a	Person of mixed European and Indian ancestry
Milpa	Planted agricultural plot or cornfield
Monte	Forest; region of scrub or brush; mountain
Nopal	Prickly pear cactus (*Cactus opuntia*)
Oficiales Reales	Royal accountants in charge of the Real Hacienda
Palma silvestre	Yucca
Pasos	Land measure
Peso	Monetary unit of eight *reales*
Principal	Member of the Indian upper class; a hereditary status
Pueblo	Indian town
Quebrada	Gorge
Real hacienda	Financial institution of the Spanish crown
Realengos	Unappropriated or royal lands
Relación	Descriptive report
Repartimiento	Labor draft
Sabana	Savanna
Sementera	Planted field

Servicio	Service, labor, or provision of goods
Sub-macegual	Persons paying tribute to a member of the Indian upper class
Tameme	Indian carrier
Tasación	Tribute or tribute assessment record
Temporal	Unirrigated cropland
Tepetate	Hardpan layer underlying soils; see also calichal
Tierras de humedad	Moist bottomlands
Tributo	Tribute
Tuna	Fruit of the prickly pear cactus
Visita	Tour of inspection; community or church ministered by nonresident clergy
Zacate	Straw; lake reeds; fodder; grass

BIBLIOGRAPHY

Ahlstrand, Gary M. "Response of Chiuahuan Desert Mountain Shrub Vegetation to Burning." *Journal of Range Management* 35:1 (1982) 62–5.

Allen, R. B., I. J. Payton, and J. E. Knowlton. "Effects of Ungulates on Structure and Species Composition in the Urewera Forests as Shown by Exclosures." *New Zealand Journal of Ecology* 7 (1984) 119–30.

Altman, Ida and James Lockhart. *Provinces of Early Mexico.* Austin, Texas, 1975.

Alvarado Tezozomoc, Hernando. *Crónica mexicayotl.* Trans. and ed. Adrián León. Mexico City, 1949.

Assadourian, Carlos Sempat. "La despoblación indígena en Perú y Nueva España durante el siglo XVI y la formación de la economía colonial." *Historia Mexicana* 38:3 (1989) 419–51.

Atlas Nacional del Medio Físico. Mexico City, 1981.

Australian Capital Territory. *Soil Conservation Council, Second Annual Report* Canberra, 1949.

Australian Encyclopedia. New South Wales, 1977.

Bakewell, Peter J. *Silver Mining and Society in Colonial Mexico, Zacatecas 1546–1700.* Cambridge, 1971.

Beadle, N. C. W. *The Vegetation and Pastures of Western New South Wales with Special Reference to Soil Erosion.* Sydney, 1948.

Bentura Beleña, Eusebio. *Recopilación sumaria de todos los autos acordados de la real audiencia y sala del crimen de esta Nueva España, y providencias de su superior gobierno.* 2 vols. Mexico City, 1787.

Bergerud, A. T. "Decline of the Caribou in North America Following Settlement." *Journal of Wildlife Management* 38 (1974) 757–70.

Bergerud, A. T., R. D. Jakimchuk, and D. R. Carruthers. "The Buffalo of the North: Caribou (*Rangifer tarandus*) and Human Developments." *Arctic* 37:1 (1984) 7–22.

Bishko, C. J. "Cattle Raising and the Peninsular Tradition." *Hispanic American Historical Review* 32:4 (1952) 491–515.

Bishko, Charles J. "The Castilian as Plainsman: The Medieval Ranching Frontier in La Mancha and Extremadura." In *The New World Looks at its History.* Eds. Archibald R. Lewis and Thomas F. McGann, Austin, Texas, 1963.

Biswell, Harold H. "Effects of Fire on Chaparral." In *Fire and Ecosystems*, eds. T. T. Kozlowski, and C. E. Ahlgren. New York, 1974, pp. 321–64.

Blasquez, L. "Hidrogeologia." *Memoria de la comisión geológica del Valle del Mezquital, Hgo.* Mexico City, 1938.

Bolton, Geoffrey. *Spoils and Spoilers: Australians Make Their Environment, 1788–1980.* Sydney, 1981.

Borah, Woodrow. *New Spain's Century of Depression.* Berkeley and Los Angeles, 1951.

The Population of Central Mexico in 1548: An Analysis of the Suma de Visitas de Pueblos. Berkeley and Los Angeles, 1960.

Brambila, M. *Mapa de Suelos de Mexico.* Mexico City, 1942.

Brand, D. "The Early History of the Cattle Industry in Northern Mexico." *Agricultural History* 25 (1961) 132–9.

Bryant, W. G. "The Effect of Grazing and Burning on a Mountain Grassland, Snowy Mountains, New South Wales." *Journal of the Soil Conservation Service* 24 (1973) 29–44.

Budowski, G. "Tropical Savannahs, A Sequence of Forest Fellings and Repeated Burnings." *Turrialba* 6 (1956) 23–33.

Butler, F. C. "Agriculture in Southern New South Wales, 1830–1958." *Agricultural Gazette.* 70:6 (1959) 281–95.

Butzer, Karl W. "Ethno-Agriculture and Cultural Ecology in Mexico: Historical Vistas and Modern Implications." *Conference of Latin American Geographers,* 17/18 (1992) 139–52.

Caillavet, Chantal. "Las técnicas agrarias autóctonas y la remodelación colonial del paisaje en los Andes septentrionales (siglo XVI)." In *Ciencia, Vida y Espacio en Iberoamérica.* Madrid, 1989.

Campbell, D. J., and M. R. Rudge. "Vegetation Changes Induced over Ten Years by Goats and Pigs at Port Ross, Auckland Islands (Subantarctic)." *New Zealand Journal of Ecology* 7 (1984) 103–18.

Canabal, Cristiani Beatriz, and Carlos R. Martínez Assad. *Explotación y Dominio en el Mezquital.* Mexico City, 1973.

Carrasco, Pedro. *Los Otomíes. Cultura e historia prehispánica de los pueblos mesoamericanos de habla Otomiana.* Mexico City, 1979.

Caughley, Graeme. "Eruption of Ungulate Populations with Emphasis on Himalayan Thar in New Zealand." *Ecology* 51:1 (1970) 53–72.

"Plant & Herbivore Systems." In *Theoretical Ecology: Principles and Applications.* Ed. R. M. May. London, 1976, pp. 94–113.

"Wildlife Management and the Dynamics of Ungulate Populations." *Applied Biology* 1 (1976) 183–247.

"What is This Thing Called Carrying Capacity?" In *North American Elk: Ecology, Balance and Management,* eds. M. S. Boyce and L. D. Hayden-Wing. Laramie, Wyo., 1979, pp. 2–8.

"Overpopulation." In *Problems in Management of Locally Abundant Wild Mammals,* eds. P. A. Jewell and S. Holt. New York, 1981, pp. 7–19.

"Vegetation Complexity and the Dynamics of Modelled Grazing Systems." *Oecologia* 54 (1982) 309–12.

"Introduction to the Sheep Rangelands." In *Kangaroos: Their Ecology and Management in the Sheep Rangelands of Australia,* eds. Graeme Caughley, Neil Shepherd, and Jeff Short. Cambridge, 1987, pp. 1–13.

Chávez Orozco, Luis. *Papeles sobre la mesta de la Nueva España.* Mexico City, 1956.

Chevalier, François. *La formación de los grandes latifundios en México.* Mexico City, 1975.

Claxton, Robert H. "Weather-based Hazards in Colonial Guatemala." *Studies in the Social Sciences* 25 (1986) 139–63.

Claxton, Robert H., and Alan D. Hecht. "Climatic and Human History in Europe and Latin America: An Opportunity for Comparative Study." *Climatic Change* 1 (1978) 195–203.

Cook, Sherburne F. *The Historical Demography and Ecology of the Teotlalpan.* Berkeley and Los Angeles, 1949.

Soil Erosion and Population in Central Mexico. Berkeley and Los Angeles, 1949.

Santa María Ixcatlán: Habitat, Population, Subsistence. Berkeley and Los Angeles, 1958.

"Erosion Morphology and Occupation History in Western Mexico." *Anthropological Records* 17:3 (1963) 281–334.

Cook, Sherburne F., and Woodrow Borah. *The Indian Population of Central Mexico, 1531–1610.* Berkeley and Los Angeles, 1960.

Essays in Population History. 3 vols. Berkeley and Los Angeles, 1971–9.

Costin, A. B. *The Grazing Factor and the Maintenance of Catchment Values in the Australian Alps.* Melbourne 1958.

"Runoff and Soil Nutrient Losses from an Improved Pasture at Ginninderra, Southern Tablelands, New South Wales." *Australian Journal of Agricultural Research* 31 (1980) 533–46.

Costin, A. B., D. J. Wimbush, D. Kerr, and L. W. Gay. *Studies in Catchment Hydrology in the Australian Alps. 1: Trends in Soils and Vegetation.* Melbourne, 1959.

Cronon, William. *Changes in the Land: Indians, Colonists, and the Ecology of New England.* New York, 1983.

Crosby, Alfred. *The Columbian Exchange: Biological and Cultural Consequences of 1492.* Westport, Conn., 1972.

"Virgin Soil Epidemics as a Factor in the Aboriginal Depopulation in America." *William and Mary Quarterly* 33 (1976) 289–99.

Ecological Imperialism: The Biological Expansion of Europe, 900–1900. New York, 1986.

Crosby, Alfred. "Ecological Imperialism: the Overseas Migration of Western Europeans as a Biological Phenomenon." In *The Ends of the Earth: Perspectives on Modern Environmental History.* Ed. Donald Worster. Cambridge, 1988.

Davies, Keith A. *Landowners in Colonial Peru.* Austin, Texas, 1984.

Denevan, William M., ed., *The Native Population of the Americas in 1492.* Madison, Wis., 1976.

Diccionario Manual e Ilustrado de la Lengua Española. Madrid, 1950.

Dobyns, Henry F. "Estimating Aboriginal American Population: An Appraisal of Techniques with a New Hemispheric Estimate." *Current Anthropology* 7 (1966) 395–415.

From Fire to Flood: Historic Human Destruction of Sonoran Desert Riverine Oases. Socorro, New Mexico, 1981.

Donald, C. M. "The Progress of Australian Agriculture and the Role of Pastures in Economic Change." *Australian Journal of Science* 27:7 (1965) 187–98.

Doolittle, William E. "Las Marismas to Pánuco to Texas: The Transfer of Open Range Cattle Ranching from Iberia through Northeastern Mexico." *Yearbook, Conference of Latin Americanist Geographers* 13 (1987) 3–11.

Drury, William H., and Ian C. T. Nisbet. "Succession." *Journal of the Arnold Arboretum* 54:3 (1973) 331–68.

Dusenberry, William H. "Ordinances of the *Mesta* in New Spain." *The Americas* 4 (1948) 345–50.

The Mexican Mesta: The Administration of Ranching in Colonial Mexico. Urbana, Ill., 1963.

Estrada Albuquerque, Anselmo. "El Valle del Mezquital: Las aguas negras matan la fauna y dan vida agrícola." *Unomásuno.* 15 August 1983, 22.

Feldman, Lawrence. "Comment on Whitmore's 'Population Decline.' " *Latin American Population History Bulletin* 21 (1992) 2.

Finkler, Kaja. "A Comparative Study of the Economy of Two Village Communities in Mexico with Special Reference to the Role of Irrigation." Ph.D. dissertation, City University of New York, 1973.

Florescano, Enrique. *Precios del maíz y crísis agrícolas en México (1708–1810).* Centro de Estudios Históricos, n.s. no. 4, Mexico City, 1969.

Estructuras y problemas agrarias de México (1500–1821) Mexico City, 1971.

"La formación de los trabajadores en la época colonial, 1521–1750." In *La Clase Obrera en la Historia de México.* Eds. Enrique Florescano, Isabel González Sánchez, Jorge González Angulo, Roberto Sandoval Zanauz, Cuauhtemoc Velasco A., and Alejandra Moreno Toscano; Mexico City, 1986.

Fox, David J. "Man–Water Relationships in Metropolitan Mexico." *The Geographical Review* 55:4 (1965) 523–45.

Frank, André Gunder. *Mexican Agriculture, 1521–1630: Transformation of the Mode of Production.* New York, 1979.

Frederick, Charles D. "Late Quaternary Sedimentation by the Rio Laja, Guanajuato, Mexico." Abstract, Department of Geography, University of Texas at Austin.

Gardner, W. *Production and Resources of the Northern and Western Districts of New South Wales.* 2 Vols. Archives of the Mitchell Library, Sydney, 1854.

Gerez Fernández, Patricia. "Uso del suelo durante cuatrocientos años y cambio fisionómico en la zona semiárida Poblana-Veracruzana, México." *Biotica* 10:2 (1985) 123–44.

Gerhard, Peter A. *A Guide to the Historical Geography of New Spain.* Cambridge, 1972.

Gibson, Charles. *The Aztecs under Spanish Rule.* Stanford, Calif., 1967.

González Quintero, Lauro. *Tipos de vegetación del Valle del Mezquital, Hgo.* Mexico City, 1968.

Grenfell, B. T., O. F. Price, S. D. Albon, and T. H. Clutton-Brock, "Over-compensation and population cycles in an ungulate." *Nature* 355 (1992) 823–6.

Handbook of the Middle American Indians. Vol. 1, ed. Robert C. West. Austin, Texas, 1964.

Hanmer, T. H. "Land Use and Erosion in the Glen Innes Area." *Journal of Soil Conservation, New South Wales* 16:4 (1960) 277–87.

Hardin, Garret. "The Tragedy of the Commons." *Science* 162 (1968) 1243–1248.

Hastings, James R., and Raymond M. Turner. *The Changing Mile: An Ecological Study of Vegetation Change With Time in the Lower Mile of an Arid and Semi-Arid Region* Tucson, Ariz., 1965.

Heathcote, R. L. *Australia.* London, 1975.

Heathcote, R. L., and J. A. Mabutt, eds. *Land, Water and People: Geographical Essays in Australian Resource Management.* Sydney, 1988.

Henige, David. "Native American Population at Contact: Standards of Proof and Styles of Discourse in the Debate." *Bulletin, Latin American Population History* 22 (1992) 2–23.

Hilder, E. J. "Rate of Turn-over of Elements in Soils: The Effect of the Stocking Rate." *Wool Technology and Sheep Breeding* 12: 2 (1966) 11–16.

Holdgate, M. W., and N. M. Wace. "The Influence of Man on the Floras and Faunas of Southern Islands." *Polar Record* 10 (1961) 475–93.

Howard, Walter E. "Introduced Browsing Mammals and Habitat Stability in New Zealand." *Journal of Wildlife Management* 28:3 (1964) 421–9.

Hughes, P. J. and M. E. Sullivan. "Aboriginal Landscape." In *Australian Soils: The Human Impact.* Eds. J. S. Russell and R. F. Isabel, Sta. Lucia, 1986, pp. 117–33.

Johanssen, Carl L. *Savannas of Interior Honduras.* Berkeley and Los Angeles, 1963.

Johnson, Kirsten J. " 'Do as the Land Bids.' A Study of Otomí Resource-Use on the Eve of Irrigation." Ph.D. dissertation, Clark University, 1977.

Jones, Rhys. "Fire Stick Farming." *Australian Natural History* 16 (1969) 224–8.

Joyce, Arthur A., and Raymond G. Mueller. "The Social Impact of Anthro-pogenic Landscape Modification in the Río Verde Drainage Basin, Oax-aca, Mexico." *Geoarchaeology* 7 (1992) 503–26.

Kaleski, L. G. "Erosion and Soil Conservation in the Hunter Valley with Special Reference to Flood Mitigation." *Journal of the Soil Conservation Service of New South Wales* 18:1 (1962) 2–9.

"Erosion Survey of New South Wales (East Central Division)." *Journal of the Soil Conservation Service of New South Wales* 19:4 (1963) 171–83.

Keith, Robert G. *Conquest and Agrarian Change: The Emergence of the Hacienda System on the Peruvian Coast.* Cambridge, Mass., 1976.

King, C. J. "An Outline of Closer Settlement in New South Wales. Part 1: The Sequence of Land Laws, 1788–1956." In *Review: Marketing and Ag-*

ricultural Economics, Department of Agriculture, vol. 25. New South Wales, 1957, pp. 3–290.

Klein, David R. "The Introduction, Increase, and Crash of Reindeer on St. Mathew Island." *Journal of Wildlife Management* 32 (1968) 350–67.

Klein, Julius. *The Mesta: A Study of Spanish Economic History (1273–1836).* Cambridge, 1920.

Konrad, Herman W. *A Jesuit Hacienda in Colonial Mexico: Santa Lucia, 1576–1767.* Stanford, Calif., 1980.

Leader-William, N. *Reindeer on South Georgia.* Cambridge, 1988.

Licate, Jack A. *The Making of a Mexican Landscape: Territorial Organization and Settlement in the Eastern Puebla Basin 1520–1605.* Chicago, 1981.

Lipsett-Rivera, Sonya. "Water and Social Conflict in Colonial Mexico: Puebla, 1680–1910." Ph.D. dissertation, Tulane University, 1988.

"Puebla's Eighteenth-Century Agrarian Decline: A New Perspective." *Hispanic American Historical Review* 70:3 (1990) 463–81.

Lockhart, James, and Stuart B. Schwartz. *Early Latin America: A History of Colonial Spanish America and Brazil.* Cambridge, 1984.

MacLeod, Murdo. *Spanish Central America: A Socioeconomic History, 1520–1720.* Berkeley and Los Angeles, 1973.

"The Three Horsemen: Drought, Disease, Population, and the Difficulties of 1726–27 in the Guadalajara Region." *Annals of the Southeastern Council on Latin American Studies* 14 (1983) 33–47.

McKay, Bonnie J., and James M. Acheson. *The Question of the Commons.* Tucson, Ariz., 1987.

McNeill, William H. *Plagues and Peoples.* New York, 1976.

Mastache de Escobar, Alba Guadalupe. "Sistemas de riego en el área de Tula, Hgo." In *Proyecto Tula.* Ed. Eduardo Matos Moctezuma, Mexico City, 1974–6.

Mastache de Escobar, Alba Guadalupe, and Ana Maria Crespo O. "La ocupación prehispánica en el area de Tula, Hgo." In *Proyecto Tula.* Ed. Eduardo Matos Moctezuma. Mexico City, 1974–6, pp. 71–8.

Matezanz, José Antonio. "Introducción de la ganaderia, 1521–35," *Historia Mexicana* 14 (1965) 133–65.

Medina, Andres, and Noemi Quesada. *Panorama de los Otomies del Valle del Mezquital: Ensayo metodológico.* Mexico City, 1975.

Melville, Elinor G. K. "The Pastoral Economy and Environmental Degradation in Highland Central Mexico, 1530–1600." Ph.D. dissertation, University of Michigan, 1983.

"Elite Formation in the Immediate Post-Conquest Era." *Proceedings, 37th Annual Meeting of the Rocky Mountain Council on Latin American Studies.* Las Cruces N.M., 1989, 91–4.

"Environmental and Social Change in the Valle del Mezquital, Mexico (1521–1600)." *Comparative Studies in Society and History* 32:1 (1990) 24–53.

"The Long-term Effects of the Introduction of Sheep into Semi-Arid Sub-

Tropical Regions." In *Changing Tropical Forests: Historical Perspectives on Today's Challenges in Central and South America.* Eds. Harold K. Steen and Richard P. Tucker, Durham, N.C., 1992, pp. 144–53.

Mendizábal, Miguel Orthón de. *Obras Completas.* Vols. 1–6. Mexico City, 1946–47.

Merchant, Carolyn. "The Theoretical Structure of Ecological Revolutions." *Environmental Review* 11:4 (1987) 265–74.

Meyer, Michael C. *Water in the Hispanic Southwest: A Social and Legal History, 1550–1850.* Tucson, Ariz., 1984.

Miranda, José. "Notas sobre la introducción de la Mesta en la Nueva España," *Revista de Historia de América* 17 (1944) 1–26.

La función económica del encomendero en los orígenes del régimen colonial. Mexico City, 1965.

"La población indígena de Ixmiquilpan y su distrito en la época colonial." *Estudios de Historia Novohispana* 2 (1966) 121–30.

Moore, R. M. "Effects of the Sheep Industry on Australian Vegetation." In *The Simple Fleece,* ed. C. Barnard, 170–83. Melbourne, 1962.

Moore, R. M., and E. F. Biddiscombe. "The Effects of Grazing on Grasslands." In *Grasses and Grasslands,* ed. C. Barnard. New York, 1964.

Morner, Magnus. "The Spanish American Hacienda: A Survey of Recent Research and Debate." *Hispanic American Historical Review* 53:2 (1973) 183–216.

Morrisey, Richard J. "The Northward Expansion of Cattle Ranching in New Spain, 1550–1600." *Agriculture* 25 (1951) 115–21.

"Colonial Agriculture in New Spain." *Agricultural History* 31 (1957) 24–9.

Motolinia (Toribio de Benavente). *History of the Indians of New Spain.* Trans. Elizabeth Andros Foster. Berkeley and Los Angeles, 1950.

Murphy, Michael. *Irrigation in the Bajío Region of Colonial Mexico.* Boulder, Colo., 1986.

Nicholson, Phyllis H. "Fire and the Australian Aborigines–An Enigma." In *Fire and the Australian Biota.* Eds. A. Malcolm Gill, Richard H. Groves and Ian R. Noble. Canberra, 1981.

Noble, J. C., and D. J. Tongway. "Pastoral Settlement in Arid and Semi-Arid Rangelands." In *Australian Soils: The Human Impact.* Eds. J. S. Russell and R. F. Isabel, Sta. Lucia, 1986, pp. 219–42.

"Herbivores in Arid and Semi-Arid Rangelands." In *Australian Soils: The Human Impact.* Eds. J. S. Russel and R. F. Isabel, Sta. Lucia, 1986, pp. 244–70.

Ouweneel, Arij. "Silent Drama in Indian Agriculture: Or, How Late Spring Droughts Ruined Maize Harvests in Anáhuac during the 1780s and 1790s." Unpublished manuscript, 1992.

Papeles de Nueva España. 9 vols. Ed. Francisco Paso y Troncoso. Madrid, 1905–48.

Parsons, Jeffrey R., and Mary H. Parsons. *Maguey Utilization in Highland Central Mexico: An Archaeological Ethnography.* Ann Arbor, Mich., 1990.

Patch, Robert. "La formación de estancias y haciendas en Yucatan durante la colonia." *Boletín de la Escuela de Ciencias Antropógicas de la Universidad de Yucatan* 4 (1976) 21–61.

Peek, James M. "Natural Regulation of Ungulates (What Constitutes a Wilderness?)" *Wildlife Society Bulletin* 8 (1980) 217–27.

Pérez Urbe, Matilde. "Rechazen suspender el uso de aguas negras en Hidalgo." *La Jornada* (Mexico City), 23 September 1991.

"Se reducirá el uso de aguas negras en el Mezquital: CNA." *La Jornada* (Mexico City) 24 September 1991, pp. 1, 16.

Piñeda, Raquel. *Catálogo de documentos para la historia del Valle del Mezquital en el Archivo General de la Nación, México.* Mexico City, 1981.

Poillon, Jacqueline Signoret. "Datos sobre algunos características ecoloógicas del mesquite (*Prosopis laevigata*) y su aprovechamiento en el Valle del Mezquital." In *Mesquites y huisaches, algunas aspectos de la economía, ecología y taxonomía de los géneros prosopis y acacia en México.* Ed. Frederíco Gómez Lorence, Mexico City, 1970.

Powell, J. M. "Conservation and Resource Management in Australia, 1788–1860." in *Australian Space, Australian Time.* Eds. J. M. Powell and M. Williams, Melbourne, 1975.

Powell, Philip Wayne. *Soldiers, Indians, and Silver.* Berkeley and Los Angeles, 1952.

Pyne, Stephen J. *Fire in America: A Cultural History of Wildland and Rural Fire.* Princeton, N.J., 1982.

Burning Bush: A Fire History of Australia. New York, 1991.

Rappaport, Roy A. "The Flow of Energy in Agricultural Society." Cited in Timothy C. Weiskel. "Agents of Empire; Steps Toward an Ecology of Imperialism." *Environmental Review* 11:4 (1987) 275–88.

Salvucci, Richard J. *Textiles and Capitalism in Mexico: An Economic History of the Obrajes, 1539–1840.* Princeton, N.J., 1987.

Sanders, W. J., J. R. Parsons, and R. Santley. *The Basin of Mexico.* New York, 1979.

Sauer, Carl O. *Land and Life: A selection from the Writings of Carl Ortwin Sauer.* Berkeley and Los Angeles, 1963.

Schwartz, Stuart B. "Indian Labor and New World Plantations: European Demand and Indian Responses in Northeastern Brazil." *American Historical Review* 83 (1978).

Scott, J. J. "Landslip Revegetation and Rabbits, Subantarctic Macquarie Island." *Proceedings of the Ecological Society of Australia* 12 (1983) 170–1.

Secretaria de Indústria y Comércio, Dirección General de Estadística. In *IX Censo General de Población.* Mexico City, 1971.

Secretaria de la Presidéncia, Comisión de Estudios del Territorio Nacional (CETENAL). Maps: Topographic, Soil Use, and Geology.

Secretaria de Programación y Presupuesto, Coordinación General de Servicios Nacionales de Estadistica Geográfica e Informática, Dirección General de Geografia del Territorio Nacional. Maps: Topographic, Soil Use, and Geology.

Serrera Contreras, Ramón Maria. *Guadalajara ganadera: Estudio regional no-vohispano, 1760–1805.* Seville, 1977.

Simpson, Lesley Byrd. *Exploitation of Land in Sixteenth Century Mexico.* Berkeley and Los Angeles, 1952.

Sinclair, A. R. E. "The Eruptions of the Ruminants." In *Serengeti: Dynamics of an Ecosystem.* Eds. A. R. E. Sinclair and M. Norton-Griffiths, Chicago, 1979, pp. 82–103.

Smith, D. I. and B. Finlayson. "Water in Australia: Its role in environmental Degradation." In *Land, Water and People: Geographical Essays in Australian Resource Management.* Eds. R. L. Heathcote and J. A. Mabutt. Sydney, 1988.

Stern, Steve J. "Feudalism, Capitalism and the World-System in the Perspective of Latin America and the Caribbean." *American Historical Review* 93 (1988) 829–72.

Stevens, Rayfred L. "The Soils of Middle America and Their Relationship to Indian Peoples and Cultures." In *Handbook of the Middle American Indian.* Vol. 1, Austin, Texas, 1964, pp. 265–315.

Strzelecki, Paul Edmund. *Physical Description of New South Wales and Van Diemen's Land.* London, 1845.

Swan, Susan. "Mexico in the Little Ice Age." *Journal of InterDisciplinary History* 11:4 (1981) 633–48.

Tamayo, Jorge L. "The Hydrography of Middle America." In *Handbook of the Middle American Indian* vol. 1 Austin, Texas, 1964 pp. 84–121.

Taylor, William B. *Landlord and Peasant in Colonial Oaxaca,* Stanford, Calif., 1972.

Tewkesbury, A. R. "Soil Erosion and Soil Conservation in Northern New South Wales." *Journal of Soil Conservation, New South Wales* 17: 1 (1961) 23–30.

Turner, J. S. "Catchment Erosion." In *The Simple Fleece.* Ed. C. Barnard. Melbourne, 1962, pp. 170–83.

Van Young, Eric. *Hacienda and Market in Eighteenth-Century Mexico: The Rural Economy of the Guadalajara Region, 1675–1820.* Berkeley and Los Angeles, 1981.

"Mexican Rural History Since Chevalier: The Historiography of the Colonial Hacienda." *Latin American Research Review* 18 (1983) 5–61.

Vassberg, David E. *Land and Society in Golden Age Castile.* Cambridge, 1984.

Vázquez Lira. "Marginación." *Unomásuno.* Mexico City, September 12, 1981.

Vivó, Jorge A. "Weather and Climate of Mexico and Central America." In *Handbook of the Middle American Indian* vol. 1 Austin, Texas, 1964, pp. 187–215.

Wagner, Philip L. "Parras: A Case History in the Depletion of Natural Resources." *Landscape* 5 (1955) 19–28.

"Natural Vegetation of Middle America." In *Handbook of the Middle American Indian* vol. 1 Austin, Texas 1964, pp., 216–64.

Walker, J., R. J. Raison and P. K. Khanna. "Fire." In *Australian Soils: The Human Impact.* Eds. J. S. Russell and R. F. Isabel, Sta. Lucia, 1986.

Wallerstein, Immanuel. *The Modern World-System: Capitalist Agriculture and the Origins of the European World-Economy in the Sixteenth Century.* New York, 1974.

The Modern World-System II: Mercantilism and the Consolidation of the European World-Economy 1600–1750. New York, 1980.

Weiskel, Timothy C. "Agents of Empire: Steps Toward an Ecology of Imperialism." *Environmental Review* 11:4 (1987) 275–87.

West, Robert C. "Surface Configuration and Associated Geology of Middle America." In *Handbook of the Middle American Indians.* vol. 1, Austin, Texas, 1964 pp. 33–83.

"The Natural Regions of Middle America." in *Handbook of The Middle American Indian* vol. 1, Austin, Texas 1964 pp. 363–83.

Whalley, R. D. B., G. C. Robinson, and J. A. Taylor. "General Effects of Management and Grazing by Livestock on the Rangelands of the Northern Tablelands of New South Wales." *Australian Rangeland Journal* 1:2 (1978) 174–90.

Whitmore, Thomas M. "Sixteenth-Century Population Decline in the Basin of Mexico: A Systems Simulation." *Bulletin, Latin American Population History* 20 (1991) 2–18.

Williams, Barbara J. "Tepetate in the Valley of Mexico." *Annals of the Association of American Geographers* 62:4 (1972) 618–26.

Williams, N. Leader. *Reindeer on South Georgia: The Ecology of an Introduced Population.* Cambridge, 1988.

Wilson, P. R., and D. F. G. Orwin. "The Sheep Population of Campbell Island." *New Zealand Journal of Science* 7 (1964) 460–90.

Wodzicki, Kazimirez. "Ecology and Management of Introduced Ungulates in New Zealand." *La Terre et la Vie* 1 (Jan.–Mar., 1961) 130–157.

Wolf, Eric, and Angel Palerm. *Agricultura y civilización en Mesoamérica.* Mexico City, 1972.

Worster, Donald, ed. *The Ends of the Earth.* Cambridge, 1988.

"Ecology of Order and Chaos." *Environmental History Review* 14:1–2 (1990) 1–18.

Wright, H. A. "Effect of Fire on Arid and Semi-Arid Ecosystems – North American Continent." In *Rangelands: A Resource Under Siege.* London, 1986.

Wright, H. A., Stephen C. Bunting, and Leon F. Neuenschwander. "Effect of Fire on Honey Mesquite." *Journal of Range Management* 29:6 (1976) 467–71.

Zambardino, R. A. "Mexico's Population in the Sixteenth Century: Demographic Anomaly or Mathematical Illusion?" *Journal of Interdisciplinary History,* 11 (1980) 1–27.

INDEX